MASTERING

BANKING

MACMILLAN MASTER SERIES

OTHER BOOKS BY THE SAME AUTHOR

Elements of Banking
Finance of Foreign Trade
Finance of International Trade
International Trade and Payments

MASTERING
BANKING

D. P. WHITING

MACMILLAN

First published 1985
Reprinted 1985

Published by
MACMILLAN EDUCATION LTD
Houndmills, Basingstoke, Hampshire RG21 2XS
and London
Companies and representatives
throughout the world

Printed in Hong Kong

ISBN 0–333–36911–4 (hardcover)
ISBN 0–333–36912–2 (paperback – home edition)
ISBN 0–333–36913–0 (paperback – export edition)

DEDICATION

To MOIRA

without whose love and encouragement
this book would not have been written

CONTENTS

CONTENTS

IV. BANKING OPERATIONS – PAYMENTS AND SERVICES

V. BANKING OPERATIONS – LENDING AND SECURITIES

CONTENTS

PREFACE

This book is intended primarily for the young banker who needs to acquire early in his or her career a sound basic knowledge of what banking is all about, in order that he or she may then build upon that knowledge through experience and through study to become fully equipped for management.

The book covers the specifications for the option modules Elements of Banking 1 and Elements of Banking 2 of the Business and Technician Education Council at National level, and is also ideal for students taking a Bankers' Conversion Course or studying banking at degree or higher diploma level.

As a foundation study, the book touches to a considerable extent upon the subjects in Stage 2 of the Banking Diploma examinations, especially Law Relating to Banking, Accounting, Finance of International Trade, and Practice of Banking. This is intentional because it is essential that before embarking on the second stage the banking student should study the industry broadly so as to be able more easily to study the individual subjects in detail at the higher level later.

For the established banker this text will serve as a useful refresher, and I hope that the style in which it is written will stimulate the reader and, who knows, possibly bring his or her knowledge up to date!

The general reader, too, should find much of interest in this book. A knowledge of the UK financial system is becoming more and more desirable for people in most walks of life, and the subject of banking has progressed a great deal from being a 'stuffy' one to a topic that is very relevant to our modern way of life.

I am most grateful to National Westminster Bank for permitting me to reproduced their group balance sheet and structure chart from their Annual Report and Accounts 1982 and a specimen cheque, and to Ray Heath and his colleagues in the Trustee Savings Bank for England and Wales for their help in producing the section on the TSBs. To my friends Rae Brimblecombe and Ted Lavender who so patiently read the typescript and made many helpful suggestions, I extend my sincere thanks.

D. P. WHITING

ACKNOWLEDGEMENTS. The author and publishers wish to thank the following who have kindly given permission for the use of copyright material: The Bank of England, Economics Division, for tables from the *Quarterly Bulletin*; The Controller of Her Majesty's Stationery Office for tables from *Annual Abstract of Statistics*.

LIST OF TABLES

LIST OF FIGURES

LIST OF STATUTES

LIST OF CASES

PART I
BANKING IN THE UK

CHAPTER 1

THE UK BANKING SYSTEM

Banks play a vital role in the economy. They predominate in the provision of money through their deposits; they are the principal institutions responsible for the circulation of the rest of the money supply, i.e. notes and coin; and, above all, they provide the means whereby resources are transferred from those who have a surplus to those in industry and commerce who can use them productively. They also provide safe and convenient payments mechanisms, both internally and internationally. Fully to understand the importance of these functions we shall have to study the banking system in detail, but before doing so it is desirable that we should determine what is meant by a bank, and then look at the broad picture of the banking system as a whole.

1.1 WHAT IS A BANK?

Until the Banking Act 1979, statute law had not been very helpful in defining a bank. In fact the existing statutes seemed to dodge the issue very nicely in that several Acts of Parliament described a bank as a company or body corporate or partnership *carrying on the business of banking*! One case in the 1960s was more helpful, however, in that the point at issue was whether a particular financial institution was carrying on the business of banking. The case was *United Dominions Trust Ltd* v. *Kirkwood* 1965. In the judgements relating to this case, three characteristics were held to be usually found in a banker's business:

1. To accept money from, and to collect cheques for, customers and to place the cheques to the customers' credit in a running account.
2. To honour cheques or orders drawn on the bankers by their customers when presented for payment, and to debit their customers in the running account accordingly.
3. To keep customers' running accounts in which credits and debits were entered.

The finding of the court in this case was that as United Dominions Trust carried out only a small amount of banking business compared with its other activities, its *banking status* was not proved, although it was agreed that the company was a bank for the purposes of the Moneylenders Act 1900.

This phrase 'banking status' became particularly important during the period following the secondary banking crisis of 1974 (which we shall examine in more detail later) and is also important in the context of the Banking Act 1979. Through their reputations those institutions which, prior to the Act, considered themselves to be banks were establishing a status (particularly in the eyes of the Bank of England), and were accorded recognition for various purposes appropriate to their particular status. It is not necessary for us to examine these concepts of 'status' and 'recognition' too closely, but simply to accept the fact that a hierarchy of bank and similar institutions already existed before the Banking Act was passed. One of the effects of the Act was to put on to a legal footing the process by which the Bank of England was already bestowing its favours on the basis of each deposit-taking institution's status. The 1979 Act imposed a general prohibition on deposit-taking without Bank of England approval, though the Act did specify a number of types of institutions which were exempted from this prohibition (see Chapter 2). Institutions already accepting deposits had to apply for permission to carry on doing so, and new institutions have to apply for approval before accepting deposits. What is particularly important in the context of defining a bank is the fact that in giving permission to an institution to accept deposits the Bank of England can differentiate between two different types of approval – as a licensed deposit-taker on the one hand, and as a recognised bank on the other. Clearly we need to know how an institution becomes a 'recognised bank', for therein lies a definition of a bank; but as we shall see the decision as to which type of permission (if any) to grant is somewhat arbitrary on the part of the Bank of England for, although the Act lays down minimum criteria for licensing and recognition, some of which are quite clear, some are left to the judgement of the Bank.

Where a licence to accept deposits is sought, the Bank of England must satisfy itself concerning the reputations of those persons who are to direct the institution's business, the size of the institution's net assets (i.e., capital and reserves); it will also look for evidence that the deposit-taking business will be conducted in a prudent manner, i.e. it will maintain adequate liquid assets and provision for bad and doubtful debts and obligations of a contingent nature.

To satisfy the requirements relating to recognised bank status, the Act lays down that:

1. The institution has for a reasonable period of time enjoyed a high reputation and standing in the financial community.
2. The institution provides a wide range of banking services or a highly specialised banking service.
3. The institution's net assets are at least £5 million (in the case of a company offering a wide range of banking services) or at least £250 000 (in the case of one offering a highly specialised banking service).

As to what is regarded as a 'wide range of banking services', the Act is quite specific:

1. Current or deposit account facilities or the acceptance of funds in the wholesale money markets.
2. Finance in the form of overdraft or loan facilities or the lending of funds in the wholesale money markets.
3. Foreign exchange services for domestic and foreign customers.
4. Finance through the medium of bills of exchange and promissory notes, together with finance for foreign trade and documentation in connection with foreign trade.
5. Financial advice or investment management services and facilities for arranging the purchase and sale of securities.

The Bank of England is empowered to disregard the fact that an institution providing a wide range of banking services does not provide one or two of these services, and to use its discretion in deciding whether or not an institution offers one or some of these services in a highly specialised way.

From our examination of the requirements of the Banking Act we are now in a position to produce a UK definition of a bank.

An institution which satisfies the Bank of England as to its reputation, size of net and liquid assets and which offers most, if not all, of the following services, or which offers one or more of them in a highly specialised way:

1. Current or deposit account facilities and overdraft or loan facilities. } and/or { Borrowing and lending in the wholesale money markets.
2. Foreign exchange services.
3. Finance through bills of exchange, together with finance and documentary services for foreign trade.
4. Financial advice or investment management services and facilities for buying and selling securities.

Readers abroad need of course to examine their own local legislation in order to establish a legal definition of a bank, but it is likely that, in substance, it will be very similar to our definition – though, in the case of the countries whose banking system is less developed, the services offered by the banks may be more restricted.

1.2 THE BANKING HIERARCHY

The principal banks in the UK are the Bank of England and the London clearing banks, and these are the institutions generally known to the man in the street – the Bank of England being at the hub of the banking system, and the London clearing banks, especially the 'Big Four' (Barclays, Lloyds, Midland and National Westminster), being the main High Street banks. However, these are by no means the only banks, as Figure 1.1 indicates. The banking system is thus quite complex (and in fact is even more complicated than Figure 1.1 suggests), because there are inter-relationships – by way of partial or complete shareholdings – between the London clearing banks and the Scottish clearing banks and with the Northern Ireland banks (indicated by the arrows in Figure 1.1), between clearing banks and merchant banks, and between the overseas banks and consortium banks. There are also links between the foreign banks and the clearing and merchant banks. All of these inter-relationships will be considered in detail as we look in turn at the different categories of banks.

Bank of England

Each country has a central bank, which operates both as the government's bank and as the banker's bank; in the UK, this is the Bank of England. We shall need to devote a whole chapter (Chapter 2) to examining these functions in detail; it will suffice at this juncture to recognise that the Bank of England is at the hub of the banking system. It has wide powers of control over the other banks. It carries out the government's monetary policy, and in doing so must have the power to restrict the ability of the banks to create credit and also to influence the level of their interest rates. It must also be in a position to manage the flow of government stocks and Treasury bills. In addition to its main office in Threadneedle Street – 'the old lady of Threadneedle Street' – it has branches in some of the main UK cities, and is also responsible for the note printing works.

Clearing banks

The London clearing banks are those which are members of the London Clearing House, where they send representatives to exchange cheques drawn on one another and giro credits payable to one another.

As can be seen by reference to Figure 1.1, there are six clearing banks plus four functional members of the Clearing House which are not strictly speaking clearing banks. Predominant amongst the clearing banks are the

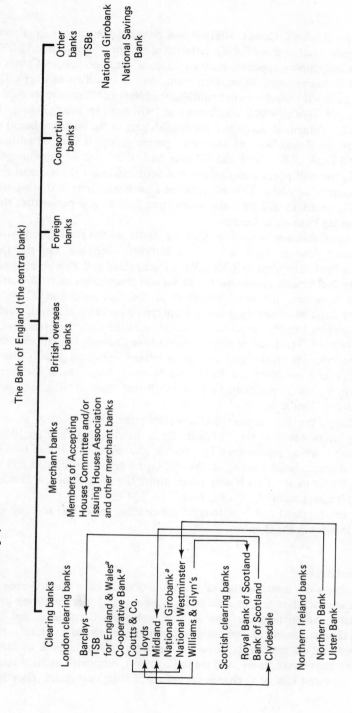

Fig 1.1 *the British banking system*

The Bank of England (the central bank)

Clearing banks | Merchant banks | British overseas banks | Foreign banks | Consortium banks | Other banks / TSBs / National Girobank / National Savings Bank

London clearing banks | Members of Accepting Houses Committee and/or Issuing Houses Association and other merchant banks

Barclays
TSB for England & Wales[a]
Co-operative Bank[a]
Coutts & Co.
Lloyds
Midland
National Girobank[a]
National Westminster
Williams & Glyn's

Scottish clearing banks

Royal Bank of Scotland
Bank of Scotland
Clydesdale

Northern Ireland banks

Northern Bank
Ulster Bank

a   With the Bank of England, these are functional members only of the London Clearing House; they are not members of the London Clearing Bankers' Committee.

Big Four – Barclays, Lloyds, Midland and National Westminter (in alphabetical order, not order of size). Between them they have nearly 12 000 branches and employ approximately a quarter of a million people. Coutts – although it has retained its separate name and is classified as a separate clearing bank – is a wholly-owned subsidiary of National Westminster Bank. Williams and Glyn's (which was formed in 1970 from an amalgamation of Glyn Mills, Williams Deacons and the English part of the National Bank) is owned by the Royal Bank of Scotland's parent group. It is expected that the Royal Bank of Scotland and Williams and Glyn's will be fully merged by 1985, and will operate in England and Scotland under the name of the Royal Bank of Scotland. This will produce a bank with over 900 branches, employing about 15 000 staff and accounting for about 8 per cent of the total banking business in Britain.

The functional members of the Clearing House are the Bank of England, the Trustee Savings Bank group, the National Girobank and the Co-operative Bank. The Trustee Savings Bank for England and Wales represents the individual trustee savings banks (TSBs) and clears items on their behalf between them and the other members of the clearing house. The Co-operative Bank has branches (money shops) in co-operative stores throughout Britain, and the National Girobank operates through the branches of the Post Office. The London clearing banks have connections with clearing banks in both Scotland and Northern Ireland – Midland wholly owns Clydesdale and the Northern Bank, and National Westminster owns the Ulster Bank, and as mentioned above, the Royal Bank of Scotland owns Williams and Glyn's.

Similarly, the few deposit banks which retain their identity as non-clearing banks – such as the Yorkshire Bank, Lewis's Bank and the Isle of Man Bank – are all now owned by London clearing banks. It can thus be seen that commercial banking in the UK (apart from that carried out by foreign banks in the UK) is very much under the control of the London clearing banks, principally the Big Four.

The development and functions of the clearing banks will be fully discussed in subsequent chapters.

Merchant banks

Traditionally the merchant banks' main function has been the provision of acceptance facilities and/or new issues business, and therefore they have comprised the members of the Accepting Houses Committee and the Issuing Houses Association, whose memberships overlap quite considerably. However, not all merchant banks are members of one or both of these. The merchant banks, as we shall see in Chapter 4, originated as institutions which accepted bills of exchange on behalf of their customers. They had extensive connections overseas as wealthy merchants, and were highly respected and trusted. If therefore these merchant 'banks' could be persuaded to add their names as acceptors on bills of exchange drawn on less well-known British merchants, these bills could be more readily discounted – the 'Bill on London' became an important means of international settlement. As joint stock companies became the most common means whereby businesses financed their operations, the merchant banks took on the function of making the arrangements for public issues of shares for companies and developed an expertise in this connection.

More recently, the merchant banks have used their skills in giving advice and other help in relation to takeovers, and also have been major institutions within the Euro-currency and other markets that have become established in London. These activities will be considered in full in later chapters.

British overseas banks

In the 1960s the London clearing banks set about making drastic changes in their relationships with banks overseas in order to meet the changing needs of their customers. Foreign trade had expanded rapidly, larger and larger international companies were becoming established, and the Euro-currency markets were developing rapidly. The banks needed to work together with the European banks to provide by joint ventures the enormous loans that were required by the multinational companies, government institutions and nationalised industries, and even governments themselves. These joint ventures – consortium banks (see below) – were one way of meeting international needs; another was to build up the banks' direct representation overseas. This was done by acquiring full ownership of British overseas banks in which the clearing banks had only part ownership, and by merging and increasing in size these overseas banks to the point where they became very large, with networks of branches and offices extending throughout Europe, North America, the Commonwealth countries and to some extent Asia. Examples of these banks are Barclays International, Lloyds Bank International and International Westminster Bank.

Foreign banks in London

London has always been a major financial centre of the world, and as such has attracted overseas banks. These banks have seen the need either to open offices in London at which to station representatives, or to open branches at which full banking services are offered. In the late 19th and early 20th century – when sterling was the main trading and reserve currency in the world and which up to 1931 (apart from 1914–25) was convertible into gold – it was very desirable to have branches in London to facilitate and to foster the trade links with Britain. However, the number of foreign banks with branches in London up to the 1950s was quite modest in relation to the number which emerged during and after the 1960s. In 1950 there were just over 50 foreign banks with offices in London, whereas in 1983 there were 390 such banks plus a further 70 with an indirect presence through minority holdings or stakes in consortium operations.

This rapid increase in the number of overseas banks (and in their total deposits) can be attributed to the existence and development of the Euro-currency markets, to the establishment of the EEC, to North Sea Oil, and to the particular needs of immigrants into the UK. US business corporations have been very active in establishing themselves in Europe, particularly since the EEC was set up. It has been their activities, plus the flow of US dollars into Western Europe through Defence Aid and Marshall Aid which have led to the emergence of the Euro-dollar market which is mainly centred in London (see Chapter 4). Expanding trade with Europe and UK entry into the EEC has further attracted the US banks to London, as well as banks from other parts of the world. Inasmuch as US oil corporations have been involved in the exploration of North Sea oil, this has served as a further attraction to London as far as US banks are concerned. The flow of funds between the immigrant communities in Britain and their countries of origin, as well as the provision of other banking services for them, has to some extent accounted for the establishment of branches in London by a number of overseas banks – for example, Indian and Pakistani banks. The investment of dollar earnings by the oil-producing countries of the Middle East has no doubt been the primary reason for the establishment of branches by banks from such countries as Iran, Abu Dhabi and Qatar.

The importance of the activities of the foreign banks can be seen from Table 1.1, which has been extracted from information published in the *Bank of England Quarterly Bulletin.*

It will be seen from Table 1.1 that foreign banks have been a very competitive force, and accounted for no less than £27 503 million of sterling deposits and £289 188 million of other currency deposits in May 1983. These foreign currency deposits far exceeded the currency deposits of the London clearing banks including their subsidiary banks.

The figures in brackets in Table 1.1 show that total sterling deposits increased more than threefold during the years 1975–83, and other currency deposits increased more than fivefold. These increases are generally reflected in the figures for the clearing banks and other British banks, but the US banks have increased both their sterling and foreign currency deposits less rapidly, whilst the Japanese banks have increased their foreign currency deposits at a phenomenal rate and the other overseas banks have achieved a sevenfold increase in both sterling and foreign currency deposits.

Table 1.1 *deposits of banks in the UK, May 1983 (£ million)*

All banks	Sterling deposits 140 935 (44 235)[a]		Deposits in other currencies 380 729 (70 321)[a]	
of which:				
London clearing banks	63 588[b]	(22 489)	22 729[b]	(3 731)
Other British banks	48 231	(14 260)	56 290	(10 574)
American banks	8 881	(4 274)	81 668	(26 678)
Japanese banks	3 768	(246)	100 265	(9 670)
Other overseas banks	14 854	(2 411)	107 255	(15 478)
Consortium banks	1 614	(555)	12 521	(4 191)

a   figures relate to May 1975.
b   includes the subsidiary banks of the London clearing banks.
Source: *Bank of England Quarterly Bulletin.*

Consortium banks
These are banks which are owned by other banks but in which no one bank has a direct shareholding of more than 50 per cent, and in which at least one shareholder is an overseas bank. In January 1979, the Bank of England named 29 such banks as listed banks – i.e., they had agreed to maintain the then $12\frac{1}{2}$ per cent reserve ratio. But these were only those consortium banks that were located in London, and there were many more located in various other financial centres of the world in which the British banks had shareholdings. However, since 1979 the number of consortium banks has diminished, and this trend is likely to continue as individual banks decide to provide the large loans required by international companies themselves, rather than do so in conjunction with competitor banks. The reader will appreciate that consortium banks may well be involved in conflicts of interest when providing services to a customer that is already a client of one of the member banks.

By joining together with a number of overseas banks and investment institutions to form a consortium bank, the UK banks have been able to participate in the past in the provision of large syndicated loans which would have been beyond the scope of an individual bank. But because the international banking activities of the individual banks have expanded over the years (as we saw above) they have become more able to provide all the finance which their customers require. Most of the syndicated loans made have been in Euro-currencies, and although most of them have been medium term there has been some financing on a short-term basis. Some of the consortium banks specialise in particular fields such as energy (e.g., the International Energy Bank), or in particular regions of the world (such as the Middle East). In addition to providing syndicated loans, the consortium banks, by being associated with individual large customers, are able to help attract investment in them and to facilitate takeovers and mergers.

Other banks

The other main banks in the UK are the TSBs, the National Savings Bank and the National Girobank. Their origins and development will be fully examined in Chapter 3. What is important in the context of this present discussion is that the activities of all of these banks (especially the Girobank and the TSBs) have been improved and extended to bring them more in line with the commercial banks. They all provide payments mechanisms for their customers in the form of drafts and cheques, and both the Girobank and the TSBs now make loans. They are thus a competitive force within the banking system, indeed they were deliberately reformed as such by government action. The TSBs have their own clearing system which is operated by the Trustee Savings Bank for England and Wales which is itself a member of the London Clearing House, though only a functional member. As such, it is able to clear cheques drawn on the clearing banks and paid into TSB accounts, and similarly, to clear cheques drawn on TSBs and paid into accounts with the clearing banks.

Finance houses

Although they are not banks (and, indeed, were not granted recognition as banks under the 1979 Act), it is desirable to look at the activities of the hire-purchase finance houses within this broad picture of the banking system, as they do provide financial services which are to some extent akin to those of the banks. Traditionally the finance houses have provided finance to enable purchases of cars, domestic appliances and other durable goods to be made on hire-purchase terms. The buyer pays back the money that the finance house has paid over to the supplier in regular instalments which include both principal and interest, and until the final payment is made the goods are legally owned by the finance house.

In more recent years, the finance houses have developed activities in addition to hire purchase. For professional people, they provide instalment loans for the purchase of goods, but without the right to repossess them. The borrower repays by bankers' standing order, and in some cases may automatically borrow a further sum once a debt has been reduced to a certain point. The finance houses have become very much involved in making term loans to industry and, more recently, in leasing machinery and equipment to industry. They also now provide mortgage-type finance for the purchase of commercial and industrial property.

From 1958 onwards, the London clearing banks deliberately sought to acquire interests in the lucrative business of instalment finance by buying either all or some of the shares in the finance houses. They did not consider this type of finance as being appropriate to them directly, but preferred instead to buy their way into this particular market; with the subsequent provision of personal instalment loans by the banks, however, the difference between the banks' own services and those of the finance houses is less distinct. There have been some buying and selling of interests in the houses over the years, but the position is now that the largest finance houses are owned by the English and Scottish clearing banks. Barclays owns Mercantile Credit, Midland owns Forward Trust, and National Westminster owns Lombard North Central. Lloyds has a major holding in Lloyds and Scottish and the Bank of Scotland owns North West Securities. The Standard Chartered Bank owns the Hodge Group.

CHAPTER 2

THE BANK OF ENGLAND

In Chapter 1, we looked at the general structure of the UK banking system, having first attempted to define a bank. We must now break down this broad picture, and look at the component parts in some detail. As we saw, it is the Bank of England which is the hub of the system, and in order to understand its present functions and its role as a central bank it is necessary to trace its origins and development. To do this, we must go back 300 years.

2.1 ESTABLISHMENT

The Bank of England was established in 1694 as a means of raising funds for an impoverished King - William III - who needed finance to pursue a war against France. A group of merchants in London who were prepared to put up £1.2 million as capital were given a Royal Charter permitting them to set up the bank. This capital was lent to the King, and the bank was allowed to issue its own notes up to that sum. The Bank of England was not the first bank to be established in England, for there were already about 50 goldsmiths operating in the City as private bankers at the time. But the Bank of England was the first bank to have *corporate status* and *royal patronage*. It began as an ordinary bank in the sense that it performed the same functions as the other banks of the time, apart from its loan to the King. In other words, it did not commence as a central bank, and only with time (and the special privileges which were gradually given over the first century and a half of its existence) did it assume the functions which are now attributed to a central bank.

In 1709, the Bank was given a monopoly over joint stock banking by the Bank of England Act of that year. This amounted to a renewal of the Royal Charter, and stipulated for the first time that no other corporate business with more than six partners could issue bank notes in England and Wales. At that time, to issue one's own notes was vital to a bank's existence so that the effect of the Act was to prevent competitor banks with more than six partners from being established – more than six partners were necessary to raise the amount of capital required to operate on the same scale as the Bank of England. As the largest note-issuing bank, it soon adopted a dominant role as far as the country's supply of bank notes was concerned, but it was not until after the Bank Charter Act 1844 that the UK's note issue came under the control of the Bank, and even then not fully until all the private note-issuing banks had been absorbed by other banks (the last merger being in 1921, see below).

In the first 50 years of its existence, the Bank of England gradually became banker to the various government departments and became responsible for the issue and management of government debt – the National Debt.

2.2 RELATIONSHIP WITH OTHER BANKS

Inasmuch as the Bank of England became the main note-issuing bank and that some of the smaller banks elected to use Bank of England notes rather than issue new notes themselves, the private banks became very dependent upon the Bank of England. They had accounts with the Bank, and kept their reserves with it, and when they ran into difficulties because of a lack of confidence as to their ability to repay depositors on demand (i.e., a run on a bank), they relied on whatever support they could get from the Bank of England.

In a crisis in 1825, many banks had to close their doors, and pressure built up in Parliament for something to be done that would enable larger and more stable banking units to be established that could more easily withstand such crises of confidence. The outcome was an Act of Parliament in 1826 (Country Bankers Act), which permitted joint stock banks to be established, and to issue their own notes, outside a radius of 65 miles of London, and at the same time the Bank of England was encouraged to open branches in the provinces. Because these new larger banks could not be established in London which was very much the main financial and commercial centre, the 1826 Act had little effect in bringing into being the larger and more stable banking units which Parliament wanted. In consequence, the restriction on joint stock banking within the 65-mile radius was lifted by a further Bank of England Act in 1833. This permitted joint stock banking within the 65-mile radius provided that the banks did not issue their own notes. At the same time that Act of 1833 made Bank of England notes *legal tender*.

By 1833, the practice of paying debts by way of cheque was becoming increasingly recognised as acceptable, and in consequence the restriction in the Act that the joint stock banks could not issue their own notes in London did not have the restrictive effect that was expected. When the new banks advanced money to their customers they did so by giving them overdraft limits, or by crediting their accounts with sums transferred from loan accounts, and encouraging their customers to draw cheques to use the sums advanced. The consequence of the 1833 Act was that the joint stock banks were quickly established from then on and, by a deliberate policy of buying up and absorbing the smaller banks, reduced banking in the UK to a relatively small number of large banks with networks of branches by the end of the 19th century.

2.3 BANK CHARTER ACT 1844

By 1844 Parliament had become concerned that there was no control over the note issues in Britain and that, furthermore, the size of these issues was not known, mostly because the note-issuing and banking functions of the Bank of England were all merged into one. Rising prices were attributed to excessive note issues, and it was thought that steps should be taken to control them. This concern was reflected in the provisions of the Bank Charter Act 1844:

1. The Bank of England should be split into *two* departments – the Banking Department and the Issue Department.
2. The Bank of England should issue a *weekly return*.
3. The *fiduciary issue* should be limited to £14 million. Every note issued beyond this limit was to be backed by gold held at the Bank of England.
4. The note issue should become centralised in the hands of the Bank of England. Existing private note issues were frozen and as the private banks became bankrupt and were amalgamated with other banks their note-issuing rights lapsed (the last surviving private note-issuing bank was Fox, Fowler and Co., which amalgamated with Lloyds Bank in 1921).

2.4 CONTROL OVER OTHER BANKS

The dominance of the Bank of England, which was reinforced by the Bank Charter Act 1844, continued to be strengthened throughout the 19th and into the 20th century by the way that the commercial banks kept accounts with the Bank of England and settled their indebtedness with one another by drawing cheques on the central bank; as the Bank's interest rate – Bank Rate – became the leading rate of interest in the UK the other banks related their interest rates to it. Furthermore, the importance of the Bank as the government's bank increased as new forms of government securities emerged and the government's borrowing requirements increased enormously, especially as a consequence of the two world wars.

Because of its importance as both the bankers' bank and the government's bank, the Bank of England has played down its role as a commercial banker, and since the First World War has ceased to compete seriously with the other banks in the provision of banking services to industry and commerce. It has some accounts for firms and individuals, but these are relatively small in number. Up until 1946 the Bank of England was privately owned, which was a somewhat difficult situation for an institution which was carrying out the government's monetary policy, for to do so it had to have the co-operation of other banks. During the Second World War, in particular, it was necessary for the government to borrow large sums of money from the banks at extremely low rates of interest ($\frac{3}{8}$ per cent per annum) by means of what were called Treasury deposit receipts, and the Bank of England had to bring its influence to bear. Bank rate was kept at 2 per cent throughout the war period (apart from a few weeks at the outset), and consequently the commercial banks were paying only $\frac{1}{2}$ per cent interest on deposit accounts. They could not pay higher rates of interest to attract deposits and also, having received deposits, could not lend them very profitably as such a large part of them had to be lent to the government at minimal rates of interest.

In 1946 the Bank of England was nationalised, the shareholders being compensated with government stock. The conduct of the Bank was placed in the hands of a Court of Directors headed by the Governor of the Bank of England, and including representatives from industry and from the trade unions. The Act nationalising the Bank gave the Bank of England very wide powers of control over the other banks, so that it no longer had to rely on their voluntary co-operation. The following extract from the Act shows just how wide these powers are:

The Bank, if they think it necessary in the public interest, may request information from and make recommendations to bankers, and may, if so authorised by the Treasury, issue directions to any banker for the purpose of securing that effect is given to any such request or recommendation:

Provided that:

a. no such request or recommendation shall be made with respect to the affairs of any particular customer of a banker, and
b. before authorising the issue of any such directions the Treasury shall give the banker concerned, or such person as appears to them to represent him, an opportunity of making representations with respect thereto.

These powers of control were reinforced in 1971 when the Bank of England produced a consultative document called *Competition and Credit Control*, and after a short period for discussions with the financial institutions concerned brought in the measures more or less as outlined in the document. These measures were designed to give the Treasury and the Bank of England better control over the banks and other financial institutions and, in particular, the amount of credit granted by them. They were also intended to stimulate competition on a fair basis between the banks by abolishing the collective agreements on interest rates and replacing the old cash and liquidity ratios with *reserve ratios* that applied not only to the commercial banks but to other banks as well. These measures, and the degree to which they have proved effective, will be discussed in Chapter 7.

The Bank of England's powers of control over banking in the UK were reinforced still further by the Banking Act 1979, one purpose of which was to bring UK banking legislation into line with that required by the EEC. As we saw in Chapter 1, the Act brought the recognition and licensing of banks under the direct control of the Bank of England, which was also given the power to withdraw recognition or licence. A further purpose of the Act was to avoid a recurrence of the secondary banking crisis of 1974, at least partly caused by the uncontrolled growth of peripheral financial institutions in the UK. The first EEC directive (77/780/EEC 1977) on the co-ordination of banking law had to be implemented by December 1979, and the Banking Act 1979 had to meet the requirements of this directive. It is quite likely that further legislation or amendments to the 1979 Act will be necessary in the future as the EEC's common banking policy develops. One feature of the first directive which made fresh legislation essential was the requirement that all credit institutions had to obtain *authorisation* before commencing activities; it also laid down certain criteria concerning capital funds, the types of business envisaged, and the reputations of those persons directing the institution's business, which had to be fulfilled before authorisation could be granted.

The 1979 Act required all institutions already accepting deposits to apply to the Bank of England for permission to do so, and from then on no new deposit-taking institution could start up without a licence to do so from the Bank. There is a clear distinction in the Act between two types of institution:

1. A recognised bank.
2. A licensed deposit-taker.

Under the first of these headings, the Bank of England gives *recognition* to sound financial institutions which call themselves banks, or propose to do so. 'Recognised banks' are supervised by the Bank of England on a non-statutory basis, and they have the right to call themselves banks. They are able to accept deposits in the same way as the institutions in category 2, but they are *recognised* rather than *licensed*.

A licensed deposit-taker is an institution which meets the criteria laid down for permission to accept deposits, but does not warrant the recognised status which would permit it to call itself a bank. All licensed deposit-takers must furnish the Bank of England with information, and accept the Bank's statutory powers of supervision.

The Banking Act 1979 lists a number of institutions which are *exempted* from the requirement to seek recognition or a licence before accepting deposits and from contributing to the deposit protection scheme (see below); these include:

1. The Bank of England itself.
2. Central banks of other EEC member states.
3. The National Savings Bank.
4. TSBs.
5. Penny savings banks and school banks.
6. Building societies.
7. Credit unions, loan societies and friendly societies.
8. Insurance companies.
9. Stockbrokers and stockjobbers.
10. Local authorities.

The second main provision of the 1979 Act does not concern Bank of England control to the same extent as the recognition and licensing procedure. However, the Bank of England was involved in the 'lifeboat operation' to rescue the secondary banks in 1974, and would no doubt be equally involved if there was a similar crisis in the future. The second provision is concerned with protecting depositors, and hence it is appropriate to consider it in the context of this chapter. The 1979 Act provided that a *Deposit Protection Fund* should be set up and financed by contributions from recognised banks and licensed institutions. In the event of failure of any of the banks or institutions, depositors will receive compensation from the fund of 75 per cent of the first £10 000 of their deposits with that institution, i.e. a maximum of £7500 per depositor per institution. The protection applies to corporate deposits as well as those of private individuals, but it does not apply to deposits by recognised banks and licensed deposit-takers themselves.

Although the amount of protection per depositor is relatively small, it would go some way towards alleviating the distress caused to them in the event of a bank failure. There is a provision in the Act for the £10 000 limit to be raised by statutory instrument in Parliament should it be considered desirable.

2.5 PRESENT-DAY FUNCTIONS

Government's bank

The functions which the Bank of England now performs can be considered under two headings, the *government's bank* and the *bankers' bank*. Whilst the distinctions between the two are not always clear cut, this is a useful and logical way of listing the functions – and, at the same time, showing the inter-relationships of these activities.

Clearly, as the government's bank, the Bank of England is responsible for running the accounts of all the government's departments, which is a colossal task in view of the sheer volume and total value of transactions carried out by the government. But this is by no means the whole story for there are many other activities which are performed on behalf of the state. Seven of these are particularly important.

Operating government accounts

The Bank of England provides bank accounts and other normal banking services for the government departments. It must be pointed out here that the clearing banks also run some accounts for government departments, but the main accounts are with the central bank.

Controlling the issue of notes and coin

In conjunction with the Treasury, the Bank of England is responsible for printing bank notes. It determines the size of the fiduciary issue of notes, which must be increased to meet seasonal needs, and must ensure that torn and dirty notes and worn out coins are replaced. There must be adequate supplies of notes and coin of each denomination to meet the needs of the community.

Issue and redemption of government stocks

The Bank is the registrar for most of the public sector's issues of stocks, and also to some extent for commonwealth stocks.

Within the public sector, it is responsible for central government stocks (and, to some extent, those of local government and the nationalised industries). As registrar, it issues and redeems stocks, records their ownership and pays the interest when it is due. These securities represent the main part of the National Debt, and their sale and redemption provides an important means whereby the Bank of England can manipulate the availability of funds and the level of interest rates in the money market.

At any one time, the Bank will have one or more *tap stocks* on issue. A tap stock is the latest issue of government stock, e.g. Treasury Stock 1995, some of which will be held by the Bank of England to be issued gradually through the government's broker on the Stock Exchange, as and when it is appropriate. In other words the Bank will 'turn on the tap', and sell some of the stock as part of its technique of controlling the availability of funds and the level of interest rates in the long-term market from day to day.

The Treasury bill issue

Each Friday, the Bank of England receives from the London discount houses and other financial institutions bids for the week's allocation of Treasury bills. These are 91-day bills issued by the Treasury in various denominations from £5000 upwards. The Treasury undertakes to pay the full face value of the bill back to the lender at the end of the period, but interest is deducted when the bill is purchased. This is done by tendering for bills at a price below their face value. If an institution tenders at a price of £97.50 (per £100), for example, it offers to lend the money to the government at 10 per cent approx. per annum (£2.50 × 4 per £100 – as 91 days is a quarter of a year, approx.). It is responsible for allocating these bills to the highest bidders, and publishes information about the average rate of interest at which the bills have been allocated at the tender. This is a key rate of interest, since it is carefully watched in the money market as an indicator as to how the level of interest rates in general is likely to move. The Treasury bill tender, like the issue and redemption of other government securities, is important in the context of carrying out the government's monetary policy.

Operating the exchange equalisation account (EEA)

By operating the EEA and maintaining the UK's gold and currency reserves, the Bank is able to influence the value of sterling and other currencies in the foreign exchange market.

The EEA was started in 1932, soon after the gold standard broke down, and was credited with the UK reserves of foreign currencies. In 1939 it was also credited with the Bank of England's holdings of gold (some £300 million) which up to that time had been held as partial backing for the note issue. The foreign currencies and gold are used to protect the pound externally by buying and selling them as appropriate. When sterling is weak, foreign currencies (and possibly gold) will be sold in exchange for sterling. This reduces the supply of sterling in the foreign exchange markets (thus tending to push up its value), and increases the supply of foreign currency (or currencies), which will tend to reduce the value of the currency concerned. When sterling is strong, the Bank of England will grasp the opportunity to buy foreign currencies for sterling and put these currencies into the reserves. If sterling is strong enough, this can be done without depressing its value unduly – or, indeed, the object may be to stop sterling appreciating too much because the higher the value of the pound in terms of foreign currencies the more difficult it is to sell UK goods overseas. The Bank of England must obviously carry out the government's wishes when intervening in the foreign exchange market as operator of the EEA.

Carrying out the government's monetary policy

This is the Bank of England's most important function. In carrying out the government's monetary policy it acts as the government's agent. As we shall see in Chapter 5, the majority of the money supply consists of bank deposits and therefore any attempt by the government to control the money supply must involve influencing (or determining) the size of *bank deposits*. Hence the Bank of England must have devices which it can use to influence and determine their size, and Chapter 7 is devoted to a study of how the Bank of England brings its influence to bear.

The Bank's international role

The Governor of the Bank of England is responsible not only for carrying out the government's monetary policy, but also for meeting with other central bank governors (there is a regular monthly meeting at the Bank for International Settlements in Basle) to discuss international monetary problems, and to decide upon joint action to deal with them. The Governor has on occasions been involved in negotiating the help of other central banks in supporting sterling when it has been weak, and in providing loans to the British government. Obviously there must be very close liaison between the government and the Treasury in carrying out this international role.

Bankers' bank

Accounts of the banks

Each of the commercial banks keeps accounts with the Bank of England, and through these they are able to settle transactions with one another, i.e. to draw cheques on the Bank. Such transactions include the daily settlement through the Bankers' Clearing House. The Bank also keeps accounts for the London discount houses, and these facilitate transactions not only between the Bank and the houses but also between the other banks and the discount houses.

The Bank of England maintains accounts for overseas banks as well as the British banks, and these include the central bank's accounts through which it is possible to carry out transactions relating to loans between countries, swap agreements, selling gold to one another, and in connection with arrangements made by the International Monetary Fund (IMF). The Bank of England also holds accounts for the IMF and other international institutions.

The balances of the London clearing banks' accounts with the Bank of England form part of their reserve assets, and are maintained at the minimum amount it is reckoned they need for the day to day transactions that are settled through the accounts. These balances can be drawn upon in cash at any time, and are indeed regarded as cash to all intents and purposes.

Provision of notes and coin

It is a function of the Bank of England to make available to the other banks the notes and coin which they require, and to replace dirty and worn out notes and coin for these banks. It is in fact through the banks that the Bank of England carries out the task of controlling the issue of notes and coin on behalf of the government, as mentioned above (coins are in fact the responsibility of the Royal Mint, but clearly their quantities and distribution are determined by the Bank).

Lender of last resort

It is vital that a central bank should act as lender of last resort to the banking system. If the commercial banking system is short of funds and is unable to borrow sufficient funds from other sources, then it must have the support of the central bank, but the central bank is able to determine the price that has to be paid for that support, i.e. the *rate of interest* charged. In the UK, the Bank of England gives this support indirectly in that it is the London discount houses and not the banks that are forced to obtain funds from the Bank of England if they are short. If the supply of funds in the London money market is insufficient, then the commercial banks call in some of the 'call money' from the discount houses, forcing them to seek assistance. This assistance may be given by the Bank directly by buying bills or, alternatively, the Bank may choose to give indirect assistance by buying bills from the commercial banks, enabling them to restore their call money loans to the discount houses or, rarely these days, lending to them. Acting as lender of last resort provides the central bank with a weapon to use as part of the government's monetary policy.

Prudential supervision of the banks

Some of the ways in which the Bank of England is responsible for controlling the banking system (other than through monetary weapons) have been discussed earlier in this chapter. Not only can it give directives to the banks, but it is also there to give advice to them and to bring its influence to bear on them. The Bank of England has been much more open about its activities in recent years and, in particular, has through its *Quarterly Bulletin* publicised the facts and reasons behind its measures to improve its supervisory role.

TOPICS FOR DISCUSSION

1. Discuss the effects of the way the Bank of England was established, and of legislation up to and including the 1833 Act, upon the development of other banks in the UK.
2. The main aim of the Bank Charter Act 1844 was to separate the Bank of England's note-issuing activities, and to bring note issuing generally within its control. Discuss the provisions of the Act in the light of this aim.
3. Discuss the ways in which the nationalisation of the Bank of England in 1946 and the Banking Act 1979 have given the Bank powers to supervise the other banks.
4. Examine the various functions of the Bank of England, and consider which of them are the most important. If you are normally resident outside the UK compare (and, if possible, contrast) the activities of the Bank of England with those of your own central bank.

CHAPTER 3

COMMERCIAL BANKING

3.1 WHAT IS A COMMERCIAL BANK?

In considering the history and development of the Bank of England in Chapter 2, we inevitably became aware how commercial banking grew. Indeed, the Bank of England was at first a commercial bank itself, and only gradually took on the role of central bank at the expense of its commercial banking activities, leaving these to the joint stock banks which flourished once the 1833 Act gave them the freedom to do so and, through amalgamations, develop into the large High Street banks of today with networks of branches and deposits running into billions of pounds. But as yet we have not considered what the term 'commercial bank' means.

Perhaps the best way of arriving at this definition is to look at those functions which a commercial bank must perform. They are threefold – the acceptance of deposits, the provision of payments mechanisms, and the provision of credit. They provide many other services besides these, but these are the essential services without which they could hardly call themselves 'commercial banks'. Of the various types of institutions we looked at in Chapter 1, all except the Bank of England, the finance houses and the National Savings Bank offer all three services and ought therefore to be regarded as commercial banks in the broadest sense of the term. The Bank of England is in a class of its own as the central bank, and the finance houses (as we saw) are not strictly speaking banks and, in any case, do not generally provide payments mechanisms for their depositors in the form of cheque books and credit giros. The National Savings Bank is, as its name suggests, a savings bank rather than a commercial bank; it accepts deposits, but apart from permitting its customers to apply for warrants payable to third parties does not at present provide them with cheque books and a giro system.

Although the TSBs still carry the word 'savings' in their title, they have developed away from being savings banks in recent years in that they now offer all three services to their customers (though as yet most of their customers are private individuals rather than business customers). The National Girobank also provides all three services, and might come within our category of commercial bank, although both this bank and the TSBs have got a long way to go yet before they match up to the more traditional type of commercial bank in providing a full and comprehensive range of services to all types of customers.

When people use the term 'commercial bank', they usually mean the large clearing banks, for it is these banks that for a century and a half have been primarily concerned with services to industry and commerce. They offer a wide range of services to private individuals, of course, and in terms of the value and volume of cheques and credit transfers – i.e., activity on their accounts, overdraft and loan facilities, and foreign trade transactions – the accounts of business customers must predominate. Throughout the rest of this chapter (and indeed in later chapters), I shall use the term 'commercial bank' synonymously with the terms 'clearing bank' and 'High Street bank'. This is not to ignore the importance to industry and commerce of the merchant banks and discount banks, but in as much as these banks play a major role in the wholesale money markets it would be appropriate to consider their activities in Chapter 4 which is concerned with the financial markets.

3.2 BALANCE SHEET

By looking at the balance sheet of a large commercial bank we can tell a great deal about its activities – in particular, its sources of funds and how these funds are employed to make a profit. The consolidated balance sheet given in full in Appendix 1 is that of one of the clearing banks (National Westminster) which is in fact a banking group and hence includes in its group balance sheet the activities not only of the main domestic banking company but also of all of its subsidiary companies as well. You would be wise to examine the balance sheet of your own bank if you are employed in one (or, as a customer of a bank, ask your bank for a copy of its balance sheet). If this is a bank abroad, all well and good as the balance sheet will help you to make comparisons between that bank and a London clearing bank. In addition to examining the figures in the balance sheet itself, look carefully at the explanatory notes accompanying the balance sheet and read through the chairman's report or statement which will no doubt give you additional information about the bank's activities, especially those of its associated and subsidiary companies (see Appendix 2).

Like any company's balance sheet, a bank's balance sheet shows the position at a particular date – usually 31 December – and, as in Appendix 1 (page 232) the figures relating to the previous year are shown side by side with the current figures. Unlike an ordinary company's balance sheet, however, the assets are shown in the opposite order – instead of showing the fixed assets (e.g., Premises) first, these are shown last and the liquid assets (commencing with Cash in hand, the most liquid of all) are shown first.

Let us now examine in turn the liabilities and the assets of our specimen balance sheet (Figure A.2 in Appendix 1). The liabilities will show us the *sources* from which the bank has obtained its funds, and the assets will show us how those funds have been *used* by the bank to make a profit.

3.3 LIABILITIES

Capital and reserves

The first item on the liabilities side in a bank's balance sheet is similar to that found in any company's balance sheet, i.e. Capital and reserves. The ordinary capital represents the amount subscribed by the *ordinary shareholders*. There may also be preference share capital, as there is in our specimen balance sheet. This is *subscribed capital*, which is entitled to a fixed rate of dividend which has to be paid before ordinary shareholders receive any dividend. The reserves are there as a result of retaining some of the profits over the years, and from the revaluation of bank premises as these values have appreciated with increases in property values generally. Whilst these three items amount to very large sums of money in themselves, they are nevertheless small as a proportion of total liabilities, whereas in the balance sheet of an ordinary industrial or commercial company these shareholders' funds would account for a large part of the total liabilities. This arises from the fact that the bank has one enormous liability – customers' deposits – which is peculiar to a deposit-taking institution.

Loan capital

This is capital that has been *borrowed*, as distinct from shareholders' funds which are subscribed and which represent the shareholders' ownership of the company. Those who lend the loan capital are not shareholders, and have no say in the running of the bank. They receive an agreed rate of interest on the capital which is lent to the bank for a set period of years.

Minority interest in subsidiary companies

The large clearing banks have subsidiary companies, and where such a company is not fully owned it is necessary to take account in the balance sheet of the fact that these are outside shareholders to which the subsidiary company is liable. They own capital and reserves, and participate in the profits of the company. If the bank shows such a subsidiary company as an asset in its balance sheet (see below) then it must acknowledge the liability to the minority shareholders amongst its liabilities.

Current, deposit and other accounts

This colossal item (£50 196 million in Appendix 1) represents the deposits which the bank has accepted – both from its retail customers and through the wholesale money market – plus a relatively small amount relating to its own internal accounts. The ratio of current accounts to deposit accounts varies, depending primarily on the rate of interest payable on deposit account; when this is high, customers are tempted to transfer from current account to deposit account. At the time of writing (January 1984) current accounts provide only about 30 per cent of the clearing banks' sterling deposits, and this is the case with National Westminster. The bank pays no interest on ordinary current accounts, but cheques may be drawn on them. The banks do pay interest on deposit accounts, which varies with the amount and the length of period for which they are deposited. The majority of deposit accounts are subject to seven days' notice. Cheques may not be drawn on deposit accounts.

Deferred taxation and other liabilities

These include provisions for taxation due to be paid to the Inland Revenue, amounts due to creditors, dividends due to be paid to shareholders and notes in circulation.

Eligible liabilities

From 1971, when the Competition and Credit Control measures were introduced (see Chapter 7), certain of the banks' liabilities were classified for reserve purposes as 'eligible liabilities'. The banks were required to keep a ratio of $12\frac{1}{2}$ per cent of reserve assets to eligible liabilities. This requirement was discontinued in 1981, but the term 'eligible liabilities' is still used, and it is therefore necessary to know what the term means. Eligible liabilities comprise sterling deposit liabilities, excluding deposits having an original maturity over two years, plus any sterling resources obtained by switching foreign currencies into sterling. Inter-bank trans-actions and sterling certificates of deposit (both held and issued) are taken into the calculation of individual banks' liabilities on a *net* basis, irrespec-tive of term. Some adjustments are also made in respect of transit items. It is not possible to calculate the eligible liabilities of the National Westminster bank from the balance sheet in Appendix 1, as the items are not shown separately.

The bank uses its shareholders' funds to *invest in assets*. However, as we have seen, the vast majority of the funds invested come not from the shareholders, but from the banks' depositors.

3.4 ASSETS

Cash on hand and balances with the Bank of England

A bank's most liquid asset is the cash it has in its tills and strong rooms, and it must ensure that it has sufficient available to meet its customers' demands at any time. Balances at the Bank of England are almost as good as cash in that they can be drawn upon to provide additional notes and coin very quickly, and also can be used to make payments between the banks themselves. An international bank would also keep balances with state banks abroad for the same purposes – to enable it to obtain additional notes and coin, and also to settle transactions with other banks; hence in Appendix 1 such balances are included in the title of this asset.

The banks use their current account balances with the Bank of England to settle the transactions with one another at the Bankers' Clearing House, as well as transactions with the Bank itself. Such balances are also a vital reserve which must be kept. Until 1971, the clearing banks had to keep 8 per cent of their total deposits in the form of cash on hand or balances with the Bank of England, but from then on they were obliged to keep only $1\frac{1}{2}$ per cent of their eligible liabilities with the Bank, and were at liberty to keep whatever additional cash and balances they wished in order to meet their day to day requirements. In 1981, this requirement was once again changed and now all banks and licensed deposit-takers with liabilities of £10 million or more must hold $\frac{1}{2}$ per cent of their eligible liabilities with the Bank of England in special *non-operational accounts*. In addition, the banks hold at the Bank whatever operational balances they think necessary. These accounts at the Bank (whether operational or otherwise) earn no interest, and neither does cash on hand, and the banks will wish to minimise the size of this asset.

Cheques in course of collection

Because as far as a Bank is concerned the cheque clearing process takes three working days, a bank will always have at any particular time an appreciable amount of money owed to it by other banks in respect of cheques which have yet to be cleared. In Appendix 1 it will be seen that this amounts to £921 million, and that is a lot of money to have 'idle', in the sense that it is earning no income. At first sight, these funds would appear to be very liquid in that they will be received within a few days and therefore their total could be included amongst the bank's liquid assets. This is not so, however, because there will be cheques in the process of being cleared that are *claims against the bank* – i.e., cheques drawn on it by customers and made payable to customers of other banks. We must assume that these amount to something like the £921 million of cheques drawn on other banks, and that therefore if the banks were to close for a few days and clear all outstanding claims this asset would disappear from the balance sheet. Clearly, therefore Cheques in course of collection should not be regarded as a liquid asset, and in the past when official liquidity ratios and reserve ratios have been in force this asset has not been included in determining how 'liquid' the bank is.

Money at call and short notice

This asset comprises money lent overnight (or at the most on up to 14 days' notice), mostly to the London discount houses, but also to money brokers, discount brokers, stockjobbers and stockbrokers and also bullion brokers. Next to cash, this is the bank's most liquid asset. Most of it can be called in next day, and the size of it will reflect the bank's needs for the day. If it expects heavy withdrawals by its customers and other needs for cash – i.e., cash on hand or balances with the Bank of England – then it will run down its money at call to provide the extra cash required. This asset produces an income to the bank, but the rates of interest received will vary with market conditions, though on average they will be *relatively* low to reflect the fact that the funds are highly liquid. When funds are short on the money market, the banks are able to demand high rates of interest but when they are plentiful the banks can command only relatively low rates. Most of the funds lent to the money market are secured by the lodgement of government stocks and bills of exchange. The activities of the banks in providing funds for the discount houses thus affect the gilt-edged and bill markets, and in order to protect the efficient functioning of these markets eligible banks are required to hold at least $2\frac{1}{2}$ per cent of their eligible liabilities in secured advances to the discount houses each day. Furthermore, over a longer period (six months or a year) secured lending to the discount houses, money brokers and gilt-edged jobbers must average 5 per cent. The term 'gilt-edged' is used to mean government and local authority stocks which, because they are issued by the public sector, are quite safe.

Bills discounted

Included under this heading are Treasury bills and commercial bills which the bank has discounted, usually with the intention of holding them to maturity. The discount charged when buying the bills represents the interest the bank receives on this asset, and this will vary with market conditions but tends to be at or somewhat higher than the banks' base rates. The banks buy the Treasury bills from the discount houses after they have held them for at least a week, and the rate of interest on these bills is determined at the weekly tender (see p. 21) and tends to be $\frac{1}{2}$ per cent or so below the banks' base rates. They are 91-day bills, and the commercial bills are usually three-month or six-month bills, though some may be of longer term.

Dealing assets

This item consists of government stocks and other investments held for dealing purposes in the money markets; as such, they are liquid assets.

Special deposits

This asset does not in fact appear in Appendix 1, as there was no call for special deposits at the time the balance sheet was drawn up. Special deposits were first brought into use in 1960 as a device to restrict the availability of liquid assets to the banks and/or make them call in some of their advances, and it was very extensively used. Although the device has not been used in recent years, the Bank of England still has the power to enforce special deposits. They amount to a call to the banks to pay over a proportion of their eligible liabilities to the Bank of England in cash by a prescribed date, to be frozen until the authorities (the Treasury and the Bank of England) decide that they shall be repaid. In view of the uncertainty as to when repayment will take place, the banks cannot regard special deposits as a liquid asset – which is of course exactly what the authorities aim to achieve by imposing them. The liquidity of the money market is reduced, and the banks must become less willing to accommodate their customers by lending them money. We shall look more closely at this in Chapter 7. The rate of interest payable on special deposits is equal to that payable by the government on Treasury bills, and it is in fact adjusted if necessary each week, after the average Treasury bill rate is announced, to the banks concerned for repayment.

Certificates of deposit

Certificates of deposit, as the name suggests, certify that a sum of money has been deposited. They are issued for substantial round amounts in sterling (or possibly US dollars), in multiples of £10 000 with a minimum of £50 000 and, normally, a maximum of £500 000. The sum deposited is repayable to bearer at a prescribed date, and it attracts interest at an agreed rate which is indicated on the certificate. As a certificate of deposit is negotiable by simple delivery it can easily be sold, and the market price for certificates of deposit is published in the press from day to day. This 'price' is in fact a rate of interest, and reflects current rates of interest in the money market generally for the outstanding term until maturity.

As we are looking at the assets side of the balance sheet, this item must represent certificates of deposit which the bank has acquired – that is, certificates issued by other banks. When they mature they will be presented to the banks concerned for repayment. In Appendix 1 any certificates issued by National Westminster Bank will be included as liabilities under the item Current, deposit and other accounts.

Investments

These are investments in government and government-backed stocks in addition to dealing assets (see above). They are of various maturity dates, and the bank will have purchased them so as to ensure that it has portfolios of stocks maturing at regular intervals, as well as some long-dated stocks which will produce a good return well into the future. These stocks produce a better income for the bank than any of the assets considered so far, but the precise yield must depend upon the price paid for them, as well as the rate of interest paid on them.

Advances

In Appendix 1, this is shown as Customers' and other accounts. This is by far the biggest asset, and the most profitable to the bank. It includes overdrafts and loans of all types - for example, straightforward loans to individuals and firms, personal instalment loans, term loans to industry, mortgage loans, and export loans. It also includes a large sum of money placed in the wholesale money markets for periods exceeding one month.

On the majority of these advances the rate of interest charged will be related to the bank's base rate or LIBOR (London Inter-bank Offered Rate), and quoted as such, possibly ranging from 1 per cent above for a large industrial customer to 4-5 per cent above base rate for the private borrower. On personal instalment loans, the rate of interest is fixed for the whole term of the loan and is charged on the whole amount for the whole term of the loan despite the fact that the advance is repaid in monthly instalments and the average outstanding loan is only half the sum advanced. The true rate of interest is thus approximately twice the nominal rate charged to the customer, as is usually the case with hire-purchase contracts. The cost of borrowing will be examined in more detail in Chapter 14, which is devoted to the subject of bank lending. A prudent bank must always provide for the fact that some of its advances may never be repaid, and thus provision for bad and doubtful debts will have been deducted from the total of advances in Appendix 1. During periods of recession, when a higher number than usual of firms and companies run into difficulties, the banks will of course make bigger provisions for bad debts.

Trade investments

These are shares and other investments in both Stock Exchange listed and unlisted companies, and represent only a very small proportion of total assets.

Investments in associated companies

These are investments in such companies as the Bankers' Clearing House, the Agricultural Mortgage Corporation, Finance for Industry and such associated businesses as credit card companies, unit trusts and insurance. In each case, the holding does not exceed 50 per cent so that the companies in which the investments are made are not subsidiary companies.

Quite apart from these investments in *associated* companies, the activities of the subsidiary companies are incorporated into the figures for the group as a whole and not shown therefore as a separate asset in the group balance sheet. They are subsidiaries of National Westminster Bank (which is the major company in the group, of course) and in Appendix 1 the asset Investments in Subsidiary Companies (£583 million) appears. The notes accompanying the specimen balance sheet list the principal subsidiaries of the bank (Appendix 3). The way in which the subsidiary and associated companies fit into the group's activities can be seen from the operations flowchart (Appendix 2).

Premises and equipment

This asset consists of all of the group's premises and equipment after allowing for depreciation and amortisation.

3.5 WHAT DOES THE BALANCE SHEET TELL US ABOUT BANK SERVICES?

On the liabilities side, the item Current, deposit and other accounts reflects one of the bank's main services – the acceptance of deposits on current and deposit accounts.

On the assets side, Cash on hand is necessary if the bank is to be able to provide the service of supplying notes and coin as and when required by its customers. Cheques in course of collection are cheques which have been paid in by customers, and which the bank is clearing on their behalf. The provision of the cheque payments mechanism is a vital service which the banks provide. The provision of Money at Call is an essential service to the money market, and to the authorities in carrying out their monetary policy. Similarly in purchasing and holding Treasury bills the banks are providing funds for the government, and assist the authorities further in pursuing their monetary policy.

The other part of the asset Bills discounted – the commercial bills which have been discounted – represents another vital service to the bank's customers. By discounting bills for them the bank is in fact providing short-term finance in anticipation of the receipt of the proceeds at maturity of the bills. This is a particularly important service for exporters. The bank's Investments are all in the public sector (apart from a small amount included under the separate heading Trade investments), and here again the banks are providing a service to both central and local government, enabling them to acquire necessary finance – and also, as far as central government is concerned, to carry out its fiscal and monetary policies.

The provision of credit to customers in the form of overdrafts and loans of various types is reflected in the item Advances. Some other services of the bank are reflected in the list of subsidiary companies which accompanies the group balance sheet (Appendix 3). We shall return to the commercial banks' services in later chapters.

3.6 LIQUIDITY AND PROFITABILITY

Appendix 1 shows that the shareholders' and depositors' funds are invested by the bank in a variety of ways. Some of the assets are held because they are liquid (i.e., are either in the form of cash or could be fairly easily turned into cash), and some are invested longer term in gilt-edged stocks, but the majority are lent out to produce the highest possible return in the form of advances and hire-purchase contracts.

A bank has the difficult task of striking a balance between using its borrowed funds in a liquid fashion in order to be able to repay depositors on demand (or within the period of notice where deposits are term deposits), and investing them in longer-term – and hence more profitable – ways. The high returns from lending enable a bank to meet its shareholders' expectations of a good dividend and a build-up of sound reserves, but the proportion of deposits invested in this way must be limited in order to stay sufficiently liquid. Experience has helped in striking the balance, of course, particularly the experience of those banks which have run into difficulties in the past in meeting depositors' demands for repayment and which have had to close their doors (or have had to be helped to survive by the other banks). Another important factor which these difficulties have highlighted is that not only must the proportion of deposits lent out as advances be limited, but also that the advances themselves must be spread out over a wide range of industries. This was clearly demonstrated during the secondary bank crisis in 1974 when some of the smaller banks (which became known as secondary banks) ran into difficulties through lending excessively to property companies. The property market was depressed, and property companies could not repay their loans without making losses on property in which they had invested. Property taken by banks as security for advances could similarly not easily be sold without incurring losses. In Chapter 14 we shall see how widely the London clearing banks spread their advances over all sectors of industry and commerce.

In the past, the Bank of England's directives have helped in establishing a reasonable balance between liquidity and profitability. Prior to 1971 the clearing banks were required to maintain a minimum cash ratio of 8 per cent (of customers' deposits) and a minimum liquidity ratio of 28 per cent of deposits, made up of cash on hand (including balances at the Bank of England) call money and bills discounted. From 1971–80, all banks were required to maintain a minimum reserve ratio of $12\frac{1}{2}$ per cent (reduced to 10 per cent in 1981), i.e. specified reserve assets as a proportion of eligible liabilities. Since 1981, the Bank of England has not specified any reserve ratio but has instead relied upon its supervisory powers – as reinforced by the Banking Act 1979 – to require an individual bank to increase its holdings of liquid assets. The Bank of England requires information about the maturity dates of assets such as government stocks held by a bank, and would soon bring its influence to bear if it was not satisfied with the liquidity situation of a particular bank.

3.7 IMPORTANT RATIOS

Although the Bank of England no longer prescribes minimum ratios which must be maintained – apart from the requirement that $\frac{1}{2}$ per cent of eligible liabilities must be held on a non-operational account with the Bank, and that at least $2\frac{1}{2}$ per cent must be in secured advances to the discount houses – a prudent bank must maintain a close check on a number of ratios.

The amount of *cash on hand* (including balances at the Bank of England) is, as we have seen, of particular significance because it is the bank's first line of defence against the day to day cash requirements of its customers. It must be able to repay current account balances on demand and other deposits at the expiry of the notice period, otherwise a run on the bank could develop. Once a depositor finds that the cash he demands is not forthcoming, and he tells other depositors or maybe the press, a lack of confidence develops and spreads very rapidly unless drastic action is taken to obtain additional cash and to convince depositors that the failure to pay would not recur. Experience has shown that the old traditional cash ratio of 8 per cent of cash to deposits is unnecessarily high, and in recent years the clearing banks have maintained a ratio of about 2 per cent of deposits.

The other liquid assets – Money at call, Bills discounted and Dealing assets – should provide an adequate stock of readily-realisable assets which could be utilised to provide additional cash if and when necessary. Apart from ensuring the discount houses have the minimum amount prescribed – $2\frac{1}{2}$ per cent of eligible liabilities, 5 per cent longer term, see above – the bank is able to vary its call money and holdings of Treasury bills and commercial bills in the light of yield advantages, but it is unlikely that a bank would consider it wise to let its liquidity ratio (Cash, Money at call and Bills discounted and Dealing assets as a proportion of Deposits) fall much below 15 per cent.

Of the other assets, those which must be regarded as longer term, Advances are the most profitable, but as has already been indicated a bank must be wary of putting too high a proportion of its resources into this asset. A bank would wish to invest a sizeable proportion of its deposits directly or indirectly into the public sector through cash (notes and coin issued by the Bank of England), balances with the Bank of England, call money (some of which is invested by the discount houses in government stocks and Treasury bills) and in Treasury bills and investments in gilt-edged stocks. Of the assets other than Advances only the bank's holdings of Commercial Bills and Trade Investments plus Investments in Associated Companies constitute a flow of funds to the private sector.

Since their involvement in the wholesale money markets in recent years the banks have been able to manage their liabilities in line with their lending; this is known as *asset and liability management*. If a bank decides to increase it advances it can buy in sufficient wholesale deposits to match its commitment and is no longer obliged to wait until sufficient retail deposits are received.

The Balance sheet (Appendix 1) has been reproduced as published in the 1982 Annual Report and Accounts of the National Westminster Bank; it therefore contains much detail which the student reader could not reasonably be expected to memorise and reproduce in answering an examination question. A simplified specimen banking group balance sheet is therefore given in Appendix 4 (page 233), and the wise student will commit this to memory so that in answering a question about a bank's need for liquidity, for instance, he or she will be able to write the balance sheet down and then use it to illustrate the written answer, drawing the facts and figures from the balance sheet to support the points made.

3.8 PROTECTING DEPOSITORS' FUNDS

From what has already been written in this chapter, it will be clear that one of the reasons why a bank seeks to strike a balance between liquidity and profitability – and must adopt a sound lending policy – is to protect depositors' funds. Similarly, the Bank of England's activities as supervisor of the banks (requiring banks to increase their stock of liquid assets, if necessary) are concerned with ensuring that a bank is able to repay its depositors. The Banking Act 1979 provided additional protection for these funds by establishing the deposit protection fund, to which recognised banks and licensed institutions were compelled to contribute about £5-6 million.

In the event of the failure of a deposit-taking institution, its customers would be compensated from the fund to the extent of 75 per cent of their deposits up to a maximum deposit for each customer of £10 000. Whilst not giving complete protection to the depositor, the introduction of this fund goes a considerable way towards doing so. The majority of depositors must surely have less than £10 000, and similarly the smaller business customers are also likely to get the maximum protection provided by the scheme. Further protection for depositors arises from the fact that by controlling the creation of credit (and hence restricting the money supply) the Bank of England pursues the government's monetary policy designed to curb inflation, i.e. a fall in the value of money. If rising prices can be minimised, serious loss in the real value of bank customers' deposits will be avoided.

We need then to know what is meant by the 'creation of credit', and how it is controlled.

3.9 CREATION OF CREDIT

Banks create credit by making loans – inasmuch as every loan that a bank makes is likely to find its way back into the banking system as a deposit – and bank deposits constitute credit. To understand this, it is necessary to follow a sum of money through the banking system, when we shall see that not only does a deposit with a bank enable it to lend money and hence create a fresh deposit, but that deposits several times the size of the original deposit may in fact be created.

A deposit of £1 000 000 with Barclays would be used (as we saw in our examination of a bank balance sheet), to acquire assets that will produce an income, but Barclays must be prudent and keep some of this as cash in order to meet requests for repayment. Let us assume for the purpose of illustration that Barclays and all the other main banks keep back 10 per cent of any fresh deposit, and lend the remaining 90 per cent by way of advances. Barclays' balance sheet will be affected in the following way:

Barclays Bank

£		£
Deposits + 1 000 000	Cash on Hand	
	and with Bank of England	+ 100 000
	Advances	+ 900 000

The customer that borrows the £900 000 will do so for a purpose. The company concerned will be wanting to acquire some assets, maybe plant and equipment; let us assume that these are purchased from a customer of Lloyds Bank. That bank will keep £90 000 in cash and lend £810 000, and the balance sheet will change as follows:

Lloyds Bank

£		£
Deposits + 900 000	Cash on Hand	
	and with Bank of England	+ 90 000
	Advances	+ 810 000

This process will continue, with a deposit of £810 000 being created by the loan of that amount. Then 90 per cent will be lent (£729 000), and 90 per cent of that, and so on until the size of the new deposit is whittled down to a negligible amount. The end result of this credit-creating process will be that the original deposit of £1 000 000 will have created deposits of £10 000 000, i.e. there will be a multiplier of 10. This particular multiplier has functioned because only 10 per cent of each fresh deposit was kept in liquid form. If the banks had decided to maintain a $12\frac{1}{2}$ per cent ratio then the multiplier would have been 8, which is calculated as follows:

$$\frac{100}{12\frac{1}{2}} = 8$$

In reality the banking system – and indeed the money markets – are extremely complex, and it is not possible to determine what the credit creation multiplier is. Nevertheless it is clear that credit creation does occur and hence it is important that the government, through the Bank of England, should control it, otherwise the money supply (which is made up mostly of bank deposits) will increase rapidly and beyond the needs of the community, with inflationary effects. At such times the Bank of England will attempt to syphon off some of the fresh deposits coming into the banks by its 'open market operations', or possibly by special deposits, and to the extent that the government prunes back its own expenditure it may ensure that less funds are flowing from the public to the private sector. In that the banks hold the deposits of the private sector, the growth in fresh deposits will thus be stemmed. The reader will appreciate that in our example of the credit creation process we assumed that 90 per cent of each fresh deposit was used to make an advance. If instead, as is most likely, only 70 per cent was advanced to the private sector and the remaining 30 per cent was used to acquire a deposit at the Bank of England, Treasury bills and government stocks, this 30 per cent would be going into the public sector. This leakage into the public sector would cut down the size of the multiplier if the funds were not used to pay for goods and services from the private sector.

Our original deposit of £1 000 000 must have originated from the public sector (or possibly from overseas) for the multiplier process to work. If the deposit was in the form of a cheque drawn by a customer of another bank, then that bank's cash base would have been eroded, and it would have been necessary for it to cut back its lending in order to maintain its cash ratio at a safe level. This would have the opposite effect to the creation of credit process started by Barclays, and as far as the banking system as a whole is concerned the net effect would be for total deposits to remain unchanged. The credit creation process thus hinges very much upon the amount of public sector spending plus the ability of the Bank of England to *control* the money markets. We will defer a more thorough examination of monetary policy until Chapter 7.

TOPICS FOR DISCUSSION

1. Discuss what is meant by the term 'commercial bank'; which banks in the UK come into this category?
   If you live abroad, which of your country's banks are commercial banks and which are simply savings banks?
2. Obtain the balance sheet of one of the large clearing banks in Britain, or in your own country, and from it discuss the manner in which the bank has struck a balance between its responsibilities to shareholders and to depositors.
3. What does the balance sheet in 2 above tell you about the services provided by the bank?
4. Discuss the credit-creation process, and why it is necessary for it to be controlled.

CHAPTER 4

UK FINANCIAL MARKETS

4.1 SHORT-TERM MONEY MARKETS

The banking system which we looked at very broadly in Chapter 1 is the major short-term money market. The banks borrow mostly on a short-term basis by accepting deposits from their customers and through acquiring wholesale funds; they also lend in the main on a short-term basis, though there is now a tendency to lend on longer term. Included in this very important money market, you will recall, are the Bank of England, the London, Scottish and Northern Ireland clearing banks, the merchant banks, British overseas banks, foreign banks, consortium banks, the National Savings Bank, the TSBs and the National Girobank.

Another important part of the short-term money market is the London discount market, comprising the discount houses, the money brokers and a number of specialist institutions. The discount houses are in fact recognised banks under the provisions of the Banking Act 1979, but they have a highly specialised role, acting as a buffer between the commercial banks and the Bank of England, and it is for this reason that they have not been included in Chapter 1 as forming part of the UK banking system. We shall need to examine their role in some detail later in this chapter, and especially their inter-relationship with other institutions.

If we take together the banks, the discount market and licensed deposit-takers such as the hire-purchase finance houses, but exclude the National Savings Bank, we arrive at the 'monetary sector', through which the monetary authorities (the Bank of England and the Treasury) pursue their monetary policy. We shall refer to this again in Chapter 7.

All the institutions in the monetary sector operate in the other short-term money markets – the bill markets, the inter-bank market, the market for certificates of deposit, the Euro-currency market, and the foreign exchange market. These are known as the Parallel Markets in that they run side by side with the financial institutions in the monetary sector. Let us now examine each of these in turn.

Bill markets

Under this heading we must consider three different markets which are nevertheless very much inter-related. These are the Treasury bill, commercial bill and local authorities markets. The Treasury bill issue was discussed in Chapter 2. It provides a market in a security which is short term in that Treasury bills are normally issued for 91 days, and as they are bought and sold in the market so the length of time to maturity shortens. They are issued by the government and are therefore an undoubted security which can easily be resold, and the rate of interest is in line with other money market rates. They are thus a *liquid asset* which the banks would want to hold, and in that they are dated at varying days of the week (even though the tender takes place on Fridays) they provide a means whereby the banks can build up portfolios of bills maturing on each day of the week, thus ensuring that they have a flow of incoming funds each morning from which to meet the day's commitments.

In the commercial bills market bills which have been drawn by companies are bought and sold. These bills are a means of obtaining finance and if they are *accepted* by the drawer's bank they become bank bills which attract a more favourable rate of discount. By *accepting* a bill, the acceptor undertakes to pay it upon maturity, and thus when a bank does this on behalf of a customer it is taking on a responsibility for which it quite reasonably will charge a fee (and, furthermore, will take it on only if it is satisfied that the customer concerned is creditworthy).

Commercial bills are issued for varying periods, usually no more than six months – for instance one month, two months or three months (maybe 30, 60 or 90 days) – and thus they are liquid assets suitable for inclusion in the banks' portfolios.

The local authorities' market is concerned mostly with bills of exchange issued by local authorities and having a tenor of no more than six months, which means that they are suitable for inclusion in the banks' holdings of reserve assets. This market is also concerned with the issue of long-term bonds, but these of course do not fall within the province of the short-term markets we are now considering.

Inter-bank market

Through this market banks with surplus funds make them available to other banks who need to raise funds. The inter-bank market has grown into the largest of the secondary markets (i.e., the markets outside the main short-term market, in other words the banks). Very large sums of money are dealt in and loans are made for periods up to six months. The

London Inter-bank Offered Rate (LIBOR) is a very influential rate of interest (see p. 195).

Market for certificates of deposit

Very closely allied to the inter-bank market is the certificate of deposit market. Certificates of deposit (see p. 31) are issued in multiples of £10 000 up to £500 000 against deposits by customers of the banks. They are deposits for fixed periods of up to a year, and at an agreed rate of interest. The holder of a certificate of deposit cannot redeem it until maturity but as it is a bearer certificate he can sell it and it will be held by a bank or other financial institution as an investment.

Euro-currency market

A Euro-currency deposit is one held by a bank operating outside the country whose currency it is. For instance a Euro-sterling deposit would be a deposit of sterling in France or some other country outside the UK. The major Euro-currency is the Euro-dollar, and the main centre for Euro-dollars is London; the London Euro-currency market is thus primarily concerned with US dollars, dollar deposits which are outside the control of the US monetary authorities and the ownership of which can freely be transferred from hand to hand on a temporary short-term basis.

The prefix *Euro* is somewhat misleading, as there are Euro-currency markets in many parts of the world in addition to Europe, but the name was derived from the fact that the first Euro-currency – the Euro-dollar – originated in Western Europe where the holders were wanting to deposit them away from the USA for political reasons, or in order to obtain higher interest rates than those available in the USA (especially when, by virtue of Regulation Q, US banks were forbidden to pay interest rates beyond a fixed level in order to attract deposits).

A very sizeable pool of dollars built up in Europe as the result of Defence Aid and Marshall aid (and more latterly as the result of the quadrupling of oil prices in the 1970s, which greatly increased the dollar earnings of the Middle East oil companies). Other factors have been the activities of large US multinational companies in Europe whose earnings have been deposited in the Euro-dollar market; the substantial US balance of payments deficits which have resulted in large US dollar payments to European countries; and (at one stage) the very strict exchange control restrictions in the UK, which made it difficult for the financing of international trade in sterling and caused banks to resort to the borrowing of dollars for this purpose.

Euro-currencies are borrowed and lent, and hence quotations for them appear in the financial press as interest rates. The quotations are 'double-barrelled' – e.g., $11\frac{1}{4}$–$11\frac{1}{2}$ per cent – the lower rate being the rate that the banks are paying on deposits and the higher rate applicable to loans of the Euro-currency concerned. The margin between the two rates is very narrow but as transactions are for large sums of money (for example, £1 million or $2 million), the profits to the banks are quite substantial.

Although currency deposits are borrowed – and hence repayable at the end of an agreed period – they can nevertheless be bought and sold as well. For instance, an exporter who is to receive a certain sum in dollars in three months' time for goods he has sold abroad can anticipate the payment by borrowing an equivalent sum in Euro-dollars for three months and selling the dollars immediately for sterling. When he receives his payment of dollars he is able to repay the Euro-currency loan. In this way he can make use of the sterling proceeds from the sale of the Euro-dollars, and the cost of doing so is the rate of interest he pays on the Euro-currency loan. He also avoids the exchange risk, because instead of selling his dollars in three months' time at whatever rate of exchange is applicable at the time, he is able to sell dollars at the *spot rate*. If he were to take the alternative course of action to avoid the exchange risk – i.e., to enter into a forward exchange contract to sell the dollars in three months' time – he would incur an expense if the forward rate was at a discount (though he would gain if it was at a premium) and, furthermore, would not have immediate access to the sterling equivalent.

Euro-currencies may be borrowed for a variety of other uses. Anyone who has an immediate payment to make (such as an importer) may find it expedient to borrow the currency required in a Euro-currency rather than in sterling, and speculators will take advantage of any Euro-currency that is relatively cheap to borrow if it can be switched into sterling at an advantageous rate of exchange and the sterling proceeds invested to produce a favourable yield. Multinational companies can also use the Euro-currency market to invest surplus funds, or to switch funds between the companies in the group.

Euro-currency loans are made for various periods of time. Quotations in the press are for overnight, seven days, one month, three months, six months and a year, but quotations are available in the market for longer terms of up to five years or more. In addition to quotations for Euro-dollars and Euro-sterling, rates of interest are also quoted for Canadian dollars, Dutch guilders, Swiss francs, Deutschemarks, French francs, Italian lira, Belgium francs, Japanese yen, Danish krone and Asian dollars (Singapore).

Some of the larger Euro-currency loans (usually referred to as *Euro-credits*), are provided by the consortium banks or other groups of banks who get together to provide possibly as much as $1000 million for up to 10 years. Such loans are usually for governments or for government-sponsored institutions, and in recent years the less developed countries

(LDCs) have been provided with considerable amounts of finance by this means.

Large business corporations, or possibly nationalised institutions or municipal authorities who need to borrow long term, and would normally do so by issuing bonds, may decide to issue them in Euro-currency if the terms of borrowing are more favourable. There is a large *Euro-bond market*, in which the banks and other financial institutions take an active part.

Foreign exchange market

The foreign exchange market in London comprises all the foreign exchange dealing departments of the banks and foreign exchange brokers, all of which are in constant touch with one another through an excellent system of telecommunications. They are also in direct contact with banks overseas. Such instantaneous contact both at home and overseas provides the nearest approach possible to the economist's concept of a perfect market. The market deals in homogeneous 'commodities' such as sterling, francs, marks and dollars, and because buyers and sellers are aware of prices being asked and charged throughout the market there tends to be only one price for a currency in terms of another currency - i.e., a rate of exchange - at any one time.

The prime purpose of the foreign exchange market is to provide the foreign currencies which importers and others with payments to make need to buy, and at the same time to provide a means whereby those who earn foreign currencies can sell them in exchange for sterling. Trading and investing overseas would be impossible without the market's provision of the means of payment, and also its determination of prices for currencies. These prices are published daily in the press in the form of spot and forward exchange rate tables, and up to the minute quotations can be obtained through the banks - though such quotations would be necessary only for very large transactions. For the vast majority of transactions, the branches of the banks receive a table of rates each morning for use during the day which reflect those quoted in the press.

With the abolition of exchange control the foreign exchange market has become one in which and through which short-term investments can be made, purchasing currencies that are likely to appreciate (or, for instance, having acquired Euro-dollars the holder could sell them for sterling and use the proceeds to invest in, say, local authority bills). He or she could at the same time buy the dollars back in the forward exchange market to be paid for out of the proceeds of the local authority bills when they mature. To the banks and other large international companies the use of the foreign exchange market has to be looked at side by side with the other short-term markets when deciding what to do with funds available for investment.

4.2 THE LONDON DISCOUNT MARKET

Development of the market

The London discount market consists of 9 discount houses (now recognised banks), plus a number of smaller houses that specialise in particular fields such as dealing in bullion or as stockjobbers. The 9 discount houses are members of the London Discount Market Association, and as such have the privilege of being able to borrow from the Bank of England as lender of last resort.

The discount houses originated as institutions that would discount commercial bills of exchange - i.e., they would buy bills of exchange for their face value less discount. The discount represented a rate of interest charged for paying over money which was not going to be recouped until the bill matured and was presented for payment. An example of an inland bill of exchange is given in Figure 10.1, and you should refer to it at this stage if you have not seen one before. Before a discount house would discount a bill, it would have to be satisfied with the *reputation* of the parties concerned with it - i.e., the drawer (and, more especially, the drawee and acceptor). It will be appreciated that the discount house relies on the integrity of the person who is expected to pay the bill at its maturity. This would usually be the drawee (i.e., the person on whom the bill is drawn), and he or she will undertake to pay it by writing an *acceptance* across the face of the bill; but he or she may arrange for some other person (or institution) such as a bank to accept the bill and it is then upon that person that the discount house relies for payment, though it nevertheless has recourse to the drawee as well. The full legal responsibilities of the parties to a bill of exchange are examined in Chapter 9, which deals with negotiable instruments.

Through the discounting of bills the discount houses provided a vital service in the UK prior to the establishment of the network of branch banks in the latter part of the 19th century. They facilitated the movement of funds by discounting for industrialists and merchants bills which they resold to the banks that were looking for ways of investing surplus funds. Once the banks took over the role of transferring the use of funds by accepting deposits of the wealthy through their branch networks and lending them to those in need of working capital (e.g., industrialists in other areas), the need for domestic bills of exchange diminished. Similarly the increased use of cheques as a means of payment also reduced the reliance on bills of exchange for this purpose. Instead the discount houses concentrated more on the discounting of bills drawn in connection with overseas trade, and this activity flourished until the outbreak of the First World War in 1914.

The disruption of international trade caused by the First World War motivated the discount houses to look for a new form of investment to replace foreign bills of exchange. At the same time the government was in need of additional short-term funds to pursue the war and their mutual needs were satisfied by the introduction of the Treasury bill (see p. 21). The discount houses invested large sums of borrowed money in these bills (and still do), thereby locking such funds up for a maximum of only three months in a security which was safe and which could be readily sold in the money market to banks and other financial institutions.

The discount houses quickly established a market in these bills making a modest turn on each Treasury bill handled, and even today a large proportion of Treasury bills put up to tender each week is acquired by the discount houses to be resold in the market. Indeed the discount houses have an understanding with the Bank of England that they will tender for all the Treasury bills in competition with one another, and with other bidders. The government is thus assured that all the bills will be taken up, and in return guarantees that it will act as lender of last resort for the discount houses, and only for them.

The government resorted to additional means of satisfying its borrowing needs during the Second World War, allowing its Treasury bill issue to decline in size, though subsequently it was restored in importance and still plays an important part in the acquisition of short-term funds by the government. The government borrowed direct from the banks by way of Treasury deposit receipts during the war period, and increased its issues of stocks. As a new outlet for their funds the discount houses set up a market in these government stocks, building up portfolios of them at varying maturity dates in order that they could satisfy the needs of the banks which at any one time would hold sufficient of each government stock to ensure that there was a steady stream of them maturing month by month and year by year.

In the postwar years, the bill of exchange re-emerged as the most important means of settlement in international trade, and also the domestic bill came back into its own mostly as a form of accommodation – i.e., a means whereby a company can get temporary finance, rather than as a means of settlement for transactions. Bills of exchange, mostly sterling bills drawn on London, now form the major part of the assets of the discount houses. Local authority bonds and bills have been issued in substantial amounts, and they are popular assets in the discount market. So too are sterling and foreign currency certificates of deposit.

Sources and uses of funds

The sources of the funds borrowed by the discount houses and the ways in which they are employed are shown in Table 4.1. The difference between the total of money borrowed and money invested represents the employment of their own capital funds.

Clearly the biggest source of funds is the UK monetary sector, from which over £5000 million was borrowed in May 1983, and the vast majority of this was on call and overnight. Call money can be called in by the banks at any time, and at best money is lent on up to a week's notice. Overnight money is lent only until the next day.

In that the discount houses borrow on such a short and tenuous basis, they must be careful to use the borrowed funds to acquire assets that are readily marketable or close to maturity. Hence we find from Table 4.1

Table 4.1 *London discount market sources and uses of borrowed funds,*
18 May 1983 (£ million)

Sources of funds	
Borrowing in sterling from	
UK monetary sector	5178
Other sources	502
Borrowing in other currencies from	
UK monetary sector	109
Other sources	28
	5817[a]
Uses of funds	
Cash deposits with Bank of England	2
Government stocks	237
Local authority investments	159
Other investments	38
Treasury bills	114
Local authority bills	146
Other sterling bills	3003
Sterling certificates of deposit	1996
Funds lent to UK monetary sector	30
Loans to local authorities	143
Other loans	31
Other sterling assets	25
Currency certificates of deposit	104
Currency bills	18
Other currency assets	17
	6063

[a] of which £5272 million was on call or overnight basis.
Source: *Bank of England Quarterly Bulletin*, June 1983.

that a sizeable amount is invested in gilt-edged securities (government and government-backed stocks, bonds and bills) which can usually be sold quite easily. Similarly certificates of deposit issued by banks are quite safe, as are loans to them and to local authorities. The large amount invested in bills of exchange will have been so invested that the discount houses have a large proportion nearing maturity, and in any case they will not buy bills unless they have good names on them as drawer and drawee or acceptor.

Buffer for the banks

The ways in which the discount houses have developed during the 20th century have led them, no doubt unintentionally, into the role of acting as a buffer between the banks and the Bank of England, and to play a vital role in the implementation of the government's monetary policy. Rather than borrow themselves direct from the Bank of England when liquidity is tight, the commercial banks have preferred instead to lend on a call money basis to the discount houses, and to squeeze them when they are short of funds. It is therefore the discount houses which have to sell bills to the Bank of England as lender of last resort.

The Bank of England can always inject funds into the money market if it wants to by buying eligible bills, and thus avoid a tight situation occurring, but there are times when it deliberately forces the discount houses to borrow from it at a relatively higher rate of interest in order to force up interest rates (or, at least, stop them from falling). This action is also connected with the weekly Treasury bill tender at which the Treasury bill rate of interest – one of the key market rates of interest – is determined. We shall come back to this subject in Chapter 7.

Transactions with the banks

Each day the discount houses are informed by the banks how much call money is to be called in, or if any further funds are forthcoming through additional call money. The banks may also be willing to buy stocks, bills, certificates of deposits, etc. from the discount houses if they need them to build up their portfolios of regularly maturing securities, but will buy only if the prices are right. The discount houses provide a service to the banks in ensuring a steady supply of these assets, but some haggling may well take place before they change hands. When funds are plentiful the discount houses are in a better position to hold on to their assets unless a better price is paid and similarly the interest rates they have to pay for call money will be lower than at other times when funds are scarce.

During the day each discount house takes stock of the situation to ascertain whether it needs to borrow more or whether it has surplus funds, and it will do this in the light of its transactions with the banks and of the forecasts from the Bank of England as to the likely shortage (or surplus) of funds in the money market generally. It will endeavour to rectify whichever of these situations in which it finds itself in order to balance its books at the end of the day. It must borrow if it is short of funds, and it will not wish to have any funds that are not invested at the close of business. Telephone calls are made to banks and other financial institutions during the day, and as a last resort the discount house must borrow from the Bank of England if the Bank will not buy bills.

The Bank of England keeps a close eye on the flow of funds during each working day, and will decide what action to take if funds are short. If as a matter of policy it decides not to force the discount houses to borrow from itself, it will give assistance – by buying bills either from the discount houses or from the banks to enable them to increase their call money loans to the discount houses. When the discount houses borrow from the banks (or, as a last resort, from the Bank of England), they must put up security for these advances by way of parcels of bills or stocks. These are transported by hand together with any bills or other securities purchased by the banks during the day.

4.3 MERCHANT BANKS

In Chapter 3, although we referred to the merchant banks as being part of commercial banking, we concentrated on the services of the clearing banks, examining a typical balance sheet of such a bank in order to highlight the bank's functions and responsibilities.

It is important in the context of this chapter to look more closely at the activities of the merchant banks, and if we compare a composite balance sheet of the merchant banks with that of the London clearing banks the differences in their modes of operation will become clearly apparent (see Table 4.2).

Acceptance of bills

The merchant banks originated as institutions which accepted bills of exchange on behalf of their customers. The bankers were themselves wealthy merchants of international repute, and so highly respected and trusted that if they could be persuaded to add their names to bills of exchange these bills became readily discountable in the London discount market at the lowest rate of interest. By accepting a bill of exchange, the acceptor undertakes to pay it at the date of maturity, and no banker is going to undertake such a task on behalf of a customer unless he is really sure of his creditworthiness. Like the American Express card such an acceptance says quite a lot about the person or firm concerned!

The merchant bank's willingness to accept bills on behalf of the customer (a British importer, maybe) was often signified in the form of a letter, and this was the origin of the *acceptance credit*, the issue of which is a major activity of a merchant bank. The bank lends its name and (but not necessarily its money) to its customer. It trusts that by the time bills which it has accepted are presented for payment, there will be sufficient funds in the customer's account to meet them, and hence no borrowing will be involved. The customer will have been able to borrow, however, by discounting the bill with a London discount house, and it is the discounter of the bill that in effect lends the money to him until the date of maturity.

The merchant bank charges a commission for opening an acceptance credit, and for accepting bills, and makes a profit from such a commission rather than from interest on lending to the importer. This is not to say that the merchant banks do not lend money – they certainly do, as we shall see later – but traditionally their function has not been to accept deposits from customers and use these funds to lend by way of loans and overdrafts.

The wealthy merchant banker found that his activities as an acceptor of bills were lucrative, and dropped his trading activities in favour of the acceptance business. The merchant banks became known as accepting houses and today they include such well-known names as Baring Bros, Lazard Bros, and Rothschild and Sons, which are members of the Accepting Houses Committee. These are not the only banks that accept bills of exchange, of course (most banks offer this facility), but acceptances account for a much greater part of a merchant bank's activities than is the case with, for instance, the clearing banks.

Other functions

The accepting houses are also members of a much larger association, the Issuing Houses Association. Issuing house services are another very important function of a merchant bank.

An issuing house has traditionally been responsible for advising and assisting corporate bodies in the issue of shares; helping partnerships and private companies to 'go public', i.e. to issue shares as public companies; and helping public companies in obtaining additional capital by issuing new shares and debentures. They have also helped governments and government institutions to obtain the finance they need. In the years since the Second World War they have been very much involved in the takeovers and mergers that have taken place, steering through the very delicate and intricate negotiations that these involve.

A private company can 'go public' in three ways. The issuing house may publish a *prospectus* inviting the general public to apply to buy shares. This prospectus is printed in the national newspapers, and gives the history of the company, including its profits in recent years, and an indication of its prospects.

Secondly the issue may be made by *placing* some of the shares with institutional or company investors who are willing to buy them, and the remainder are offered for sale to the general public.

The third method is an *offer for sale*, and involves the issuing house in buying all of the shares and then offering them to the general public later. In effect the issuing house acts as an underwriter in this instance, in that it undertakes to buy the shares and the new company is assured that it will receive all the capital it requires.

When shares are sold by prospectus the services of an underwriter are also required, and this will not necessarily be an issuing house. The underwriter agrees to take up any shares which are not applied for by the public and charges a fee for its services.

When an issue of new shares is about to take place, an application is made to the Stock Exchange Council for the company to be listed, and if this is agreed to the shares will be quoted on the Stock Exchange from a few days after the shares have been allocated to the successful applicants who are from then on able to resell the shares through the Stock Exchange.

Other activities of the merchant banks include borrowing and lending in the Euro-currency markets, making and arranging medium- and long-term loans, issuing and dealing in certificates of deposit, foreign exchange dealing, gold and silver bullion, commodity dealing, insurance broking and managing investment portfolios for both private and corporate customers. They are also involved in factoring and in leasing.

Whilst in the past those merchant banks which are members of the Accepting Houses Committee specialised in lending their names rather than money – i.e., accepted bills of exchange – this is no longer the case. Their total deposits both in sterling and in other currencies have risen quite rapidly, and so too have their advances. At the same time, the London clearing banks have become involved (either directly or indirectly) in merchant banking so that the distinctions between the two types of banks are now much less apparent – though, as Table 4.2 shows, the distinctions still exist. The table compares the combined balance sheet totals of the 17 accepting houses with those of the London clearing banks, and shows that both types of institution have enormous sums of money deposited with them. As is to be expected in view of their relative sizes and differences in emphasis, however, the total sterling deposits of the accepting houses are only about a tenth as large as those of the clearing banks. The total of other currency deposits of the accepting houses is, however, half the size of those of the clearing banks, and demonstrates the importance of transactions in foreign currencies to the accepting houses.

Table 4.2 balance sheet totals London clearing banks and accepting houses, 18 May 1983 (£m)

	Clearing banks	% of assets	Accepting houses	% of assets
Liabilities				
Sterling deposits				
UK monetary sector	7 543	8.0	1 552	7.0
UK public sector	1 028	1.0	94	0.4
UK private sector	47 366	48.0	4 323	21.0
Overseas	4 419	4.0	866	4.0
Certificates of deposit	3 232	3.0	465	2.0
	63 588	64.0	7 300	35.0
(of which sight deposits)	(22 157)		(1 645)	
Other currency deposits				
UK monetary sector	3 406	3.0	3 492	17.0
Other UK	2 252	2.0	1 122	5.0
Overseas	15 502	16.0	6 494	31.0
Certificates of deposit	1 569	2.0	225	1.0
	22 729	23.0	11 333	54.0
Other liabilities	13 163	13.0	2 389	11.0
Total liabilities	99 480		21 023	
Eligible liabilities	50 668		3 300	

Assets				
Notes and coin, balances with Bank of England, bills	2 683	3.0	59	—
Market loans				
LDMA (secured)	2 885	3.0	207	1.0
Other monetary sector	7 743	8.0	2 903	14.0
Certificates of deposit	609		739	3.0
UK local authorities	276	1.0	605	3.0
Overseas	126		254	1.0
Advances	47 359	47.0	3 280	16.0
Investments	5 339	6.0	605	3.0
Other currency assets	23 911	24.0	10 913	52.0
Other assets	8 549	8.0	1 457	7.0
	99 480		21 023	
Acceptances	1 357		2 800	

Note: Because some of the figures for individual items have been rounded up or down the columns do not add up to the totals given in some cases.
Source: *Bank of England Quarterly Bulletin*, June 1983.

Two other important facts emerge from Table 4.2:

1. The accepting houses take far less private sector sterling deposits than the clearing banks. This is a reflection of the fact that the clearing banks are the High Street banks which offer services to the general public, whereas the merchant banks accept more of their deposits on a wholesale basis, especially those in foreign currencies.
2. The accepting houses keep much smaller cash balances and bills than the clearing banks. This is a further reflection of the fact that they do not have branch networks through which customers require cash transactions.

4.4 TRUSTEE SAVINGS BANKS (TSBs)

Origin and development

The Savings Bank Act 1817 marks the origin of the TSBs though there were some small savings banks in existence prior to that Act. The Act made it compulsory for depositors' funds to be invested in a separate account at the Bank of England and managed by the National Debt Commissioners. A fixed rate of interest was paid on these funds to the banks. The managers or trustees of the banks looked after their depositors' funds on a voluntary basis, and had legal responsibilities laid down by a subsequent Act in 1863.

Whereas in 1819 there were 465 individual banks, by 1974 these had been reduced by amalgamations to 72. In that year dramatic changes both in the structure of the TSBs and in the services that they provided took place, which brought the banks much more in line with the commercial banks though their services are still primarily for the private individual. It is appropriate, therefore, to examine these changes in some detail.

The movement of these banks towards commercial banking is highlighted by the fact that although they are listed in the Banking Act 1979 as exempted institutions, it was intended that this should be only a temporary arrangement, and that therefore they may soon have to become licensed institutions (and, most likely, recognised banks). They will then be brought within the direct control of the Bank of England and also have to contribute to the deposit protection fund.

The *Page Report*'s recommendations, which were put into effect from 1974, included a provision that the 72 TSBs should be drastically reduced so as to form a small number of regional banks with branches. They were in fact reduced to 18 banks plus a central TSB. Further amalgamations have since taken place and now there are only four banks – the TSB England and Wales, the TSB Scotland, and banks in Northern Ireland and the Channel Islands operating under a holding company called the TSB

Group. It is expected that the banks will go public in 1985, but before this can be done a further Act of Parliament will be necessary.

The Trustee Savings Bank Act 1976, which put the Page Report recommendations into effect, freed the TSBs from having to invest their depositors' funds with the National Debt Commissioners, and instead permitted them to invest these deposits in a wide variety of ways, including advances to their customers. The fact that the banks are now able to *lend money* (and have done so very extensively) has done more than anything to bring the TSBs much more in line with the clearing banks. Previously they were very much only savings banks and (even though they had been providing their current account customers with cheque books since the 1960s), they were held back from competing seriously with the high street banks by the lack of this third main facility.

TSB services

The TSBs have brought their accounts very much in line with the other banks, offering current and deposit accounts. Many of the old ordinary accounts still exist on which customers earn interest at 4 per cent, but the tax-free concession was removed in 1979.

Cheques can be drawn on current accounts, and provided a customer maintains a minimum balance of £100 no charge is made on the account. The banks have their own internal clearing system and the TSB England and Wales is a functional member of the Bankers' Clearing House in London.

Deposit accounts attract interest at a rate tied to the bank's base rate; seven days' notice is required for withdrawals. Term deposits attract higher rates of interest, depending upon the term involved, and the interest may either be fixed at the outset for the whole period or variable with base rate.

Money may also be deposited on Marketlink account, subject to a minimum deposit of £10 000. Interest is calculated on a day to day basis at 1 per cent below base rate. The balance must remain above £10 000 or the interest reverts to the ordinary deposit rate. There is also a contractual savings scheme over a five-year period which includes guaranteed life cover and on which the rate of interest is around $1\frac{1}{2}$-2 per cent above the normal deposit rate.

Loans and overdrafts are provided for customers in very similar ways to those of the clearing banks. The rate of interest charged varies with base rate, and the margin above this rate depends upon whether the advance is secured, the purpose of the loan and the status of the customer, and ranges from 2-7 per cent above. On home improvement loans and personal loans interest is charged on the whole amount for the whole period of the loan, but this does not apply for improvement loans above £5000, where normal loan terms would be charged.

Depositors may enter into a Moneyplan whereby they arrange for an automatic transfer of a set amount each month to a Moneyplan account, and are granted a credit limit of 30 times the monthly amount. They receive interest on any outstanding credit balance and pay interest on a debit balance on a day to day basis.

The TSBs were amongst the first of the banks to offer house mortgage loans, and a substantial proportion of deposits has been invested in this way. Loans are made at a rate of interest which is competitive with those of other banks and of the building societies, and this rate is changed only when necessary to bring it in line, i.e. it does not automatically follow changes in base rate.

In addition to cheque guarantee cards, issued on a similar basis to those of the clearing banks, the TSBs issue Trustcards. These are credit cards comparable to Barclaycards, and are also part of the international VISA network, and if the credit card holder chooses not to pay his monthly account in full within the prescribed period he is charged interest at, for example, $1\frac{3}{4}$ per cent per month on the outstanding balance. He is, of course, given a credit limit and a minimum monthly repayment is prescribed.

Other services which the TSBs offer, and which are provided on a similar basis to those of the clearing banks, are shown in Table 4.3.

Table 4.3 *TSB services*

Travellers' cheques and other travel facilities – foreign currency and travel insurance

Bankers' drafts, MT and TT (see Chapter 12)

Purchase and sale of stock exchange securities

Standing orders and direct debits

Credit transfers

Insurance services

Safe custodies

Cash dispensers

For solicitors wishing to remit funds on behalf of their clients on the completion of house purchases, the TSBs run the Speedsend service, whereby in a matter of minutes recipient branches can be informed of transfers so that the vendor's solicitors can complete the conveyances. In addition, the TSBs completely own United Dominions Trust (UDT), and hence are able to offer hire-purchase facilities to customers; Swan National (the car rental company) are a subsidiary of UDT.

The TSB Unit Trust has been in existence for some years, and its services are of course available through the bank branches.

Future developments

Since 1974 the TSBs have been transformed into a small group of banks with a total of 1650 branches and 24 000 staff, and £7000 million in funds. They have 13 million accounts held by 6 million individual customers. Of the four banks obviously the TSB England and Wales and the TSB Scotland predominate as major competitors respectively to the English and Scottish clearing banks. Developing as they have done from savings banks to 'commercial' banks they are still primarily concerned with the accounts of personal customers.

However, their commercial business is expanding quite rapidly, and it remains to be seen how these activities develop. Progress in the sphere of electronic banking has been good and many branches (especially in the Midlands and the North) have automatic service tills. As yet there have been no link-ups with other banks or building societies in this connection, but it is clearly a possibility (see also Chapter 17).

4.5 NATIONAL GIROBANK

In 1968, the Post Office introduced the National Giro (renamed National Girobank in 1978) in order to provide a means whereby depositors with the system could arrange transfers to the accounts of other depositors and might draw cheques in favour of payees who are not Girobank account holders. Account holders may also make transfers by standing orders to other Girobank accounts and to clearing bank and TSB accounts. They can also arrange to have their salaries credited to their giro accounts. The giro was originally essentially a money transmission service, and was meant to be primarily for the benefit of small account holders who previously had no bank account. Being run by the Post Office Corporation it was seen (together with the system of postal orders and money orders) as a means of transmitting money through the Post Office.

Following the transformation of the TSBs by the Trustee Savings Bank Act 1976, the government decided to improve the status and services of the National Giro. It was renamed National Girobank, permitted to make loans and overdrafts, and provide the wide range of services that the TSBs now provide. It was given listed status by the Bank of England, which meant that it had to maintain the $12\frac{1}{2}\%$ reserve ratio when it was enforced and comply with calls for special deposits as did the other banks.

A number of local authorities, government departments and large business firms now use the bank's services – the Manpower Services Commission (MSC), for example, uses the system to pay out unemployment benefits and training grants.

The National Girobank was listed as an exempted institution in the Banking Act 1979, on the grounds that it is part of a public corporation (the Post Office) and subject to supervision by the Treasury and Department of Trade and Industry. However, it is understood that although exempted it will be subject to the same prudential criteria applied to other deposit-taking institutions. It has not contributed to the deposit protection fund, but has been required to contribute an amount to the Treasury equal to that which would have been payable under the system if it had been a member of it.

4.6 LOAN AND SAVINGS AND CAPITAL MARKETS

These markets are concerned with the use of savings, and for investment on a longer-term basis than would be the case in the short-term money markets. Included under this heading are the building societies, insurance companies, pension funds and investment trusts and unit trusts. We shall examine the functions of each of these in turn.

Building societies

These are non-profit making societies owned by the shareholders, who receive interest and not dividends on their investment. There are still some deposit account holders who technically (because they are not shareholders) do not participate in affairs of the society, and in the event of liquidation they would be treated as creditors and be given preferential treatment over shareholders. However, the majority of accounts are share accounts.

Up to April 1985 building societies had one big advantage over other institutions competing for deposits, in that they paid an agreed rate of income tax on funds to be distributed as interest and hence paid interest which was free of tax. They were also open for longer hours each day than the banks and also on Saturday mornings and these two facts – interest net of tax and longer opening hours – made the building societies very competitive with the High Street banks. However, the banks now pay interest net of tax and some of them are open on Saturday mornings.

The building societies have 6500 branches and 36 million depositors, and although they do not normally issue customers with cheque books, some societies have now done so, although they have no direct access to the Bankers' Clearing House and have to use the services of a clearing bank in order to get their cheques cleared; the societies individually (and collectively through the Building Societies Association) are actively exploring electronic banking techniques in order to offer easier cash withdrawal and deposit transfer to customers. It is possible that a shared cash dispenser network will be established in the near future, and one society has already established a Homelink facility whereby customers (through a Prestel link) can view their accounts on their television sets, and pay household bills with some suppliers directly.

The supervision of the building societies is carried out by the Chief Registrar of Friendly Societies, and their range of activities is limited by the Building Societies Act 1962. They are precluded from making loans other than for property purchase, may not lend on an unsecured basis, and cannot issue cheque guarantee cards.

Building societies accept their shareholders' savings mostly on a short-term basis. On ordinary share accounts deposits are repayable on demand and the society's basic rate of interest is paid. However, somewhat longer-term deposits are attracted by offering rates of up to $1\frac{1}{2}$ per cent above the basic rate for longer-term deposits, depending upon the terms on which the deposits are taken. On a deposit subject to seven days' notice the rate of interest would possibly be $\frac{1}{2}$ per cent above the basic rate, whereas a two- or three-year deposit would attract the highest rate. Even these longer-term deposits will be repaid earlier if the depositor so requests, but usually a period of notice is required (maybe one, two or three months) and interest is lost for this period. The building societies were given power in the Finance Act 1983 to raise money through the wholesale money market by the use of certificates of deposit, and hence they now compete with the banks for these funds.

Some building societies have achieved *trustee status* by maintaining at least a minimum ratio of cash and investments to total assets. This status attracts deposits from trustees looking after other people's money who must by law invest such funds only in certain approved forms of investment.

Whereas deposits are short term (or relatively short term), the building societies lend on a long-term basis by way of mortgages against house property. Mortgages are for varying periods of years, but the most usual is 25 years. To borrow short and lend long is obviously more risky than to lend on a short-term basis, but although share accounts can be withdrawn at short notice in practice these funds stay in for several years.

The banks have offered serious competition to the building societies in recent years by offering house mortgages. They have collectively lent very substantial sums of money in this way, but after the initial spurt they tended to clamp down on this form of long-term lending and now provide such finance on a much more selective basis.

Assurance companies

Very substantial sums of money are collected by the assurance companies each year from policy holders and investors in their various schemes, and their funds are employed mostly on a long-term basis – especially the life assurance funds, repayment of which will be spread over the years ahead.

Assurance companies are very active in the financial markets, and they are of considerable importance.

Pension funds

Many of the assurance companies run pension schemes for employees, and also there are a large number of pension funds administered by companies and institutions themselves. These superannuation schemes receive regular monthly contributions from both employers and (usually) employees, which are tantamount to savings, to provide pensions upon retirement. The funds can therefore be invested on a long-term basis. To some extent the funds are invested in government securities, but in the main the pension funds buy stocks and shares in industrial and commercial companies quoted on the Stock Exchange.

Unit trusts and investment trusts

A *unit trust* collects together the savings of a large number of subscribers and invests these funds in stocks and shares on behalf of them jointly. Each subscriber's capital is thus spread over a wide range of industrial and government investments in a way that would be impossible if he or she were directly to invest any modest funds.

The investor is allocated units according to the amount of the subscription, and the daily valuation of units is calculated and published on the basis of the total worth of the trust divided by the number of units issued. Investors may subscribe to the trust for blocks of units or, in many cases, agree to subscribe a regular sum each month which may well be linked with assurance cover. The trust is not a limited company and has no share capital of its own. The managers look after the unit holders' funds, with an obligation to invest them as wisely as possible in order to produce a good return and capital growth. They receive a fee from the subscribers which is deducted from the income distributions. Units may be redeemed by selling them back to the trust.

Investment trusts are limited companies which invest in stocks and shares, the share capital subscribed by their proprietors. The investment trust's shares are quoted on the Stock Exchange and thus shareholders may redeem their capital by selling their shares on the market (and not by selling them to the trust itself, as is the case with unit trusts). The trusts sometimes raise additional funds by issuing loan stocks, and these funds are invested in stocks and shares. The income from the trust's holdings of stocks and shares is used to pay interest on loan stock and dividends to the shareholders. The value of the trust's own shares is determined in the market by the forces of supply and demand.

Share issues

Here we are concerned with the channels through which industry, commerce and the public sector obtain their long-term capital, as distinct from loans.

When a small business is developing, it may well manage with its own capital and retained profits plus loans from individuals, banks, hire purchase finance companies and as it gets bigger possibly an assurance company or pension fund may be prepared to nurse it along by an injection of loan capital. However, once a business has fully stretched these sources of such capital and wants to expand further, a public issue of shares must be considered.

Both the major clearing banks and the merchant banks act as *issuing houses*. Many of the merchant banks have for many years functioned as issuing houses, and the major clearing banks also have new issues departments which specialise in this activity – they advise company customers on the best means and appropriate terms for a new issue, and they will undertake (for a commission) to receive the applications from the public for the shares and to allocate them. Once the shares have been issued they will be quoted on the Stock Exchange, through which future sales and purchases can take place. We shall examine the functions of the Stock Exchange in detail in Chapter 6.

Government stocks are issued by the Bank of England following a newspaper advertisement and are taken up by the banks and other financial institutions. Some of the stocks are held back as tap stocks as we saw in Chapter 2, and will be sold by the government broker through the Stock Exchange from time to time in line with government monetary policy. Some stocks are also sold through the Post Office Register. Once stock has been issued, future purchases and sales are channelled through the Stock Exchange.

As we saw in our examination of the assurance companies, pension funds, unit trusts and investment trusts, the major part of their funds is invested in British and foreign companies through the acquisition of stocks and shares, and in government stocks. To some extent these may be obtained direct, but mostly they are purchased through the Stock Exchange. These institutions are an important source of long-term capital for industry and commerce.

4.7 BANK INTER-RELATIONSHIPS

Besides their relationships with the discount houses and the Bank of England already described in this and other chapters, the banks have an important relationship with all the other institutions which comprise the London financial market. The relationship is that of banker and customer.

Without the banks the building societies, assurance companies, investment trusts, hire-purchase finance houses, etc. would find it difficult to function. Their receipts of cash and cheques are paid into the banks and their loans and investments are carried out by drawing cheques on their accounts with the banks. A person who withdraws money from a building society by cheque will in fact be handed a cheque drawn by the building society on one of the commercial banks.

To some extent, the banks are involved in another way with some of the other institutions, in that they hold shares in them or may own them completely as subsidiary companies.

Other inter-relationships between the various financial institutions in London exist through the various parallel markets such as the Euro-currency market, the inter-bank market, the certificates of deposit market, and the local authority market. The institutions buy and sell, or borrow and lend, in all of these markets. They are also brought in contact with one another indirectly through the actions of money and deposit brokers who act as intermediaries between them, and who also bring about switches of funds from one market to another as interest rates fluctuate.

There are also relationships between the banks and other financial institutions with the Stock Exchange. Through that institution the banks, assurance companies, etc. buy and sell securities, and they have a special relationship with the government broker who acts on behalf of the Bank of England in feeding tap stocks on to the market.

TOPICS FOR DISCUSSION

1. Trace the inter-relationships which exist between the various financial institutions which make up the London money market in its broadest sense.
2. Discuss the activities of the various parallel financial markets.
3. Compare the functions of the building societies with those of the banks. In what ways can it be said that the building societies are becoming increasingly competitive with the High Street banks?
4. Consider the importance of the assurance companies and the pension funds in the London money market and in the UK economy as a whole.
5. Contrast the activities of the merchant banks with those of the clearing banks.
6. Discuss the developments that have occurred in the TSBs since 1974, and consider why the government at the time of the *Page Committee's Report* considered it desirable to act on the advice of the committee.
7. Consider why it is that the discount houses are allowed to continue in existence, bearing in mind that the clearing banks could carry out their functions themselves.

PART II
THE ECONOMIC BACKGROUND

CHAPTER 5

THE USE OF MONEY

5.1 INTRODUCTION

In order fully to appreciate the importance of the banking system within the economy it is necessary to consider the functions of money, and what constitutes 'money' in modern UK society. The size of the money supply and the methods of controlling it have become highly important factors to a government in pursuing its economic policy and especially so during the 1980s when the monetarists in both the UK and in the USA have succeeded in convincing their respective governments that control of the money supply must be the key factor. Their contention is that by restraining the growth of the money supply the rate of inflation can be reduced and competitiveness with the rest of the world improved. However, as events have indicated, the price is likely to be a high level of unemployment.

At the end of Chapter 3 we examined the process by which credit is created, and saw how an increase in the cash base of the banks can lead to a rise in bank deposits by several times as much. As we shall see, bank deposits account for the majority of the UK money supply, and therefore control over the *credit-creating* process is vital if the money supply is to be controlled.

5.2 ORIGINS OF MONEY

The coinage
If we were all self-sufficient and preferred not to trade with one another there would be no need for money. In a primitive society this might be possible, of course, but it is inconceivable that we could live like this today even in the small communes that are established from time to time. Some *direct* exchange of goods – barter – is likely to be inevitable, and if trading becomes at all extensive then barter must give way to *indirect* exchange involving the use of money.

This is how money originated. Barter became impossible because of the problems associated with it. How was the value of one commodity in terms of others to be measured? How could one overcome the problem of large indivisible units offered in exchange for small items? How could one transport and store commodities (especially perishable ones) in order to be able to exchange them?

To overcome such problems one commodity which was particularly sought after by the community, and which was reasonably durable and divisible, came to be used as the *medium of exchange*. Examples of such commodities are shells, salt, spears, cloth and grain, which have all been used at times as a 'money supply'. They were indeed money, because they were acceptable as a means of payment for goods: not ideal forms of money, perhaps, but nevertheless that is what they were. Later the precious metals – gold and silver, bronze and copper – were recognised as being ideally suitable as money. They were valuable, and therefore only small quantities were required when paying for goods; they were durable; and, what is particularly important, they could be cut, weighed and marked and recognised as *units of particular value*. Hence the origin of coins. Many of our modern coins derived their names from the names of weights, such as the pound and the pennyweight.

In our modern community, coins form the small change, and as a proportion of the total money supply are not very significant. However, we cannot do without them, nor are we likely to do so in the so-called 'moneyless society' of the future (see p. 223). Some coins fall out of use, of course, and are 'demonetised' – such as old pence and shillings (and, before long, the halfpenny piece) – but generally they are useful, a fact that is demonstrated by the recent introduction of the £1 coin which, although it is gold in colour, is not made of gold nor is its intrinsic value £1.

Our original coinage used to be worth its intrinsic value, i.e. the gold or silver from which it was minted was worth the face value of the coin. When the pound was first used as a unit of account, the pound of silver was minted into 240 pennies. The silver penny was to all intents and purposes the only coin in circulation in Britain until the end of the 13th century, and it was recognised in Europe as a coin of consistent fineness of silver and thus readily acceptable.

It was not until 1489 that the gold sovereign was minted though some gold coins (particularly nobles, which were worth a third of a pound) were in circulation prior to that date. Gold and silver coins circulated side by side, but when in the 18th century silver became worth more than the mint price very few silver coins were minted and the gold standard really came into its own. The gold guinea was the standard gold coin at first, until the gold sovereign became the standard coin after 1817. The mint price of gold remained at £3.17s.10½d. per standard ounce for most of the time up to 1914, and the gold standard was based on this until then. The link with gold was temporarily restored from 1925 until 1931 when the gold standard was finally abandoned. Since then, the UK coinage has been purely 'token money', with an intrinsic worth generally less than the face value, though the value of the metal in both 'silver' and copper coins got very near to face value on occasions, and now coins are made of less valuable alloys. The £1 coin first issued in 1983 is gold in colour, but it is made from copper, zinc and nickel and is thus a token coin; it is resistant against tarnishing, and has a milled edge to discourage counterfeiting. Whereas a £1 note has an average life of about nine months it is expected that the £1 coin will last for 40 years. The coin is twice as expensive to produce, but obviously it will prove much more economical in the long run.

Bank notes

The first bankers in Britain were the goldsmiths, who in addition to their trade as craftsmen in gold and silver, found that they could profit from accepting gold and silver coins for safe keeping. They gave *receipts* for such deposits, and gradually these began to be passed from hand to hand – they were after all issued by well-known and highly-respected goldsmiths, who could be trusted to pay over gold and silver coins against receipts should the holders choose to present them. Consequently the early bankers found that once deposited the coins lodged with them remained intact whilst the evidence of the debts which existed between them and their depositors circulated and rarely came home to roost. They therefore *lent* some of the coins lodged with them, and charged interest on the loans, and these coins tended to find their way back in the bank as fresh deposits to be lent and re-lent. Clearly this became a very profitable activity, and to encourage holders of their receipts to pass them from hand to hand the goldsmiths started to issue them in convenient denominations – e.g., £1 and £5 – and thus the *bank note* originated.

The goldsmiths then gave up their work as craftsmen, and devoted their time to the development of their banking business. They were followed by other merchants in corn and worsted cloth and other commodities who similarly accepted deposits and issued their own notes against them and made advances on the basis that they needed to keep only a proportion of their customers' deposits in gold and silver coins. Thus the private note issues flourished, and by the beginning of the 19th century concern began to be expressed about the size of the note issues, culminating in the Bank Charter Act 1844 which centralised the note issue in the hands of the Bank of England as we saw in Chapter 2.

Bank deposits

By the early 19th century, cheques were becoming quite widely used as a means of payment, and their use was further stimulated by the commencement of 'deposit banking' – a term used to describe the type of banking which involved the acceptance of deposits and the granting of loans and overdrafts which could be utilised by drawing cheques instead of taking the advance in the form of bank notes. Deposit banking was the answer to the 1833 Act which permitted joint stock banks to be established in the London area provided they did not issue their own notes. It had been considered essential up to that time for a bank to issue its own notes, for how otherwise could it lend money? The new joint stock banks were deposit banks. Through their rapid growth the cheque system flourished, and as it flourished so joint stock banking grew.

Cheques are used to *transfer the ownership* of bank deposits; they originated from the practice of account holders with the private banks writing notes to their banks instructing them to pay over sums of money from their deposits to the bearer of the note, who was possibly a manservant. This overcame the inconvenience of having to attend personally at the bank in order to make withdrawals, and became recognised also as a convenient means of making payments to other persons in settlement of debts.

The modern-day cheque is no more than a written instruction to the bank to pay a set sum of money to a prescribed person, or to such other person as he may instruct by indorsing the cheque. We shall need to examine the legal aspects of such transactions later, but what is of significance in the context of this chapter is the fact that by means of the cheque bank deposits became part of the money supply. It is not the cheque itself which is money, but the *deposit against which it is drawn*. The majority of transactions of industry and commerce and of the public sector, plus a sizeable proportion of the transactions of individuals, are carried out by way of cheques, and without them the development of the UK as a nation with a high standard of living would not have been possible.

5.3 FUNCTIONS OF MONEY

Money is used as a means of indirect exchange, as we have seen, and therefore one of its functions must be to act as a *medium of exchange*. In order to fulfil this function money must be acceptable to those who have goods and services to sell. To be 'acceptable', the money supply must have certain qualities. Primarily it must be reasonably *stable in value*, so that the holder knows that he or she will be able to obtain roughly the same quantity of goods and services with it when he or she chooses to spend it as was the case when he or she accepted it. The money must also be *durable*, or it may perish in the hands of the recipient before he or she can make use of it. Money must also be *divisible*, in order that it can be used in convenient amounts, and must also be easily *transferable*; finally, it must be *recognisable* as money. Whereas the commodities first used as money lacked some of these qualities and hence were replaced eventually by silver and gold coins (and later bank notes and bank deposits), the present day money supply has all these properties – with one possible exception, and that is stability. If inflation becomes rampant and the value of money falls very rapidly, then it may no longer be acceptable as a means of payment and some other form of money will be sought after.

A second function of money is to be a *unit of account*. Without such a measuring rod it would be impossible for a modern community to function. It must be possible to measure the value of goods and services in terms of a common unit of account, in order to establish prices, and in order to record transactions. We must be able to compare the value of the commodity with that of another, and thus to establish which goods we will buy with our limited supply of money. With a unit of account it becomes possible to measure the value of production, and of the national wealth.

Two further functions of money derive from these first two, for if money was not a medium of exchange and a unit of account it could not fulfil the function of being a *store of wealth*, and *a standard for deferred payments*. To be a store of wealth the value of money must be stable. This does not mean that the value must remain completely unchanged during the time it is held. Even during periods of quite severe inflation the pound sterling has continued to function as a medium of exchange and has been used to store wealth. It is only when the inflation becomes excessive and the situation becomes impossible (as in Germany in 1922-3), that the money is no longer usable and a new form of money (such as cigarettes, for example) becomes the medium of exchange until a new currency issue is made.

During a period of such hyperinflation, the medium of exchange may be different from the unit of account. In Germany in the 1920s, for example, the Swiss franc was often used as the unit of account for contracts. Money will also be used as a standard for deferred payments – i.e., goods are sold on credit and book debts are recorded – only if the money supply remains acceptable as a medium of exchange and unit of account. The reader will appreciate that unless book debts can be recorded in terms of some acceptable form of money with which to measure value, it would be virtually impossible to supply goods on credit.

Money also performs one other vital function in a modern community, in that it is the mechanism through which most goods and services are *distributed*. To some extent (and possibly a great extent in a communist state) the government must be responsible for the allocation of some goods and services such as firearms, drugs, education and medical care, but in the main it is the person who is able (and prepared) to pay the price for a commodity who receives it.

5.4 CONFIDENCE

The present-day UK money supply consists of Bank of England notes, coins produced by the Royal Mint, and bank deposits. None of these has an intrinsic value of any significance. Bank notes are worth nothing as paper, and the UK coinage is now worth little as metal. Nor is the note issue any longer backed with gold, and therefore if someone was to take a £5 bank note to the Bank of England and ask for it to be changed he would be given five £1 notes or some coins. No longer can £5 worth of gold be demanded in exchange. All modern money is therefore based on *confidence* – confidence that it will remain acceptable as a means of exchange; as we have seen, this confidence is likely to remain intact provided that the value of money remains reasonably constant. To protect the value of the money supply the government must pursue sound economic policies (including monetary policy) which seek to keep both the supply of, and demand for, goods in equilibrium. If demand exceeds supply, there will be inflation and hence a tendency for the value of money to continue to fall. In Chapter 7 we will examine the objectives of monetary policy, and the means by which they may be achieved.

5.5 PRESENT-DAY MONEY SUPPLY

Fiduciary issue

In the Bank Charter Act 1844 the fiduciary issue (that is, the part of the note issue which is not backed by gold but is based on *trust*), was set at £14 million, with the proviso that when banks closed down or were amalgamated two-thirds of their note issue could be taken over by the Bank of England. During the First World War the Treasury issued its own notes and by the end of the war in 1918 the total fiduciary issue had risen to £320 million. By virtue of the Currency and Bank Notes Act 1928, the Bank of England took over the Treasury note issue and the fiduciary issue was set at £260 million. The Act also provided that the Treasury could authorise the Bank of England to issue notes beyond this limit for a period of up to six months and a subsequent series of Currency and Bank Note Acts authorised further additions to the fiduciary issue culminating in the Act of 1954 which empowered the Treasury to alter the note issue by laying formal minutes before Parliament. The note issue has in fact been allowed to increase year by year, and now stands at about £11 500 million. From time to time questions have been asked in Parliament about the continued expansion of the note issue and some considerable alarm has been voiced concerning it. However, the note issue must be seen in the light of the money supply as a whole – it constitutes only 28 per cent of the UK money supply in its narrowest sense (M_1, as discussed below), and it is important that notes (and coin) should be made available to meet the needs of the community. It would be ludicrous if bank customers had to be told that they could not withdraw deposits in cash because of a shortage of notes and coin, and could withdraw only by issuing cheques to third parties. The important thing is that the money supply as a whole should be controlled.

Until 1939, the country's reserves of gold were used by the Bank of England as backing for part of the note issue (that part which was not fiduciary), but in that year the gold was transferred to the Exchange Equalisation Account (EEA) as backing for the pound externally, and the whole of the note issue was made fiduciary.

Legal tender

This term denotes those forms of money which must be accepted by law in settlement of a debt. Table 5.1 shows the components of legal tender in the UK.

Table 5.1 *UK legal tender*

Bank of England notes and £1 pieces for any amount	
50p pieces up to	£10
Other cupro-nickel coins up to	£5
Bronze coins up to	20p

Bank deposits as money

We can thus see that the modern UK money supply comprises bank deposits in the main, plus the Bank of England's note issue and the coinage. As to which of the bank deposits to include there is some controversy (and, indeed, the government's various official aggregates of the money supply vary in the extent to which deposits are included).

Not all bank deposits are a means of payment, for whereas current account balances can be drawn upon instantly at will by drawing cheques, deposit accounts cannot. Banks now accept deposit account balances on various terms, the most common still being the seven-day account – i.e., withdrawals can be made by giving seven days' notice. These deposits (and similarly those deposited on even longer terms), cannot be withdrawn on demand, and hence it is doubtful whether they should be included in the money supply.

When we pay for goods in a shop we do so in the main by handing over notes and coin, or by drawing a cheque. If we draw a cheque, we are in effect transferring the ownership of a bank deposit. To us, then, our current account balances are *as good as cash*, and we regard them very much in that light.

If we have money on deposit account we may well regard it as virtually cash, and take that balance into account when calculating our liquidity position. We know that before we can make use of the deposit account balance we have to give the appropriate amount of notice, and that we cannot draw cheques against it. However, with foresight and good management a deposit account customer is able to give notice of withdrawal at the appropriate time and have the current account credited, or withdraw in cash to meet the anticipated cash requirements. Hence a short-term deposit account balance is very near to being money, and the term *near money* is used to denote this type of asset. This applies similarly to a deposit in a building society, or money invested in national savings certificates and to any other short-term investment which can be fairly easily liquidated. However, two important factors distinguish these 'near money' assets from money. These are first that notice of withdrawal or encashment must be given and, secondly, that the asset has to be converted into money – i.e., notes and coin or a bank deposit (as evidenced by a cheque) – before it can be used as money.

This concept of *liquidity* is important, because it affects the actions of the community in demanding goods and services, and it is for this reason that the government's official definitions of money take near-money assets into account. The reader will appreciate that these liquid assets are held not only with banks but also with non-bank financial institutions (NBFIs), and also in bills and bonds and other securities issued by both the public and private sectors of the community. The values of some of these assets vary from day to day, and are determined by market forces through supply and demand.

The astute reader will have realised that when buying goods in a shop there are ways other than using notes and coin or drawing a cheque. A credit card could be used, for instance, a hire-purchase agreement might be entered into, or the store might be prepared to send the bill at the end of the month. These methods delay payment (and, possibly, provide for money to be borrowed by the purchaser). In either case, money in the form of notes and coin or bank deposits will be required or acquired to settle the debt, so that our definition of money is not affected.

Official measurement of the money stock

The Bank of England publishes information concerning the UK money supply and uses a number of different measures ranging from what is called M_0 (the narrowest measure) to PSL_2 (the broadest measure). We now need to consider each one in turn, and to establish the purposes for which they are compiled. Each one of these monetary aggregates is important in itself as a tool for the government in carrying out its monetary policy, and also as an indicator to those who study such statistics as to the success (or otherwise) of this policy.

In October 1983, the government introduced M_0 as a measure of the actual cash held by the community and the banks. It therefore does not include any bank deposits other than the banks' working balances. This new aggregate comprises notes and coin plus the banks' holdings of cash and their operational balances with the central bank, but it does not include their obligatory non-operational balances with the Bank of England, as these cannot be withdrawn.

The money aggregate M_1 includes notes and coin in circulation and private sector sterling sight deposits with the monetary sector. As mentioned in Chapter 4, the monetary sector includes the recognised banks, licensed deposit-taking institutions, the TSBs and the National Girobank. It also includes the banking department of the Bank of England. The important factors are that it includes only *private sector* deposits, and that these deposits are those in sterling and repayable on demand, i.e. sight deposits. It does include some large wholesale deposits on which interest is paid and which are not strictly speaking held for transaction purposes, but, generally speaking, M_1 is a measure of the money stock *immediately available* for use in carrying out transactions.

The government has now also introduced a narrower version of M_1, which excludes interest-bearing sight deposits. It is called $NIBM_1$, and is sometimes referred to as 'retail M_1', in that it is the wholesale sight deposits which, generally speaking, attract interest.

The money aggregate M_2 was introduced in 1982, and is an attempt to produce a finer measure of the availability of money for transactions than M_1. Wholesale sight deposits are excluded as they are in the nature of short-term investments rather than transaction balances, and so too are balances of more than £100 000. Balances up to that sum on current account and deposit account with terms of withdrawal of less than a month held by banks in the private sector are included, although in the case of deposit balances they cannot be withdrawn immediately. They can, however, be drawn fairly quickly and might be regarded by their holders as money which could be used for transactions. To these balances the total of cash in circulation is added and, more recently, building society deposits and ordinary deposits with the National Savings Bank, which can be withdrawn fairly quickly, have been included in arriving at M_2. The relationship between all the narrow measures of the money stock is illustrated in Figure 5.1.

Fig 5.1 *composition of narrow monetary aggregates 19 October 1983 (£ billion)*

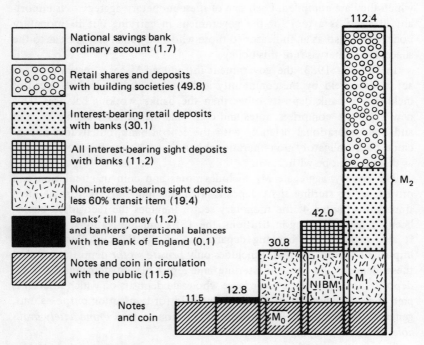

National savings bank ordinary account (1.7)

Retail shares and deposits with building societies (49.8)

Interest-bearing retail deposits with banks (30.1)

All interest-bearing sight deposits with banks (11.2)

Non-interest-bearing sight deposits less 60% transit item (19.4)

Banks' till money (1.2) and bankers' operational balances with the Bank of England (0.1)

Notes and coin in circulation with the public (11.5)

Notes and coin

Source: HM Treasury, *Economic Progress Report*, December 1983

The third official measure of the money supply is M_3, which was the total of cash in circulation plus sterling and foreign currency deposits with banks held by UK residents in both the private and public sectors of the community. In 1984 the composition of Sterling M_3 and M_3 was changed to exclude public sector deposits. This measure is now usually refined as Sterling M_3 to exclude foreign currency deposits, and less use is made of the broader M_3. Sterling M_3 is a measure of the money stock that receives particular attention by the authorities as it is closely related to changes in the assets of the banks. It is obviously a much broader measure of the money stock than M_1, but is roughly equal in size to M_2, and by measuring changes in it and analysing their causes the authorities are better able to pursue a successful monetary policy. We shall look more closely at Sterling M_3 in Chapter 7.

Since 1980, the Bank of England has published two additional aggregates – PSL_1 and PSL_2 – which take into account liquidity held by the private sector in forms other than cash and balances with the banks. PSL_1 comprises cash in circulation with the public, together with sterling deposits with banks held by UK residents in the private sector (but, unlike Sterling M_3, excludes such deposits by the public sector). It also excludes deposits with a maturity of more than two years. To this total are added the private sectors' holdings of treasury bills, banker's acceptances, deposits with local authorities and certificates of tax deposit. The money aggregate PSL_2 includes PSL_1 plus deposits of the private sector with building societies and the National Savings Bank, plus investments in National Savings securities (but deposits and securities which cannot be realised within one year without significant loss are excluded). Figure 5.2 shows how the broader measures of the money stock compare with one another.

Finally, we must consider the concept of Domestic Credit Expansion (DCE). This is a measure of the increase in Sterling M_3, plus any deficit in the balance of payments minus any surplus in the balance of payments. It

Fig 5.2 *measures of the money stock, August 1983 (£ million)*

M_1, Sterling M_3 and M_3		*Not seasonally adjusted*
Notes & coin in circulation		11 527
Sterling sight deposits (private sector)		29 705
		41 232 = M_1
Sterling time deposits (private sector)		55 549
Sterling deposits (public sector)		2315
		99 096 = Sterling M_3
Deposits in other currencies		13 780
		112 876 = M_3
PSL_1, PSL_2		*Seasonally adjusted*
Money	94 686	94 686
Other money market instruments	3129	3129
Savings institutions savings & deposit accounts		60 750[a]
Certificates of tax deposits	1929	1747
	99 744 = PSL_1	160 312 = PSL_2

a including building societies £56 412 million.

Source: *Bank of England Quarterly Bulletin*, September 1983

is a measure of the increase in the money stock resulting from *domestically-generated credit*, and excludes the effects upon the money supply of the balance of payments. An adverse balance of payments reduces the money stock because UK residents pay for the deficit from their holdings of money and therefore this deficit needs to be added back to the increase in Sterling M_3 in order to find the true increase in Sterling M_3 attributable to growth in domestic credit. A balance of payments surplus has the opposite effect, of course, and must be *deducted* from Sterling M_3 to arrive at DCE. It is important for domestic demand to be restrained in order to avoid excessive imports, and therefore it is useful to have DCE as a measure of the domestic money supply – any excessive rate of increase in DCE could result in an adverse balance of payments. But the deficit in the balance of payments could to some extent rectify the situation, in that it could reduce the money stock.

TOPICS FOR DISCUSSION

1. Consider how, and to what extent, the functions of money are affected by inflation.
2. Discuss the importance of controlling the fiduciary issue.
3. What is the purpose of each of the official measures of the money stock. Why is it necessary to publish more than one of these?
4. Consider what is meant by the 'whole liquidity position' of the community.

CHAPTER 6

SAVINGS AND INVESTMENT

6.1 IMPORTANCE OF SAVINGS AND INVESTMENT

The term 'saving' is usually used to mean 'refraining from spending'. If, instead of using some of our income to buy goods and services we put it aside - possibly by depositing it with a bank or building society, or even placing it in a vase on the mantlepiece - we are *saving*. The important aspect of this from a national point of view is that we are refraining from spending, and making the goods and services that we might have bought available to others. This is vital if the community is to carry out investment in capital assets.

We save for a number of reasons - for holidays, or to buy a car or some other particular item we want to acquire, or simply to have something to fall back on when we retire or should some emergency occur. To some extent saving is imposed upon us through national insurance contributions - we have to deny ourselves present-day consumption of goods and services in order to pay these contributions, and in return receive sickness and other benefits including the state pension when we retire.

'Investment' is a term that has two meanings, and this often causes confusion. We talk of investing in stocks and shares, in national savings certificates or in premium savings bonds. In this way we are investing *money capital*. In the other meaning of the term we are carrying out *capital investment* - in the form of real assets such as factories, shops, roads, offices, and plant and equipment. This is sometimes referred to as 'capital formation'. Such capital assets are used in the production of goods and services, but are not themselves consumed, except in the sense that they depreciate and wear out. Those people who are involved in constructing or manufacturing capital assets earn incomes which they need to spend on consumer goods and services, although they are not themselves producing any. There is thus a gap in the community between the total of incomes and the total output of consumer goods, and this gap has to be bridged by savings – savings must equal investment. Hence the importance of savings. If the necessary volume of savings does not occur the government must step in and impose additional taxation to reduce purchasing power, or alternatively let inflation occur in which case money will ration out the goods and services to those willing (and able) to pay the higher prices.

Investment, too, is important. Capital assets are used to produce further goods and services and therefore the quantity of those assets – i.e., the level of capital formation – must be sufficient to generate enough output to meet our needs (and, if at all possible, to bring about a continuing increase in output which will enable our standard of living to rise, i.e. our real incomes to increase). Our real incomes are 'incomes' in terms of goods and services, not simply money incomes which may be eroded by inflation. If the physical output of goods and services increases whilst the population remains unchanged, then our real incomes per head will rise. If this is to happen, the amount of capital formation must increase sufficiently not only to increase the output of goods but also to permit capital assets to be replaced or maintained in good order.

The types of assets in which capital formation was carried out in 1981 are shown in Table 6.1, and also the industries which carried out the investment.

6.2 WHO SAVES?

Saving is carried out not only by individuals, but also by companies (and, on occasion, by central and local government and by public corporations). Personal saving takes the form of deposits in banks, building societies, national savings certificates, etc., in addition, two other forms of saving are often overlooked. When an individual pays premiums on life or endowment assurance policies, he or she is saving. He or she is denying immediate expenditure to the extent of the premiums in order to reap the benefit later when the policy matures. Similarly, superannuation contributions are a form of saving. Pension funds receive enormous sums of money from both employers and their employees, and these funds are invested indirectly in industry and commerce through the acquisition of stocks and shares.

If a local authority does not use some of its rates income in a particular financial year, then that money is saved by placing it into reserve. However, overall, local authorities now tend to spend more than their income, borrowing the difference by the issue of local authority bills and other securities. Similarly, public corporations and central government consistently spend more than their income, and borrow to bridge the gap.

In 1981, personal saving amounted to £22 604 million, but after allowing for depreciation, stock appreciation and addition to tax reserves this

Table 6.1 *Gross domestic fixed capital formation 1981 (£ million)*

By type of asset	
Buses & coaches	279
Other road vehicles	3 759
Railway rolling stock	151
Ships	253
Aircraft	145
Plant & machinery	15 581
Dwellings	5 186
Other new buildings & works	12 313
Transfer costs of land & buildings	1 710
	39 377
By industry group	
Agriculture, forestry & fishing	843
Petroleum & natural gas	2 847
Mining & quarrying (excl. petroleum & natural gas)	837
Manufacturing	6 227
Construction	582
Gas, electricity, water	2 376
Transport & communication	4 090
Distributive trades	2 601
Other service industries	7 524
Dwellings	5 186
Social services	1 805
Other public services	2 749
Transfer costs of land & buildings	1 710
	39 377

Source: *Annual Abstract of Statistics*

amount was reduced to £16 013 million, which was $7\frac{1}{4}$ per cent of total personal income in that year.

Companies and financial institutions saved a somewhat similar gross amount (£24 813 million), but as is to be expected, their provisions for depreciation, stock appreciation and additions to tax reserves was very much greater, and reduced their net saving to £1533 million.

6.3 SAVINGS MEDIA

By looking at the financial markets in Chapter 4 we have considered in some detail many of the institutions which provide the media through which savings are channelled to industry and commerce and to the public sector. To the individual who wishes to invest savings, each of these institutions offers investment opportunities which may or may not be attractive, depending upon whether he or she is looking for easy access to the money with, possibly, the convenience of a payments mechanism; a good rate of interest, a possible capital gain, or simply a sound form of investment with no danger of losing the money.

Let us now look at these institutions once again in the light of these criteria, and also consider the forms of national savings and the activities of the Stock Exchange.

Banks

To many millions of people, bank accounts provide a convenient medium for at least some of their savings. We have our incomes - whether they be salaries, pensions, or interest and dividends - paid into our current accounts, and draw on these incomes for day to day expenditure. To the extent that credit balances remain outstanding (and bearing in mind that usually a minimum balance of £100 must be maintained in order to avoid charges) the banks have enormous sums to invest in both the private and public sectors. The London clearing banks alone had over £22 000 million of sterling sight deposits in May 1983 - not all deposited by private individuals by any means, but nevertheless a substantial proportion was. To keep such a balance is convenient in that it secures payments mechanisms for the account holder whether the bank be a clearing bank, a TSB or the National Girobank. However, the current account earns no interest, and therefore the majority of account holders will transfer to deposit account or to some other form of remunerative investment, any balances beyond what is needed for normal day to day requirements. For modest amounts the banks pay comparatively low rates of interest (about 4 per cent below base rate), but for larger deposits - £5000 or £10 000 or more depending upon the bank - higher rates of interest can be obtained. The London clearing banks had no less than £41 000 million of term deposits in May 1983, i.e. deposits other than on current account.

Building societies

Share and investment accounts with building societies are a popular form of saving, particularly as the interest is paid free of basic rate of tax and in consequence the rates of interest paid compare very favourably with those obtainable elsewhere. Balances on ordinary share accounts are immediately accessible and, depending upon the terms on which deposits are made, funds on term deposit can usually be withdrawn within two or three months, though there may be some loss of interest.

The building societies also encourage regular savings by running Save-as-you-earn (SAYE) schemes and other rather similar arrangements, whereby the saver is committed to monthly savings of, say, £20 a month for a period of five years (in the case of SAYE) or for possibly a shorter period and receives a higher rate of interest than on normal term share accounts with a bonus at the end of the period. The SAYE schemes are standard amongst the societies but the arrangements for other build-up accounts vary between societies.

Depositors' funds are invested by the societies in property, of course, by providing mortgage finance for house purchase and, to some limited extent, for the acquisition of business premises.

Compare these services of a building society to personal depositors with those of a bank given in Chapter 13 (pp. 173-7).

Assurance companies

The main activity of the life assurance company is the provision of assurance policies that will provide a sum of money in the future to the assured and/or protect any dependants should he or she die in the meantime. Monthly (or maybe weekly) premiums are received by the assurance company regularly over a set period of years, or until the assured dies, and up to March 1984 the policy holder was able to claim allowances at the standard rate against income tax. This rate of tax was deducted from the premiums by the assurance company. The lump sum benefits upon maturity of the policy are free of tax, and both tax benefits have been an obvious attraction to the saver quite apart from the assurance element.

Endowment policies can be taken out for various periods of years to suit the needs of the particular policy holder. The amount of the premium depends upon the term of assurance and also the sum assured, and naturally a young person who is able to spread the cover over a long period of years will be able to obtain it for a relatively small premium, whereas an older person wanting to save for retirement will have to pay higher premiums. In the event of the policy holder's death during the term of the policy, the sum assured is payable to the next of kin plus any accrued profits and premiums cease to be payable.

Policies can be with profits or without profits. The former type gives the policy holder a share in the profits accruing to the assurance company through investing premiums, and provides a hedge against inflation in that upon maturity of the policy he or she receives the sum assured plus the profits that have been allocated. The assurance companies have very large sums to invest, and can do so on a long-term basis, and they are able to take advantage of the capital gains that may accrue through holding investments over a long period.

Generally the assurance companies have performed well over recent years, and been able to pay out good profits to those insured. The companies give no firm promises as to what the profits will be, and they may or may not succeed in keeping abreast with inflation, but clearly with profits policies are a better proposition than without-profits policies if the assured can afford the higher premiums.

Whole-life assurance policies are similar to endowment policies, and can be with profits or without, but no term of years is stipulated and instead payment under the policy is made only when the policy holder dies. There may be a set period of years for the payment of premiums after which the policy becomes a paid-up policy, or the premiums may be payable during the whole of the person's life.

In addition to life and endowment cover the assurance companies offer many other ways of investing savings, such as annuities, personal pension plans, insurance bonds and unit trusts with an insurance element. Up to now the assurance companies have laid emphasis on the tax-efficiency of their schemes in selling them to the public – i.e., they have stressed the exemptions from income tax (and, possibly, capital gains tax) which were permitted, and how their concessions were of particular value to investors in the higher income tax brackets.

The term 'assurance' is applied to life and endowment cover, whereas the term 'insurance' is applied to other types of cover for risks such as fire, theft and damage which may (or may not) occur.

The assurance companies invest their clients' funds in best gilt-edged stocks and equities. They also invest directly in companies (for instance, 'nursing' private companies up to the point when they are able to go public), and are involved in the acquisition and lending out of commercial and industrial premises.

Pension funds

Closely allied to the activities of the assurance companies are the pension funds. Indeed very many companies use pension schemes run for them by the assurance companies, and only the large institutions operate their own superannuation funds. An indication of the amount of money flowing through the hands of pension funds from employers and employees and being invested by the funds mostly in stocks and shares is given by the fact that in 1981 the net income – after administrative costs and payment of pension benefits – of funded pension schemes (including those of life assurance companies) was £12 824 million. Clearly the pension schemes are of considerable national importance in that they provide so much capital each year for industry and commerce, but also of course in that they are there to provide incomes at retirement (which must considerably reduce the burden upon the state which might otherwise arise through claims from the elderly for financial assistance).

Unit trusts and investment trusts

The main advantage to the saver of investing in a unit trust is that the risks are spread over a range of companies in the same industry, or over a whole range of industries.

Some unit trusts invest funds in particular countries such as the USA and Japan, where they endeavour to take advantage of more favourable yields and/or capital growth. A saver with only a modest amount of capital to invest is unable to acquire a whole range of shares to spread the risks or to improve the chances of selecting shares which prove to be especially successful, and therefore such a saver is wise to put money into a unit trust.

Unit trusts have been very popular, particularly amongst small investors, and 'league tables' are published in the press indicating the degree of success of the trust managers in increasing the values of their unit holders' funds. The total value of a trust's portfolio of stocks and shares is divided by the number of units held, and the bid and offer prices published daily in the newspapers are based on this valuation. The *bid price* is that at which the unit trust is prepared to buy back units held by investors, and the *offer price* (the higher of the two) is the price at which it is willing to sell units. The margin between the two prices goes towards the costs of running the fund and, in addition, the managers deduct a small percentage of the dividend earnings of the shares in which the fund's resources are invested as an annual charge towards these expenses. The dividends, net of expenses, are allocated to the unit holders on the basis of their holdings and these allocations are either distributed half-yearly to the holders or credited to them as additional units, depending upon the arrangements made at the outset.

Blocks of units are offered for sale from time to time through advertisements in the press and, in addition to this, the trusts receive a regular inflow of funds from those unit holders who enter into a scheme to subscribe a regular amount (usually monthly, by banker's standing order). In this way small savers are able to build up their investments out of income. Quite often such schemes have an assurance element which insures the policy holder for the total investment planned over the term of the scheme, and in the past has permitted the instalment to be paid net of income tax.

The banks have been very active in the unit trust field since the 1960s and all the big banks, including the TSBs, have established their own trusts. The banks were also (and still are) trustees of other unit trusts for many years previously, and therefore have a great deal of expertise in managing such investments. Customers are able to invest in the whole range of unit trusts through their banks, and to obtain information concerning them.

Assurance companies also run unit trusts, and have the advantage of being able to attach assurance cover to their schemes.

Investment trusts, like unit trusts, invest their funds in stocks and shares. However, they differ from unit trusts in that they are public companies who use their shareholders' capital (plus the proceeds of debenture issues) to invest in the shares of other companies. Shares in investment trusts are therefore bought and sold through the Stock Exchange and therefore the comments below concerning the services of the Stock Exchange apply equally well to investment trusts. As far as the saver is concerned, he or she must have a sufficient sum to invest through a stockbroker in investment trust shares to make it an economically worthwhile exercise.

National Girobank

This bank was originally primarily concerned with money transmission facilities rather than collecting savings. However, its services have been developed so as to provide a wide range of banking services to both personal and business customers, and (to the extent that balances are left outstanding on accounts with the bank), they provide an important channel through which savings are passed to the public sector (and, through advances, to the private sector). For further details concerning the National Girobank, see Chapter 4.

TSBs

As we have seen, these banks are no longer only savings banks in that they offer a wide range of banking services, primarily to personal account holders but also to an increasing number of commercial and industrial concerns. They still attract savings, of course, and remain an important channel through which savings are collected and made available to those who need to borrow. In that the banks no longer have to place their deposits with the National Debt Commissioners, only a relatively small proportion is lent to the public sector and the majority is lent to the private sector by way of loans and overdrafts (see also Chapter 4).

Finance houses

The hire-purchase finance houses accept deposits from the general public, but are interested in larger deposits than those, for instance, deposited with building societies. They therefore pay better rates of interest for large sums of, say, £1000 or more and these rates are particularly favourable when deposits are lodged for fixed periods of a year or more. Their main source of finance is the wholesale money market. Some of the finance houses are of course subsidiaries of the banks.

National Savings Bank

This bank was known as the Post Office Savings Bank until 1969 when it was put under the control of the Department of National Savings (a government department). Transactions are still carried out through the 22 000 Post Offices and sub-Post Offices, however, thus providing the small saver with a local agency for paying in and drawing out money, and the convenience of being able to do so during the whole of the opening hours of the Post Offices including Saturday mornings.

The bank collects mostly small savings in its ordinary accounts, on which only a modest rate of interest is paid but this is free of tax up to £70 of interest per annum. Investment accounts, on the other hand, attract a very favourable rate of interest which (although subject to income tax) compares quite well with rates of interest paid by the building societies. These accounts require a month's notice for withdrawals.

The National Savings Bank does not offer the wide range of banking services of the National Girobank or the TSBs, but warrants payable to third parties can be obtained and transfers can be made to National Giro-bank accounts. Standing orders and direct debits are also possible. The activities of the National Savings Bank form part of the national savings movement (see below).

6.4 NATIONAL SAVINGS

The government encourages personal saving by offering various forms of investment through the Department of National Savings. These are listed in Table 6.2, from which it will be seen that the total amount outstanding in 1982, including accrued interest, was £20 319 million. The government has stepped up its efforts in recent years to attract personal savings by offering favourable rates of interest.

Table 6.2 *National savings year ended 31 March 1982 – amounts remaining invested (including accrued interest) (£ million)*

NSC	12 333
SAYE	657
Other securities on the NSS register	842
National savings bank	
Ordinary A/cs	1 702
Investment A/cs	2 992
Premium savings bonds	1 506
British savings bonds	286
National savings stamps & gift tokens	1
	20 319

Source: *Annual Abstract of Statistics*

National savings certificates

The most popular of the national savings instruments is the national savings certificate. The current issue of certificates requires investors (and the government) to commit themselves for a period of five years if they are to achieve the maximum compound rate of interest of approximately $7\frac{1}{2}$ per cent per annum tax free on average. Certificates can be surrendered earlier, but at a penalty because the certificates increase in value mostly in the fourth and fifth years. They are issued in multiples of £25 with a maximum holding of 200 units, and each unit is worth £35.90 at the end of the five-year period. National savings certificates do not have to be redeemed at the end of the period, but attract interest at a lower rate from then on. In addition to being free of income tax they are also exempt from capital gains tax.

As the general level of interest rates change, the Department of National Savings brings out new issues with more appropriate yields.

One of the issues of national savings certificates is *index-linked*. This means that the growth in the value of the certificates is linked to the Index of Retail Prices. At the end of the five-year period, the indexes at the beginning of the period and at the end are compared, and the value of the certificates at surrender is increased in the same proportion as the index. When the rate of inflation was greater than the general level of interest rates the issue of certificates was particularly popular, but as the rate of inflation at the time of writing (January 1984) is only about 5 per cent the yield is poor in comparison with interest rates paid by, for instance, the building societies. Consequently the government has been paying an annual bonus to the certificate holders to make the yield more competitive.

The government's Save-as-you-Earn (SAYE) scheme is run on a somewhat similar basis to this index-linked issue of national savings certificates, but instead of being paid for in a lump sum they are subscribed for on a regular monthly basis over the five-year period. The minimum amount is £4 per month, and the maximum is £50. The growth in value of the units is calculated on a monthly basis so that, for instance, an instalment of £20 paid in in the first month of the second year of the scheme would grow in proportion to the increase in the retail prices between that month and the end of the five-year period of the scheme. Here again, the government has been paying a bonus to make the scheme more attractive.

Premium savings bonds

These bonds offer the incentive of a chance to win a prize in a monthly draw. At each draw a sum equal to a rate of interest of 7 per cent per annum (at January 1984) is used to pay out a large number of prizes varying in size from one of £250 000 down to a very large number of £50. In addition, there is a weekly draw for prizes of £100 000, £50 000 and

£25 000 (one of each). The winning numbers of bonds are selected by an electronic device which is able to select numbers at random. All prizes are free of income tax and capital gains tax, and they are sent through the post to successful bond holders. Bonds may be encashed for their face value within a few days.

The high prizes that might be won are of course an attraction to investors, but there are inevitably also a large number of bond holders who receive no reward for their investment. Holders gamble the interest on the bonds, but unlike other forms of gambling they do at least get their investment back intact whether they win or not!

Income bonds

These bonds are designed to provide a regular monthly income to investors who have £2000 or more (maximum £200 000) to invest. The rate of interest is high in relation to other rates (at January 1984 $11\frac{1}{2}$ per cent), but it is subject to tax, although tax is not deducted at source and therefore the bonds are attractive to those individuals or organisations not subject to tax. It is paid direct to a bank account, or can be sent by warrant through the post.

Holdings may be withdrawn subject to either three months' or six months' notice, with interest rate penalties that depend upon the period of notice and length of time the bonds have been held. On a bond that has been held for at least a year and for which six months' notice of withdrawal has been given, interest is paid in full.

National savings income bonds may be held for a guaranteed initial period of 10 years.

Deposit bonds

The British savings bonds listed in Table 6.2 are no longer available, but instead it is possible to buy national savings deposit bonds which are intended for people who wish to invest lump sums at a high rate of interest (at January 1984 $11\frac{1}{2}$ per cent) with no tax deducted at source. In this respect they are like income bonds, but the interest is paid annually and not monthly. The minimum holding is £500 and the maximum is £50 000. Repayment is subject to three months' notice, and no interest is lost provided the bond has been held for at least a year.

Other securities on the national savings stock register (NSSR)

It is possible to buy and sell a wide range of the government stocks quoted on the Stock Exchange through the national savings stock register. Forms and envelopes are obtainable from post offices, and the form is sent by post to the bonds and stock office in Blackpool. The advantages of buying or selling stocks by this method are that tax is not deducted from the interest paid, and that commission charges are attractive especially when small investments are involved. Interest can be credited to a bank account, or will be sent through the post if required.

Prices at which stocks are bought and sold are of course those prevailing in the market from day to day, but allowance must be made for the fact the applications to buy or sell are made through the post, and the prices quoted in the press may have changed in the meantime.

A maximum of £5000 may be invested in any one stock on any one day, but there is no limit to the total amount of stock that may be held.

6.5 THE STOCK EXCHANGE

Buying and selling stocks and shares

Many savers prefer to invest their money directly in stocks and shares rather than invest through a unit trust or investment trust. They are prepared to take the risk that the particular shares they choose turn out to be less successful than they expected, in terms of the dividends that are paid and growth in the value of the shares. On the other hand, they are free to buy and sell shares as they please, and stand to get a great amount of satisfaction from managing their own portfolio of stocks and shares. However, buying and selling shares can be expensive for the small investor because stockbrokers, although they charge a fee based on the value of the shares, impose a minimum charge. Stamp duty has also to be paid when shares are purchased.

A stock exchange is a market through which such purchases and sales can be arranged, and the London Stock Exchange is amongst the largest in the world. All British government stocks (usually referred to as British funds) are quoted on the London Stock Exchange and also shares in public companies which have applied for (and been granted) permission for their shares to be listed. Such a listing imposes an obligation upon the company to abide by the code of conduct laid down by the Stock Exchange Council concerning the way in which the company's affairs are conducted and dealings in its shares. If the Council are not satisfied, they have the right to suspend or discontinue the quotation of the company's shares.

When a company 'goes public' or wishes to raise additional capital its shares are offered for sale (see Chapter 4), and this will be done before the shares are quoted on the Stock Exchange. The exchange therefore deals in second-hand shares but, nevertheless, it is a convenient channel through which savings can be invested in industry and commerce. Similarly, government funds are first issued by the Bank of England, but in that a large proportion of each issue is usually taken up by the Bank of England itself in order to use the stock as a 'tap issue' (see below) the public sector can raise fresh funds through the Stock Exchange.

There are two types of dealers on the Stock Exchange – stockbrokers and stockjobbers. The *brokers* act as agents between the investors and the stockjobbers, for which they charge a commission. The *jobbers* deal in particular types of stocks and shares – e.g., shares in electrical companies – and trade on their own account. They buy from and sell shares to stockbrokers, taking as their profit the difference between the buying price and the selling price. Contracts between jobbers and brokers are agreed verbally, and are followed later by a written contract. Payments from the investor to the stockbroker in respect of government stocks are made as soon as the broker's client receives a contract note, but payments in respect of company shares are due on 'settlement day', which is normally about 10 days after the end of the account period (which lasts two weeks).

Completion of the transfer of ownership of the stocks and shares is done by the registrar of the company concerned, who issues a *share certificate* to the new owner indicating his or her name and address. This is not necessary for what are called 'bearer securities', which simply pass from hand to hand without registration of names.

One of the firms of stockbrokers acts as agent for the government, and is known as the government broker. Through this firm the Bank of England, acting for the government, will buy and sell government stocks. As mentioned above, the Bank of England handles new issues of government stocks and invites applications for them from the public direct (i.e., not through the Stock Exchange), and the banks and other financial institutions do buy large amounts of them. Some of the latest issue of stock will always be kept by the Bank of England, however, to be made available for sale on the Stock Exchange through the government broker as and when it is strategically appropriate to do so.

This particular stock is called the 'tap stock', a name which is derived from the fact that the government broker 'turns on the tap' and makes more of the stock available when it is decided to do so. This device is useful in controlling the quantity of stocks available for sale on the Stock Exchange at any particular time, and through that influencing the prices of gilt-edged stocks and their yields. Inasmuch that government stocks are usually long-dated – i.e., they have many years to maturity – the government is thus able to influence the level of long-term interest rates through the government broker, as well as short-term interest rates through the government buyer in the discount market.

The national newspapers list the dealing prices for British funds and company shares as at the close of business each day. For each stock the stockjobber will quote two prices – one is the price at which he or she is willing to sell; the other (lower) price is the buying price. The prices quoted in the press are the middle prices (and therefore, assuming that share prices have remained unchanged since the prices were quoted, the stockbroker's client must expect to pay a few pence more per share if he or she is buying and receive a few pence less per share if he or she is selling).

Investors are able to instruct their banks to buy or sell shares on their behalf, and they will do this through their brokers, but stockbrokers will deal direct with investors if their portfolios of shares (and hence likely transactions) are large enough to make it worthwhile opening an account for them. Stockbrokers will give advice to their clients about the suitability of particular stocks and shares for their particular requirements, and investors carrying out transactions through their banks are usually able to obtain such brokers' reports through the agency of the bank. There are also firms which publish news sheets on stocks and shares, which may be subscribed to.

Importance of the Stock Exchange

The Stock Exchange plays a very important role in the community in that it provides an efficient market for existing securities, through which securities can be converted into cash or into other assets. It enables savers – including the institutions such as pension funds, insurance companies and unit trusts which collect other people's savings – to lend their money to industry and to the government. Borrowers and lenders are brought into touch with one another through the market.

Prices of stocks and shares on the Stock Exchange, together with their yields and information concerning the progress of the companies concerned, are published in the national press, and this information assists savers in deciding how to invest their funds. Movements in share prices are determined by supply and demand, and are a useful barometer of opinion as to the future prospects for industry and commerce and of the likely future trend for interest rates. A favourable opinion concerning the prospects for a particular company will cause the price of its shares to rise, and will make it easier (and cheaper) for the company concerned to raise new capital through a new share issue should it wish to do so.

There is a strict code of conduct on the Stock Exchange concerning the activities of both the jobbers and the brokers and, in addition, a company's shares will no longer be listed if the Stock Exchange Council is not satisfied with the way its affairs are being conducted. Investors are therefore protected.

Both the government and industry have access through the Stock Exchange to the community's savings which they are able to tap respectively through the issue of bonds and shares.

TOPICS FOR DISCUSSION

1. Discuss the need for capital investment within a community, illustrating how vital the level of savings is in this connection.
2. Compare the ways in which assurance companies and pension funds channel savings to industry and commerce.
3. Apart from the National Savings Bank, and to some extent the TSBs, the banks do not generally run savings accounts as such. Consider, then, how the banks provide a channel through which savings can be passed on to industry and commerce.
4. Why should the government bother to collect savings through the national savings movement when it issues such an enormous quantity of British stocks?
5. Consider the value of the Stock Exchange to savers, to industry and to the government.

CHAPTER 7

MONETARY POLICY

7.1 OBJECTIVES

The purpose of monetary policy is to control the money supply and the cost and availability of credit, so as to regulate demand and through this influence the rate of inflation, economic growth and employment.

Monetary policy must, however, be seen in the context of a government's economic strategy as a whole, which includes the employment not only of a particular monetary policy but also of an appropriate fiscal policy - i.e., the policy concerned with the government's income (taxation) and expenditure - and, possibly, direct controls such as a prices and incomes policy as well. All of these policies must be pulling in the same direction if the government's objectives are to stand some chance of success. It would, for instance, be futile to attempt to restrain the level of monetary demand by firm control of the money supply with the objective of reducing the level of inflation if at the same time the fiscal policy was to reduce taxation and increase also the level of government spending.

The objectives of a government's economic strategy may conflict, and force the government to decide which objectives are more important; the most likely areas of conflict are between a high level of economic growth with full employment on the one hand, and control of inflation on the other. This has been clearly demonstrated since the late 1970s when so much attention has - rightly or wrongly - been given to controlling inflation. The annual rate of increase in prices has certainly been reduced, but the price of this has been only a very modest amount of economic growth and a very high level of unemployment. It would be wrong to imply, however, that one is the only cause of the other for clearly there are many factors affecting the level of economic growth in the UK, not the least of those being the level of demand in other countries, especially those in North America and Western Europe.

The responsibility for the monetary policy lies firmly in the hands of the government, but it is the Bank of England which is primarily responsible for putting it into effect though it does so in very close liaison with the Treasury. Indeed we have already used the term 'the authorities' in earlier chapters to mean the Treasury and the Bank of England working together. The degree to which the central bank is allowed to act independently from the government varies considerably from country to country. In the UK they work closely together whilst in the USA the central bank (the Federal Reserve), works much more independently.

7.2 THE QUANTITY OF MONEY

In order to understand the aims of monetary policy it is necessary to appreciate the connection between the quantity of money and the prices of goods and services, for it is the basic claim of the proponents of the theory that increases in the money stock lead to higher expenditure and this in turn can lead to rising prices.

The original quantity theory of money was that the money stock in the community x the number of times it changed hands in a given period (the velocity of circulation) = the total value of transactions, and that any change in the money stock (unless it was offset by a change in the velocity of circulation) would affect the level of transactions and/or their prices. This could be expressed by the equation $MV = PT$, where:

M = Money supply.
V = Velocity of circulation.
P = Prices.
T = Transactions.

This was a very simplistic approach to the problem, for the equation states nothing more than a truism in that the money supply x its velocity of circulation must = the total value of transactions. However, it is a useful starting off point for our examination of the theory.

It is not possible to measure the velocity of circulation of the money stock apart from measuring the turnover of bank deposits by the value of cheques passing through the London Clearing House. If we divide the total annual value of these cheques by the amount of bank deposits, and then compare the answer year by year, an acceleration or deceleration of the velocity of circulation will become apparent – but this is a very crude measure, in that the total of Clearing House business includes vouchers for very large payments between banks (and between banks and other financial institutions) which would possibly give a false indication of the trend in velocity of circulation between the community in respect of transactions in goods and services. But in any case we cannot measure the velocity of circulation of the rest of the money supply, i.e. notes and coin.

If we take T as being fixed – which it would be in the short period – only if it could be shown that V is independent of M could it then be said that an increase in M will bring about an increase in prices. However, there is every likelihood that an increase in M will be accompanied by a fall in V. The theory is a weak one therefore if it can be supported only by the equation of exchange. Later economists sought new ways of relating the theory to reality, however, and now using the income approach, the theory can be more usefully applied.

Let us take the equation $Y = k\,M$, where:

Y = Money income of the community.

M = The money stock.

k = The average no. of times each unit of money is received as income.

Here, we are concerned with a new form of velocity, we are no longer concerned with the velocity of circulation of money in the broad sense that we were in looking at the equation $MV = PT$. We are now concerned with that *proportion of total income* which the community wishes to hold in money form which determines the size of k, and if this proportion remains stable we then have a reliable link between money and income. If (assuming no change in k) the money supply is increased whilst the national income remains static, prices will rise. Only if there are under-used resources is national income likely to rise quickly enough for the increase in the money supply to be required to maintain the ratio k, and therefore it is not very likely that an increase in the money stock will *in itself* trigger off an increase in the national income.

We have assumed that k remains unchanged, which may not be the case, especially during a period of inflation. If prices are rising steeply, holders of money may choose to keep less of it and to buy goods as a hedge against inflation, and in consequence k may well rise. The extra spending would stimulate production so that Y would increase and therefore the existing money stock may still be required to achieve the new proportion of income to be held as money. If production (national income) does not rise under such circumstances, prices will rise still further and stimulate the tendency to buy goods rather than hold money. The inflation will then breed upon itself.

If when the money stock increases, the community decides to buy more goods to restore their holdings of money to what they were previously, they spend some of the money in acquiring financial assets such as government stocks, the demand for these assets will force up their prices and therefore the yields on them will decline. There is thus a useful link between the money stock and interest rates, and in any case it is reasonable to assume that the higher the rate of interest the greater will be the attractiveness of financial assets other than money. A rise in interest rates will therefore reduce the demand for money to hold - i.e., increase k. As there is an obvious link between interest rates and capital investment by industry (though economists vary in their opinions as to the strength of this link), the size of the money stock can affect investment as well.

The money stock is therefore a very useful target for the government's monetary policy in that it influences expenditure and hence incomes and the level of employment, interest rates and the level of capital investment. But as to whether controlling the money supply is the best intermediate target for a government to use in carrying out its monetary policy, controversy reigns. The 'monetarists' would of course claim that this is the best target. Incidentally, 'intermediate target' is used rather than simply 'target' of monetary policy in that the variables controlled are the means whereby the end is to be achieved. If the purpose of monetary policy is to control expenditure, for instance, a number of monetary variables could be controlled in order to achieve this - such as interest rates, credit and the money stock. Each of these variables can be used as an intermediate target in an attempt to achieve the main aim.

7.3 OTHER INTERMEDIATE TARGETS

Monetary variables
As has just been mentioned, in addition to the money stock there are a number of other monetary variables which can be used as intermediate targets for monetary policy. These are credit, interest rates, exchange rates, and possibly expenditure itself. We have dealt at some length with the money stock and will be coming back to it, but we need now to look briefly at each of the others in turn.

Credit
There is a case for using bank credit as the intermediate target rather than the money stock, inasmuch as an increase in bank lending (which is, of course, what we mean by bank credit) is certain to lead to an increase in expenditure. The increase in bank lending may well increase the money stock by creating fresh deposits, but this is by no means certain. If credit is used as the intermediate target, then changes in the supply of credit generally would need to be measured, and not only that provided by the banks.

Exchange rates
Controlling the value of sterling in terms of other currencies - i.e., exchange rates - could be a useful target for monetary policy, but past experience has shown that endeavouring to maintain fixed exchange rates can result in

the country's economic policy having to revolve round the exchange rate. It becomes a case of 'the tail wagging the dog', in that maintaining the exchange rate becomes the purpose of monetary policy, and the intermediate targets such as the money stock are the means towards the end of maintaining exchange rates. This does not mean that the exchange rate should not be used as one of the intermediate targets, but it should not be relied on too much. By influencing exchange rates (bringing them down, for instance), exports could be made more competitive thus increasing economic growth; but at the same time imports become dearer in terms of sterling which would be advantageous from the point of view of discouraging them, but higher costs of imported raw materials and foodstuffs would cause domestic prices to rise.

Interest rates

Using the level of interest rates as an intermediate target in controlling the level of expenditure is fraught with difficulties because of its uncertain effect. There is some considerable doubt as to whether businessmen are greatly influenced in their investment decisions by interest rates, and therefore what the effect of a change in interest rates will be upon expenditure generally. However, it is certain that lower interest rates will affect business decisions to some extent, and in that industry and commerce owe such an enormous amount to the banks and other financial institutions a 1 per cent reduction in interest reduces industry's costs very considerably and this must enable them to moderate their price increases and improve their profit figures, with consequential effects upon business confidence and future investment.

Expenditure

Control of expenditure can be used as an intermediate target as part of the monetary policy, instead of being itself the purpose of using other targets. If the objective is to control the money stock, then attempts could be made to control expenditure as a means of achieving this objective. However, changes in the level of expenditure take time to measure and hence weapons to stimulate or reduce its growth may be used too late to have the necessary immediate effects upon the objective. It would be easier (and quicker) to influence and measure the size of the money stock than to bring about a desired change in the level of expenditure (and to measure it).

7.4 WEAPONS OF MONETARY POLICY

Introduction

The central bank has a number of weapons in its armoury with which to fight the battle of limiting the money stock as an intermediate target in controlling the level of expenditure. In that bank deposits account for a major part of the money supply – the proportion depending upon which money aggregate is used (see Chapter 5) – the main effort must be towards limiting the growth of bank deposits. However, as we saw when looking at the money aggregates, the whole liquidity situation of the community is also of vital importance in that it influences expenditure decisions, and therefore the authorities (in wishing to control the size of bank deposits) may also turn their attention to the deposits of other financial institutions as well. The introduction of the new M_2 aggregate in 1982 as a finer measure of the availability of money for transactions points to the awareness of the authorities of the need to measure the growth in deposits in building societies and the National Savings Bank as well as the deposits of the commercial banks.

The 'traditional' weapons of control are the central bank's base rate of interest (originally known as Bank Rate and more recently as Minimum Lending Rate (MLR) in the UK), open market operations and reserve ratios. To these have been added direct controls in the form of directives to the banks concerning the level of advances and special deposits. These weapons, and the extent to which they have been used, will now be considered. Although the term 'central bank' is used synonymously with the Bank of England in this chapter, the reader will understand that much of what is written applies equally as well to central banks abroad.

Central bank's base rate

Up to 1972, the Bank of England published its Bank Rate, which was the minimum rate of interest at which it was willing to discount bills for the discount houses as lender of last resort. The clearing banks had collective interest rate agreements, and related the rate of interest they paid on deposits to Bank Rate and similarly their interest charge for loans. Deposit rate was usually $1\frac{1}{2}$–2 per cent below Bank Rate, and the interest on advances ranged from $\frac{1}{2}$ per cent above Bank Rate for major companies to 3 per cent or more above for unsecured lending and lending to personal borrowers. The Bank of England was thus able directly to influence the level of interest rates generally, and used the weapon of raising Bank Rate not only to increase other interest rates but as a strong psychological weapon as well.

From 1971–81 Bank Rate was replaced by MLR, with the intention that it would follow market rates rather than lead them. It was to be adjusted in the light of Treasury bill rate, which was itself a barometer of interest rates in the money market. However, this did not work in practice for long, and the MLR was used to lead interest rates in the same way as its predecessor, Bank Rate, had been. In 1971 the banks abandoned their agreements on interest rates and started to publish their own base rates, but in practice these have followed one another very closely and also followed MLR during the time that it was in force.

Since 1981, the Bank of England has refrained from setting a MLR, though it has declared the intention of reintroducing it should it be considered desirable. The bank now attempts to keep interest rates within unpublished bands which are subject to change in consultation with the Chancellor of the Exchequer in the light of the growth of the money aggregates and other developments in the economy. When the Bank of England buys bills from the discount houses the rates of interest charged are within the unpublished bands, and are sometimes higher than those in the market. This means that the discount houses may still be penalised when they are forced to seek finance from the Bank as lender of last resort.

The reason why a central bank would wish either directly to lead the level of interest rates or, alternatively, strongly influence them, is that by making money dearer, borrowing (and hence credit expansion) is discouraged, whilst if interest rates are reduced borrowing is encouraged. The Bank of England endeavours through the interest rate intermediate target to attain that level of interest rates that will bring forth that amount of bank lending which would bring the money stock up to the desired level. This assumes that the private sector (particularly businesses) will respond in the expected way to a change in the price of money – i.e., to borrow more of it when it is cheaper and less when it is dearer. However, this may not always be the case because other factors (especially future prospects for profits and also the expected level of inflation) will affect the desire to borrow. There is also likely to be a time lag between the raising or lowering of interest rates and the respective reduction or increase in the level of borrowing, because it takes time to reduce spending commitments or to acquire new capital equipment and stocks.

At times in the past, there has been conflict between the use of the interest rate weapon for domestic and for external purposes. For instance, when it has been desirable to bring about a reflation of the economy by encouraging investment through lower interest rates, and at the same time it has been necessary to avoid an outflow of short-term capital which is attracted abroad by the relatively high rates of interest in other countries. Such a conflict can place a government on the horns of a dilemma and make it virtually impossible to achieve that flexibility in interest rates which is necessary if such rates are to be used as a monetary target.

If interest rates are used as a monetary weapon, it is usually necessary for the government to make the rates effective by its *open market operations*.

Open market operations
By selling and buying bills of exchange in the open market, the Bank of England can reduce (or increase) the amount of central bank balances held

by the banks, and through this endeavour to make its interest rate policy effective. However, it cannot have it both ways – either it controls the price of money, or it controls the volume of securities available in the market, but not both – although it can hope to achieve a correct balance between the two. When the central bank sells bills to the private sector, they are paid for by cheques drawn by the banks or on the banks, and when these have been cleared the banks' balances with the central bank are reduced. To restore these balances, the banks may have to borrow from the central bank (or in the UK squeeze the discount houses, who must in turn borrow from the Bank of England) which is able to impose higher rates of interest for such borrowing if it wishes to do so. Similarly, when the central bank buys bills from the banks (or discount houses) it increases the central bank balances of the banks and interest rates then tend to fall.

Open market operations can also be used to make the reserve ratios of the banks effective by reducing the availability of liquid assets. If these are short the banks may have difficulty in maintaining the reserve ratio (if one is in force) and therefore have to reduce the level of their advances in order to increase cash balances.

Reserve ratios

In the UK the clearing banks were required to maintain reserve ratios up to 1981, and even after that, as we know, they have been required to keep a set proportion of their eligible liabilities on a non-operational account with the Bank of England. Up to 1971, the clearing banks were expected to keep at least 8 per cent of their deposits in cash or on account with the Bank of England (the cash ratio) and a minimum liquidity ratio of 28 per cent of deposits (this had earlier been maintained at 30 per cent). The liquid assets were Cash on Hand and Balances at the Bank of England, Call Money and Treasury and Commercial Bills. These two ratios were not *legally* enforced, but no doubt if the banks had not maintained them pressure would have been brought to bear upon them by the Bank.

The existence of these higher ratios greatly restricted the ability of the banks to increase their advances, and once the ratios were replaced in 1971 by the reserve assets ratio of $12\frac{1}{2}$ per cent (which was common to all banks), the clearing banks were able to switch a large amount of liquid assets into advances (for details of the reserve assets ratio, see Chapter 3).

As already mentioned, the central bank can endeavour to make effective such reserve ratios by its open market operations, and possibly force the banks to reduce their advances. Similarly, the central bank can endeavour to achieve this objective by controlling the more narrow cash base – i.e., the cash ratio.

This is known as *monetary base control*. If the central bank can make it difficult for the banks to maintain an adequate balance at the central bank the banks may be obliged to sell some of their assets and restrict their lending in order to build up the cash base. If they sell securities to the private sector (excluding the monetary sector) bank deposits will fall, and the cash base ratio will be restored – or, alternatively, if they raise interest rates on deposits so as to attract deposits from other banks and other financial institutions, they would need to also charge higher rates of interest on advances, which would discourage borrowers. The use of monetary base control was considered by the Bank of England when the new methods of monetary control were introduced in 1981, but so far the device has not been implemented though the imposition of the $\frac{1}{2}$ per cent compulsory non-operational balances at the Bank of England provides the first step for any future implementation of this form of control.

Direct controls

The three traditional methods of control which we have considered are all *indirect* controls, in that the central bank imposes them in the hope that it will achieve its objective of controlling the expansion of bank credit. The same may possibly be said of special deposits (and of the supplementary special deposits that were imposed in Britain for a short period), in that the Bank of England uses them as a means of achieving the same end of controlling bank advances. However, special deposits are a direct control in the sense that the banks are given a direct request – which may well be regarded as an instruction – to hand over in cash to the Bank of England a set proportion of their eligible liabilities (see Chapter 3). If the banks hand over special deposits they may well have to restrict their lending in order to build up their central bank balances to the point where they are able to hand over the required amount and yet be left with an adequate balance for their day to day needs. They may also achieve the extra cash by selling securities to the private sector and reducing the general liquidity situation, which would discourage expenditure.

The central bank may achieve its objective of controlling bank credit by the means of the most direct method of all. This is to instruct the banks not to increase their advances or to limit their growth to, say, 5 per cent during the next year. On one occasion (July 1955), the banks were actually asked to make a substantial reduction in their advances. Direct controls of this nature have not been imposed in the UK since the introduction of the Competition and Credit Control measures in 1971, but 'qualitative controls' on bank lending still remain in existence. These are concerned with the *types* of bank advances. On occasions, for instance, the banks have been given a directive to give priority to advances to industry and for exports, and to restrain lending to private individuals and to property developers.

From 1974–80, the Bank of England endeavoured directly to control the growth of bank interest-bearing deposits by imposing supplementary special deposits (see below).

7.5 MONETARY TARGETS IN THE UK

Targets for growth of the money stock have been set year by year in the UK since 1976, and although they have not always been achieved, they have been regarded as the main lynch-pin in the government's economic policy, though more recently the government has been showing increasing interest in both exchange rates and interest rates as economic indicators. The targets are set as a range (for instance, 8–12 per cent) in order to allow some flexibility. The aggregate in which the target was expressed up to 1981 was sterling M_3 and subsequently the government referred to both M_1 and PSL_2 as well in setting its targets.

Since 1980, the government has published a medium-term financial strategy (MTFS) in addition to its annual monetary targets. This strategy reflects the government's intentions on public spending and taxation as well as monetary policy for three years ahead. Projections are given for public expenditure, taxes and public borrowing, with particular emphasis on the public sector borrowing requirement (PSBR). The PSBR projection has been as a proportion of national income, and the government has endeavoured to reduce this percentage each year so as to reduce interest rates which should encourage industrial investment. If the PSBR is high then high interest rates must be given on government stocks to encourage investors to buy them; if the PSBR is reduced, interest rates can be reduced.

7.6 COMPETITION AND CREDIT CONTROL

In 1971, the Bank of England brought into force the new system known as Competition and Credit Control. Whereas in the previous two decades the authorities had relied on direct controls to restrict the level of bank lending the new form of control was to rely on the use of *market forces*. Competition between the banks was to be encouraged by their having their own base rates and by the abolition of the interest rate agreement between the banks, and the banks were all to be treated equally as far as the imposition of the new $12\frac{1}{2}$ per cent reserve ratio and special deposits were concerned (whereas previously they had applied only to the clearing banks).

The new methods of control were to rely on the use of interest rates to regulate the growth of the money supply. To help enforce this, the Bank of England deliberately started to put up more Treasury bills for tender each week than were necessary so as to take more from the central bank balances of the banks. To relieve the shortfall in these balances, the banks restricted their loans to the discount houses, who were then forced to borrow from or sell bills to the Bank of England. The Bank of England gave their assistance at rates which suited it, and in consequence it was better able to control the level of interest rates. The clearing banks were also required to keep a minimum of $1\frac{1}{2}$ per cent of their eligible liabilities in balances at the Bank of England, which also helped the Bank of England in enforcing its control of interest rates through the over-issue of Treasury bills.

In the event, the Competition and Credit Control measures were not very successful. This was partly the result of the rapid increase in oil prices in 1973-4, which caused a high level of inflation and made control of the money supply more difficult. Through the removal of the old 28 per cent liquidity ratio and its replacement with the $12\frac{1}{2}$ per cent reserve ratio the clearing banks were presented with the possibility of greatly increasing their advances, and hence a rapid increase in the money supply was to be expected. Furthermore, these banks were able to be more competitive and thus to acquire deposits which were previously in the hands of competitor banks and other financial institutions, and this too enabled them to increase advances and through the expansion of credit bring about an increase in the money stock.

There was a need to make credit more available to stimulate industrial investment and its growth might well have been contained through the Bank of England's interest rate policy had the oil crisis not occurred. When inflation became excessive, extremely high interest rates would have been required to make the weapon effective. Even though interest rates reached record levels, they did not rise quickly enough or sufficiently high to contain the money growth. Excessively high interest rates would, it was feared, discourage industrial investment.

Another event which occurred affected the public's confidence in the banking system which, although it did not have any direct effect upon the government's monetary policy, must have had serious indirect consequences in that it called for a massive joint support operation by the Bank of England and the clearing banks. This was the secondary bank crisis. The smaller banks lent excessively to property companies against the security of (in the main) industrial and commercial property. But the demand for such properties fell and property values slumped, and therefore the advances could not be repaid without selling properties at a loss. In consequence confidence in the secondary banks' ability to repay depositors was lost and the so-called 'lifeboat operation' (involving the setting up of a £1200 million fund to prevent these banks going into liquidation) was necessary.

In an attempt to improve control over the money supply the supplementary special deposits scheme was used at various times during the years

1974–80. This became known as the 'corset', no doubt because it was designed to stop bank deposits from expanding! Under the scheme, the Bank of England prescribed a limit to the extent to which the banks' interest-bearing deposits could grow. The reader will appreciate that with their new freedom to bid higher rates of interest to attract deposits they were able not only to obtain them but at the same time push up the general level of interest rates. To stop both things happening, the Bank of England penalised individual banks which exceeded the prescribed limit for growth of interest-bearing deposits. This was done by requiring them to hand over supplementary special deposits on which no interest was paid even though the banks were paying interest on deposits to their customers: the more a bank exceeded the quota, the more steep was the penalty in the form of the call for supplementary deposits.

The corset was not popular in that it was completely contrary to the spirit and intention of Competition and Credit Control and, although it may have assisted the authorities in achieving their targets for growth in the money stock, it caused distortions in the market and led to the diversion of credit into less orthodox channels.

The fact that the corset had to be used indicated that Competition and Credit Control did not work successfully and the authorities brought out a new discussion document called *Monetary Control*, which was to form the basis for new measures introduced in 1981.

7.7 1981 MONETARY MEASURES

The monetary control measures introduced in 1981 involved the abolition of the corset, the reserve asset ratio and the requirement that the clearing banks should hold at least $1\frac{1}{2}$ per cent of their eligible liabilities in balances at the Bank of England; they also involved the suspension of MLR. The removal of the corset needs no explanation for it was clearly an unpopular form of control. The removal of the reserve asset ratio of $12\frac{1}{2}$ per cent may seem more surprising, however, for the banks are now able to maintain whatever stock of liquid assets they feel appropriate, but it must not be forgotten that the Banking Act 1979 gave the Bank of England the ultimate weapon of withdrawing a bank's licence if it is not run on prudential lines and does not heed the advice of the Bank of England. The $1\frac{1}{2}$ per cent balance at the Bank of England has been replaced by a requirement that applies to all banks, and not only to the clearing banks. All banks and licensed deposit takers beyond a minimum size must now maintain a non-operational account at the Bank of England with a balance which amounts to $\frac{1}{2}$ per cent of their eligible liabilities. This is of course much fairer on the clearing banks.

The suspension of MLR gives the authorities more flexibility in influencing the level of short-term interest rates. They are now kept within unpublished bands, and can thus be adjusted quickly when necessary (as, too, can the bands themselves should the need arise). Although the MLR is no longer published the authorities still use interest rates as an important monetary target. The Bank of England enforces it with regard to short-term rates by its open market operations, buying and selling bills as appropriate, whilst long-term rates of interest are determined more by the market itself.

To give itself more scope for carrying out open market operations in bills the Bank of England has made more banks eligible banks – that is, banks whose acceptances the Bank of England is willing to buy. In this way the volume of accepted bills in the money market is now greater, and to ensure that the discount houses have sufficient funds to buy bills, the Bank of England requires all eligible banks to hold at least $2\frac{1}{2}$ per cent of their deposits in secured loans to the discount houses each day. Furthermore, on a daily average basis over six months or a year, they must lend at least 5 per cent of their deposits to the discount houses (and certain other specialised intermediaries).

Intervention by the Bank of England in the money market is designed to even out the uneven flow of funds from day to day between the public sector and the private sector and vice-versa. Each day, the clearing banks inform the Bank of England what balances they require in order to meet their commitments for the day and by combining this knowledge with its own information about flows of funds between the banks and the public sector, the Bank of England is able to estimate the likely shortage (or surplus) of funds in the money market. It announces this estimate in the morning and revises it at midday if necessary.

When there is a shortage of funds, the Bank of England will buy bills from the discount houses. They will offer the bills at whatever rates of interest they choose to apply, but if the Bank of England considers the rates too low it will refuse to buy the bills, and the discount houses are then obliged to offer bills at higher rates to obtain the finance they require. It is in this way that the Bank of England enforces its interest rates policy. Sometimes the Bank of England buys bills from the discount houses with an agreement that the houses will buy the bills back on a stipulated day; this may be selected by the Bank of England deliberately so as to offset an expected surplus of funds in the market on the day in question.

To bring about a fall in interest rates, the Bank of England lowers its dealing rates in the bill market – i.e., it increases the price it is willing to pay for bills when it buys them. If there is a surplus of funds in the market, the Bank of England sells Treasury bills to the banks and discount houses.

TOPICS FOR DISCUSSION

1. Discuss the need for control of the money supply in order to prevent inflation. What other means are open to the authorities for controlling inflation?
2. Consider the ways in which a central bank can influence or control the level of interest rates. What is the purpose of raising or lowering interest rates?
3. Why might a central bank consider it necessary to enforce a minimum reserve assets ratio upon the commercial banks?
4. Discuss the usefulness of direct controls over bank lending. Why might they have to be imposed, and why are they so unpopular with the banks?
5. Which of the measures adopted under Competition and Credit Control were aimed at (i) increasing competition and (ii) controlling the banking system?
6. The Bank of England no longer publishes its MLR, yet its controls are still centred round its influence over interest rates generally. Consider how it can achieve the latter influence without the former weapon.
7. What consitutes the government's medium-term financial strategy (MTFS)? Why is the size of the PSBR of particular importance in this connection?

PART III
THE LEGAL BACKGROUND

CHAPTER 8

BANKER-CUSTOMER RELATIONSHIPS

8.1 BASIC CONTRACTUAL RELATIONSHIP

There is no statutory definition of a 'bank customer', and therefore it is necessary to rely on case law in order to establish whether a person is a customer or not. In *Great Western Railway* v. *London and County Banking Co.* (1901), it was stated that a customer must have a current account or deposit account or some similar relationship. However not all 'customers' of banks deposit money and may, for instance, deposit valuables other than money, yet the banks regard such people as customers. In *Woods* v. *Martins Bank Ltd and Another* (1959) it was considered that Woods became a customer when he made an investment in a company on the advice of the manager, even though his account was not opened for some weeks thereafter.

The length of time during which there have been dealings with a person does not appear to affect the situation, for in *Ladbroke and Co.* v. *Todd* (1914) and *Commissioners of Taxation* v. *English, Scottish and Australian Bank Ltd* (1920), it was established that a continuous dealing relationship was not essential to a definition of a customer and that the relationship began immediately an account was opened and funds paid into it.

The time of commencement of the banker–customer relationship is important because the contractual duties of a banker do not begin until then and, furthermore, to gain the protection of s.4, Cheques Act 1957 when collecting a cheque the bank must receive payment *for a customer*. When an account is to be opened suitable references must be taken up, but this does not preclude a banker opening the account on a conditional basis on the understanding that it will be closed if references are unsatisfactory. However, if cheques are collected for the account holder in the meantime, the legal position is not clear. It is quite likely that the account holder has not become a customer, in which case the collection of cheques was a risk.

No written contract usually exists between banker and customer, the account being opened by verbal agreement without any precise statement as to the terms and conditions (though there may be a mandate giving signing instructions). It is therefore an implied contract based on the duties and rights of both parties as established by both banking practice and case law. The terms of the contract have been gradually determined and modified as banking practice has developed over the years. The contract is that of debtor and creditor, the bank being the debtor and the customer the creditor when the account is in credit, and vice-versa when the customer has borrowed from the bank. In addition, the banker is agent to the customer when, for instance, the banker collects bills of exchange and cheques, makes payments for third-party cheques, remits funds abroad and buys or sells stocks and shares for the customer.

The duties of a banker were reviewed in the judgement in *Joachimson* v. *Swiss Bank Corporation* (1921):

1. The banker must receive money from and collect cheques and other bills of exchange for the customer and repay the money against the customer's written order. The order must be addressed to the branch where the account is kept and repayment made at that branch during normal working hours (banking practice has changed since then, of course, in that, for instance, such orders may be given by pressing the keys at a service till after hours).
2. The banker must give reasonable notice before closing an account in order that the customer may make other arrangements and also so that any cheques that may have been drawn may reach the bank.

From (1) above it will be seen that the customer (the debtor) must seek out the creditor (the bank), which is the opposite to the normal legal requirement that the debtor must seek out the creditor.

The duty of a customer is to exercise reasonable care in drawing cheques, and this applies even if he or she employs someone to write them. In *London Joint Stock Bank* v. *McMillan and Arthur* (1918), an employee of a customer wrote out a cheque for £2 but did not insert the words and left sufficient space either side of the '2' for the amount of the cheque to be altered after signature to £120. It was held that the bank's customer (the employer) did not exercise reasonable care in making the written order, and therefore lost his case against the bank.

A banker has the implied right to charge interest on advances, and reasonable commission for other services performed for a customer. He or she is also entitled to be reimbursed for any expenses incurred when acting on the customer's behalf. The banker has the right to repayment on demand of any overdrawn balance and has the right to exercise a lien over any of the customer's property lodged with the bank other than those simply deposited for safe custody (see below). The lien covers negotiable instruments such as cheques and bills of exchange, and any other document which provides for money to be paid to the customer, such as an insurance policy.

In the vicarious capacity as agent for the customer, the banker must obey the principal's lawful instructions with reasonable competence and diligence. He or she must personally perform the tasks, and not delegate them. However, there may be an express or implied agreement that work may be delegated and it is, for instance, understood that the bank employs clerks to carry out most of the work. As agent, the banker must render an account to the principal whenever it is required. The banker must also avoid being placed in a position where the banker's own interest would clash with that of the principal, and must not make any secret profit over and above the commission which the principal pays. The banker must also keep the principal's affairs secret.

8.2 BOND OF SECRECY

Bank customers have always expected their affairs to be kept secret - quite apart from the legal responsibility of a bank to do so - and generally speaking this bond is rarely broken. However, there are occasions when a bank must divulge information about its customer's account even without express consent. In the case of *Tournier* v. *National Provincial Bank Ltd* (1924), it was decided that the duty of secrecy is not absolute, and that there are four instances when disclosure may be justified:

Under compulsion of law
A bank may be directed by a court to produce copies of a customer's account. Subsequent legislation has also compelled banks to divulge information, for instance, to inspectors authorised to investigate the affairs of companies, and to the Inland Revenue about deposit account interest in excess of a certain amount credited to a customer in any one financial year.

Duty to the public
Where it is vital to the community - for instance, where a customer is known to be trading with the enemy.

In the interests of the bank
Where, for instance, the bank is demanding payment from a guarantor of a customer's overdrawn account.

Where the customer's interest demands disclosure
Where, for instance, a bank replies to a status enquiry concerning its customer: here, it is assumed that the bank has implied authority from

its customer. Similarly, where the bank is dealing with the manager of a business, there may be an implied consent on the part of the owners of the business to divulge information concerning the account.

8.3 STATUS ENQUIRIES

The banks answer status enquiries concerning their customers received from other banks and credit reference agencies and take the possible risks of breach of contract and of being sued for libel or slander by a customer who considered the banker's opinion defamatory. However, the bank may claim that it has express authority when the customer gives someone a banker's name as a referee or instructs a bank to answer an enquiry from another bank. The bank might possibly succeed in court on the basis of implied authority, on the assumption that the customer knew of the practice between banks of answering such enquiries when he or she opened the account.

As far as the danger of defamation is concerned, the banks are especially cautious in framing their replies to enquiries. They do not divulge the balance on the customer's account and endeavour to give a general answer from which the enquirer can deduce a response, which nevertheless shows the customer in a true light. The banks always include a disclaimer of responsibility in their replies, and mention the fact that the bank is not a credit reference agency under the Consumer Credit Act 1974 (if they were an agency, they could be called upon to disclose their opinion). As far as the disclaimer is concerned, there is some doubt as to whether this would protect a bank if it were challenged under the Unfair Contracts Act 1977.

A banker may also incur liability for fraud or for negligence when giving an inaccurate opinion in a reply to a status enquiry. A claim of fraudulent misrepresentation could be made only if the reply was signed, and it is for this reason that replies are not signed. To claim negligence on the part of the responding banker the enquirer would have to establish that the bank had some contractual or fiduciary relatiohship with him.

8.4 BANKER AS BAILEE

When banks take charge of deed boxes, parcels of deeds, stocks and shares and other securities on behalf of their customers they are *bailees*. If the banker is paid for this service he or she is a paid bailee, but otherwise the banker is a gratuitous bailee and this distinction between the two types could make some difference should there be an accusation of negligence against a bank by a customer as bailor of property lodged with the bank for safe custody – a gratuitous bailee must take *reasonable* care of property entrusted, but a paid bailee must take the *maximum possible* care, including modern security devices, when looking after property. However, the distinction between the two types of bailees has become less important because the banks do take very good care of property left with them, whether they are paid for the service or not. In either case, it is incumbent upon the banker as bailee to prove that the loss of any property bailed was not the fault of the bank or its agents.

If an item left in safe custody is delivered to the wrong person, the banker could be sued for conversion which is an unauthorised act which deprives another person of his property.

When property is deposited with a bank for safe custody the bailor (the customer) retains ownership of it, and the bank cannot claim a lien on it except to the extent of any unpaid fees in respect of the bailment itself.

Banks prefer boxes to be locked and packages to be sealed before they are lodged for safekeeping and the bank's receipt usually states that the contents are unknown. These precautions may lessen the bank's liability for any loss or damage.

8.5 CUSTOMERS OF THE BANK

Married women

A married woman can now own property in the same way as if she were unmarried, and she can enter into any contract and be sued for a debt or a tort. She is subject to the law relating to bankruptcy as if she were a single person. A married woman may therefore open and run an account, borrow money and pledge security to the bank and avail herself of all the other banking services. However, if she is a minor the rules for opening and running an account for a minor will of course apply (see below).

Despite the Sex Discrimination Act 1975, some banks still require to know the name of a married woman's husband, his employer's name and his occupation, when opening an account for her. This is because of the decision in *Savory and Co.* v. *Lloyds Bank Ltd* (1932), in which the bank was found negligent in not finding out these details when opening a wife's account. Quite apart from this, the bank will want the usual references. When a married woman deposits security on behalf of another person banks usually arrange for her to be independently advised by a solicitor. This is particularly desirable where she is lodging security in respect of her husband's account.

Minors

A minor is a person under 18 years of age, and as such is not bound by contracts. He or she cannot give a guarantee, nor borrow against the guarantee of an adult, although to take a form of indemnity as security is possible.

When opening an account for a young person, the banker must endeavour to ascertain his or her age, and record the date of the 18th birthday. Normally the account should be kept in credit, but bankers do on occasions use their discretion in allowing a small overdraft, even though legally they have no claim for repayment.

A minor may be a partner, and can operate on a partnership account and even incur an overdraft, as agent for the partnership. He or she is not personally liable, however, until he or she reaches the 18th birthday, except for his or her own share of the partnership assets in the event of bankruptcy of the partnership.

Similarly, a minor may be a party to a joint account but would not be liable for any overdraft on the account incurred before he or she reached 18.

Joint accounts

When an account is opened in the names of two or more persons, the bank requires its standard form of *mandate* to be signed. This must indicate whether one, some, or all of the parties are to sign on the account and to withdraw items of security from the bank.

Even though not all of the parties need to sign on the account to make withdrawals, the mandate will establish that they are all liable in respect of any money borrowed from the bank. This liability is always *joint and several* - i.e., there is a right of action against all of the parties to the account jointly, and then on an individual basis against each partner until the whole debt is recovered. There is a right of set-off between the private accounts of the individual parties and their joint account, and death does not release the estate of a deceased party for debts owing on the joint account.

When one of the parties to a joint account dies, the bank would by common law obtain a good discharge by paying over a credit balance to the surviving parties or by taking a new mandate on the account signed by the surviving parties. The rule of survivorship must apply, but this becomes a matter for the surviving parties to sort out between themselves, provided that the bank's mandate establishes quite clearly that the intention of the parties was that upon the death of one of them the balance should vest in the survivors. Safe custodies are usually handed over against the signatories of the surviving parties to the account and of the personal representatives of the deceased party.

The bankruptcy of one party determines the mandate, and the account must be stopped and the credit balance released on the signatures of the solvent party(ies) and the trustee or official receiver. If there is an overdraft, the bankrupt's security will be released only if the remaining parties repay the overdraft or undertake (with the bank's approval) to do so. Safe custodies will be released on the joint authority of the remaining parties and the trustee or official receiver.

Mental incapacity also determines the mandate on a joint account, and the account must be stopped. A credit balance can be released against the signatures of the remaining parties and the Court of Protection. The incapacitated party's securities against an overdraft will be released only if the other parties to the account repay the overdraft, and safe custodies will be released against joint signatures in the same way as a credit balance.

Personal representatives

The personal representatives of a deceased person are executors if there is a will, or administrators if there is not. Executors are appointed in the will, administrators are appointed by the court. Where executors refuse to act (or are incapable of acting) administators may be appointed.

An executor's powers to act are confirmed by *probate*, which is an official copy of the will with a certificate that the will has been proved. Letters of administration are granted to the administrator(s). These documents must be presented by the personal representative(s) before a credit balance and securities and safe custodies of the deceased can be withdrawn. If the account is overdrawn, the personal representatives may choose to pay off the overdraft in order to obtain release of securities, or to sell off the securities for the purpose of repaying the overdraft.

If executors or administrators are unknown, the usual references must be obtained before opening an account for the personal representatives. The account is opened in the names of the executors or administrators, with an indication in the title of the account that they are either executors or administrators of the deceased. The mandate indicates whether one or all of the personal representatives are to sign, and always establishes joint and several liability in respect of any advance. As capital transfer tax has to be paid before probate or letters of administration can be obtained personal representatives very frequently require bank finance to enable the tax to be paid.

Club and society accounts

Unincorporated associations have no separate entity, and therefore cannot be sued in their own name. They are non-profit making associations, and as such are not partnerships. The members are not liable in respect of any borrowing by the club or society unless they have given their own personal assent, and the appointed officers would therefore be normally liable for any borrowing.

When the account is opened, the bank requires its appropriate mandate form to be signed which confirms that a meeting of the association resolved that the account should be opened and that certain officers should sign on the account. Usually the mandate bears the signature of the chairman or president as well as those of the persons to sign on the account. A copy of the society's rules will also be required.

Borrowing is not usually involved, and if it is should be allowed only if the association's rules permit it. Security should be taken if at all possible, such as a guarantee of one (or some) of the members.

Partnership accounts

The Partnership Act 1890 defines a partnership as 'the relation which subsists between persons carrying on business in common with a view of profit' (s.1). There need be no written agreement or deed between the partners, it can be simply a verbal or implied agreement. There must not be more than 20 partners, except where the partnership consists of practising solicitors or accountants or persons carrying on a business as members of a Stock Exchange.

A partnership has no separate entity (except in Scotland) and therefore any action against the partnership must be taken against the *partners themselves*. All partners are responsible for the firm's debts, and may be made bankrupt to pay for them. It is no longer necessary for a firm carrying on business under a business name to register that name with the Registrar of Business Names, all that is required is that the names of all the partners appear on business notepaper, circulars, etc. and for the names and addresses of the partners to be displayed.

In opening an account for a partnership, a banker cannot therefore rely on the certificate of registration for confirmation of the names of the partners and may need to see the firm's notepaper or other business documents for confirmation, or visit the premises. A banker must be cautious at the outset because the bank will doubtlessly be collecting cheques payable to the firm and could conceivably be sued for conversion should they be paid into a bogus account in the firm's name by someone who pretended to be the true owner of the firm.

Every partner is an agent of the firm unless the partnership agreement provides to the contrary, and binds the partnership unless the person dealing with the partner concerned is aware of his lack of authority. In a trading firm (one involved in buying and selling goods) there is an implied authority for any partner to bind the firm in respect of bills of exchange (including cheques), promissory notes, contracts of borrowing, and a pledge or sale of the firm's assets except on transactions under seal. In a non-trading firm, a partner cannot bind the firm in respect of these items apart from cheques unless they are part of the firm's usual business. A partner cannot without express authority bind a firm by deed nor execute a guarantee in the firm's name, unless giving guarantees forms part of a firm's usual business. All partners must therefore normally be involved in signing a guarantee.

When opening an account for a partnership, the banker will require a mandate signed by all the partners which covers the drawing of cheques and, borrowing and charging of securities, and will include a clause in which the partners accept joint and several liability. Signatures on the account may be in the name of the firm or on behalf of the firm.

When collecting cheques for a partner's private account drawn on the partnership, the bank is not put on enquiry unless the cheques are exceptionally large or there is some doubt about the partner's integrity. However, a bank is put on enquiry when cheques payable to the partnership are paid into a partner's account, and likewise if the cheques are drawn by the partnership and payable to third parties and indorsed.

Upon the death of a partner, an account that is in credit may be continued by the remaining partners in order to wind up the business, but a new mandate is required. If there is a debit balance it is desirable to claim against the deceased's estate and for this reason the account should be stopped.

Company accounts

A company is a corporation – i.e., a legal person which by law exists and has rights and duties quite separate and distinct from the members of the corporation. Apart from companies set up by Royal Charter and nationalised corporations established by Act of Parliament, the majority of companies are set up by registration under the Companies Acts 1948–81. They are incorporated by registering specified documents with the Registrar of Companies.

Companies may be *unlimited*, which means that in the event of insolvency the members are liable for the company's debts without limit and their own personal assets may have to be used in settling the company's debts. Alternatively, the company may be *limited by shares or by guarantee*. In the first of these two types of limited company the liability of the members of the company is limited to the amount of their shareholdings, and this is the situation with the vast majority of companies. In the second type, the liability of each individual member is limited to the amount of the guarantee which he has given to the company.

Companies also fit into one of two other categories, public companies and private companies. A public company may offer its shares and debentures to the general public, but a private company may not. Both types of company must have at least two members but there is no upper limit on the number of members (although private companies tend still to restrict the size of membership and to restrict the transfer of their shares).

Whether a company is public or private the procedure for incorporation is the same. Five documents must be registered with the Registrar of Companies:

1. Memorandum of Association.
2. Articles of Association.
3. A statement giving the names of the directors and of the secretary, and accompanied by their written consents to act. Included in the statement must be the address of the registered office.
4. A declaration of compliance with the Companies Act 1948 concerning registration.
5. A statement of the company's capital, if there is to be any.

Of these documents, the first two are particularly important and need to be examined in detail.

The *Memorandum of Association* is the company's charter with the outside world, and the company can act only within the powers laid down in it. The memorandum contains the name and registered office of the company. The name must end with the word 'Limited' (Ltd) if it is a private company, and Public Limited Company (plc) if it is a public company (or the Welsh equivalents). In addition, the objects of the company must be given, the company's powers, the fact that liability is to be limited, and the authorised capital of the company.

The *objects clause* must give details of the purposes for which the company has been formed. If any transaction entered into by the company after its incorporation exceeds those authorised in the objects clause, it may be *ultra vires* (beyond the powers) and such an act cannot be rectified by the members of the company. However, the European Communities Act 1972 provides that anyone dealing with a company can enforce an *ultra vires* contract against it if he dealt in good faith and if the transaction was decided on by the directors. The same act stipulated that a third party may assume that the powers of directors to bind the company are not limited under the memorandum and articles of association, that he need not enquire as to the capacity of the company to enter into the transaction or about the powers of the directors. He is presumed to have acted in good faith unless it can be proved that the contrary is the case. However, it is doubtful whether a bank could claim protection under these provisions, in that it would receive a copy of the memorandum and articles when the account was opened. The company's *powers* - such as to borrow money and acquire businesses - will usually be listed in addition to its objects.

The *Articles of Association* are concerned with the relationship between the company and its members. They are concerned, for instance, with the rights of shareholders to vote at the company's meetings, the issue and transfer of shares, the powers of directors and the conduct of meetings.

The memorandum and articles of association are both public documents, and may be inspected at the office of the Registrar of Companies.

When the Registrar of Companies is satisfied with the documents filed with it, he issues a *certificate of incorporation* which brings the company into existence. A private company may then commence business, but a public company must not do so (nor borrow any money) until it has been issued with a certificate that the share capital requirements have been complied with. This certificate is called a *trading certificate*. A public company will also need to seek permission from the Stock Exchange Council to be listed on the Stock Exchange.

When opening an account for a limited company, the bank will need to see the certificate of incorporation (plus, in the case of a public company, the trading certificate); it may open an account for the receipt of subscriptions only, pending the receipt of the trading certificate. The bank will also require a certified copy of the resolution appointing the first directors of the company, unless they are named in the articles of association. The bank's mandate form will also need to be signed by the chairman and secretary of the company after a meeting of the board of directors has been held passing the resolution contained in the mandate form. This mandate will include the names and signatures of those persons who may sign on the account. Anyone signing cheques and other instruments on behalf of the company must sign 'per pro' or 'for and on behalf of', indicating the name of the company and, after the signature, the capacity in the company – i.e., secretary or director.

The bank must examine the company's memorandum and articles of association, and be satisfied that the company's activities are generally in conformity with them. If the company is to borrow money, the bank must examine the memorandum to see if it is specific about borrowing money, and also the articles to see if the directors' borrowing powers are limited.

8.6 LIEN, HYPOTHECATION AND PLEDGE

Banker's lien

A *lien* is the right to retain property belonging to another person until a debt due from the owner of the property to the holder of the property has been paid. It is an *implied* right, not an express right. The ownership of the property remains unchanged, but the lender has possession. The possessor cannot sell the property, but the owner cannot get it back until he pays the debt.

A banker has an exceptional lien over his customer's property, in that he or she has the right of sale after reasonable notice to the customer – but, of course, this lien exists only if the customer is in debt to the bank. The banker's lien is a general lien over property of the customer which comes into the banker's hands in the ordinary course of business – such as cheques and other bills of exchange, promissory notes and coupons. Where property is handed to the bank for a special purpose, however (such as for safe custody or for selling through a stockbroker), the lien does not apply. When a bank takes securities from a customer to back an advance it will avoid any possible dispute as to the purpose of depositing the securities by taking its usual form of charge in which the right of lien is incorporated; furthermore, it will include the right of sale.

A bank which has possession of an article over which it has a lien must not let it out of its possession, because in doing so it would lose its lien.

Pledge

A *pledge* is an express agreement (unlike the lien, which is an implied agreement). It delivers goods (or documents of title to goods) to a creditor as security for a debt or some other obligation, on the understanding that the goods or documents will be returned to the pledger when the debt has been paid or other obligation completed.

As with a lien, the ownership of the property remains with the borrower, but possession passes to the creditor. However, if the debtor does not repay by a stipulated time for repayment (or after a demand for repayment), the pledger then has the power to sell the property concerned.

Letters of pledge are used by bankers as the normal practice when they lend against produce which has been bought or sold, especially in international trade. They usually hold the shipping documents, including the bill of lading which is a document of title to the goods, for release when the borrowing is repaid.

Where it is impossible for the banker to take a pledge over goods or documents because they have yet to be received (from overseas, most likely) the bank may take a *letter of hypothecation*. This is an agreement to give the bank a pledge over the goods (or documents of title to the goods) when they become available. Such an agreement is by no means as secure as the pledge itself, and gives the bank little control over the documents or the goods themselves.

TOPICS FOR DISCUSSION

1. Discuss the contractual relationship between banker and customer and the extent to which it is (i) a debtor–creditor, and (ii) principal–agent relationship.
2. A bank has a bond of secrecy with its customer and yet is willing to answer status enquiries. How can these two facts be reconciled?
3. Discuss the role of a bank as bailee for the valuable possessions of its customers.

4. Consider what is meant by 'joint and several liability', and why a bank desires to establish it when lending to joint borrowers.
5. A firm is not a separate entity, yet a company is. Discuss the concept of 'separate entity' and how it affects the operation respectively of partnership and company accounts.
6. Consider the differences between a lien, a pledge and a letter of hypothecation.

CHAPTER 9

THE CONCEPT OF NEGOTIABILITY

9.1 WHAT IS 'NEGOTIABILITY'?

The term 'negotiability' is applied to instruments used to transfer money – such as bills of exchange, cheques, promissory notes, dividend warrants, bearer debentures, and Treasury bills. These instruments are in fact called 'negotiable instruments'.

The full legal title to a negotiable instrument is transferred by delivery (or by indorsement and delivery) to the person receiving it, provided that he or she has a good title to it, even if a previous holder had a bad title. The recipient must be acting in good faith, and be unaware that a previous holder's title was a bad one. This puts a negotiable instrument in a rather different category from an article – because if someone bought a car, for instance, in good faith and not knowing that it had been stolen before it was sold, the rightful owner could repossess it. The purchaser would have to endeavour to get his or her money back from the vendor, and if he was unsuccessful he or she would have to bear the loss.

There are four essential characteristics of a negotiable instrument:

1. The legal title to the instrument can be transferred by simple delivery, or if it is payable to order by indorsement and delivery.
2. The person to whom the instrument is negotiated can sue on it in his or her own name.
3. Provided that the instrument is apparently in good and regular order, the person to whom it is negotiated obtains a good title to it. However, he or she must have taken it in good faith and for value without any knowledge of defect in the title of the transferor. The recipient's good title is not affected in any way if it is discovered that, in fact, the transferor had a defective title (or no title at all).
4. There is no need to give notice of transfer to the person liable on the instrument, i.e. the drawer of a cheque or bill of exchange. A bill of

exchange (or cheque, which is a type of bill of exchange) is a written promise by the drawer that anyone who takes it in payment will be paid in cash when it is presented to the person (or bank) on whom it is drawn, provided that it is presented at the appropriate time and place.

If I receive a cheque payable to me and I indorse it and leave it about, then I do so at my own risk because, if it is stolen and fraudulently passed on by the thief to someone in settlement of a debt, I would have no redress against that person. He or she could pay the cheque into a bank account, and thus receive value for it, provided that he or she had taken it from the thief or some subsequent holder in good faith and without any reason to suspect that the thief's title was not good.

The concept of negotiability makes an instrument acceptable as an alternative to notes and coin. Anyone who sells goods against a cheque, for instance, which has already been negotiated, has the satisfaction of knowing that he or she has the right to present the cheque for payment without cause to worry about any previous defect in title – always assuming, of course, that he or she has no reason to be suspicious about any previous holder's title.

9.2 NEGOTIABLE INSTRUMENTS

Important Definitions

Negotiable instruments are *choses in action*, which means that they are property the right to which is enforceable in a court of law. The subject of negotiability is covered in the Bills of Exchange Act 1882 which, together with the Cheques Act 1957, constitutes the statute covering not only bills of exchange (including cheques), but promissory notes as well. The two Acts are clearly of considerable importance to the banking student, and you would be wise to familiarise yourself with them. The comments that follow contain, where appropriate, references to the relevant sections of the Acts.

A *bill of exchange* is defined by the Bills of Exchange Act as an unconditional order in writing, addressed by one person to another, signed by the person giving it, requiring the person to whom it is addressed to pay on demand or at a fixed or determinable future time a sum certain in money to, or to the order of, a specified person, or to bearer.

A *cheque* is defined in the Act as a bill of exchange drawn on a banker payable on demand.

A *promissory note* is defined as an unconditional promise in writing made by one person to another signed by the maker, engaging to pay, on demand or at a fixed or determinable future time, a sum certain in money to, or to the order of, a specified person or to bearer.

There are many similarities between the three definitions, especially between that of a cheque and a bill of exchange. The definition of a cheque in fact states that it is a bill of exchange, so that the definition of the latter applies to the former: but with two amendments – that a cheque is always drawn on a banker, and that it is always payable on demand. Therefore looking at the definition of a bill of exchange in detail we will be covering many factors that are applicable to all three of the instruments.

Unconditional order (or promise)

A bill of exchange (cheque or promissory note) must be *unconditional*. Therefore the instrument must not have built into it a clause which says (or implies) that the bill or note must not be paid unless a certain action has been performed. If, for instance, it contained a statement to the effect 'provided that I find the car to be in good working order', the instrument would not be legally valid. Such a clause would of course put an unbearable restraint upon a banker cashing a cheque, for he could hardly be expected to have to check on whether the drawer was satisfied before he made the payment. A cheque which includes a receipt form and an instruction that it must be signed is nevertheless unconditional provided that the instruction is not made an essential requirement for payment by the bank.

Order in writing

A bill or note must be *in writing* (the term 'writing' includes typewriting and printing). The essential point is that it must not be only a verbal instruction or promise. The Bills of Exchange Act does not say that it must be written on paper, and therefore cheques which have been chiselled into stone, or even written on the back of a cow have been presented to (and paid by) banks!

Addressed (made) by one person to another

The word 'person' includes not only an individual or partnership of people but any company or institution which is a *legal person*. In the case of a cheque, it must be addressed to a banker. In the case of a promissory note, it is a promise not an instruction, therefore it is made to (and not addressed to) a person.

Signed by the person giving it (by the maker)

The person who gives the instruction (or makes the promise) must put his *signature* to it. Therefore a bill, cheque or promissory note which is not signed is not legally valid.

To pay on demand or at a fixed or determinable future time

A cheque, as we have seen, must be payable on demand – i.e., on presentation to the person on whom it is drawn at an appropriate time, e.g. during banking hours. A bill of exchange or a promissory note, on the other hand, could alternatively be made payable at a *future* date. It then becomes known as a 'usance' or 'term' bill (or note). This 'future date' must be actually stated, or at least determinable. A bill which is made payable 'one month after date' is payable at a determinable future date, and so is one payable '30 days after date'. If the bill was dated 13 May it would be payable respectively on 13 June and 12 June. Similarly, a bill which is payable at a given period 'after sight' is payable at a determinable future time, even though at the time the bill is drawn the date of sighting is not known. The date of sighting is usually, though not essentially, the day on which the bill is presented to the drawee for acceptance, and the stipulated period of time is calculated from then.

Note that when a bill (note) is payable a set number of months after date or sight, it is payable on the day of the month the bill is dated (or sighted) unless there are some days lacking in the month. A three-month bill dated (or sighted) on 15 June is payable on the 15 September, but one dated 31 January is payable on 30 April. A three-month bill drawn on 30 November would be payable on 28 or 29 February (depending upon whether it is a leap year or not). Where a bill (or note) is payable at a number of days after date or sight, the date of maturity must be calculated precisely. A 90-day sight bill which is sighted on 10 January would be payable on 10 April; this is calculated as follows:

> 21 days left in January
> 28 days in February
> 31 days in March
> 10 days in April
> 90

(the bill would be payable on 9 April if it was a leap year). Where a bill (or cheque) is undated, or an acceptance of a bill is undated, it may be dated by a holder.

A sum certain in money

S.9, Bills of Exchange Act says that this sum can include interest, be by stated instalments, or be by stated instalments with a provision that upon default the whole shall become due. The sum can also be calculable at an indicated rate of exchange, or according to a rate of exchange to be ascertained as directed by the bill. Where the sum payable is expressed in words and also in figures, and there is a discrepancy between the two, the sum denoted by the *words* is the amount payable. It is, however, usual practice for banks to return cheques where there is a discrepancy with the comment 'Words and figures differ'.

To, or to the order of, a specified person, or to bearer

A bill, cheque or note can be made payable simply to a specified person – e.g., pay S. Robinson – but it is more usual to make it payable to his *order*, and in fact cheques have the words 'or Order' printed on them. The payee could in either case make the instrument payable to his order by indorsing it on the back with his signature and writing above his signature 'Pay Tom Brown'. The instrument can be made payable to two or more payees jointly, or it may be made payable in the alternative to one of two, or one or some of several payees (s.7).

A bill is payable to bearer if it is drawn payable to bearer, or is indorsed in blank, or is payable to a fictitious or non-existing payee. 'Indorsed in blank' means that the payee (or a subsequent holder) signs the bill without designating an indorsee.

9.3 ACCEPTANCE, INDORSEMENT AND DISCHARGE

Acceptance

A bill of exchange (but not a cheque or a promissory note) must be accepted as a signification by the drawee of his assent to the order of the drawer. The acceptance must be written on the bill, and signed by the drawee or his agent. The mere signature of the drawee without additional words is sufficient (s.17). An acceptance may be general or qualified, the latter being a conditional acceptance stipulating acceptance subject to the fulfilment of a condition stated in the acceptance; or it may be partial, i.e. accepting to pay only part of the amount; or it may be local, which means that it is an acceptance to pay only at a particular specified place, but to be a qualified acceptance it must state that the bill will be paid there and not elsewhere. A qualified acceptance may also be qualified as to time, or it may include the acceptance of one or more of the drawees (but not all).

Indorsement

A bill, cheque or promissory note is *negotiated* when it is transferred from one person to another in such a manner as to constitute the transferee the holder of it. When the instrument is payable to bearer, it is negotiated by delivery, but where it is payable to order it is negotiated by the indorsement of the holder completed by delivery. Where the holder of an instrument payable to order transfers it for value without indorsing it, the transfer gives the transferee such title as the transferor had in it, and the transferee in addition acquires the right to have the indorsement of the transferor.

To be in order an indorsement must comply with six conditions:

1. It must be written on the bill itself and signed by the indorser. The simple signature of the indorser without additional words is sufficient.
2. It must be an indorsement of the whole instrument.
3. Where the instrument is payable to the order of two or more payeees or indorsees who are not partners, all must indorse, unless the one indorsing has authority to indorse for the others.
4. Where the payee or indorsee is wrongly designated or his name is misspelt, he may indorse as described, adding, if he wishes, his proper signature.
5. Where there are two or more indorsements, each indorsement is deemed to have been made in the order in which it appears on the bill.
6. An indorsement may be made in blank or special. It may also contain terms making it restrictive.

A special indorsement specifies the person to whom (or to whose order) the instrument is to be payable. Where an indorsement is in blank, any holder may convert the blank indorsement into a special indorsement by writing above the indorser's signature a direction to pay the bill to or to the order of himself or some other person.

An indorsement is restrictive which prohibits the further negotiation of the instrument, or which expresses that it is a mere authority to deal with it as thereby directed and not a transfer of the ownership.

The Cheques Act 1957 deals specifically with the indorsement of cheques, and was designed greatly to reduce the need for indorsements.

S.1(1) of the Act states 'Where a banker in good faith and in the ordinary course of business pays a cheque drawn on him which is not indorsed or is irregularly indorsed, he does not, in doing so, incur any liability by reason only of the absence of, or irregularity in, indorsement, and he is deemed to have paid it in due course'. This is a very sweeping provision, and goes beyond what had been recommended (which was to abolish the need for indorsement where a cheque is paid by its payee into his account). However, it does say *in the ordinary course of business*, and to make it clear what they regarded by this term the Committee of London Clearing Bankers published a list of instruments which still require indorsement:

1. Order cheques which are paid into an account other than that of the payee.
2. Cheques presented for encashment at the counter other than those made payable to Cash or Wages.
3. Bills of exchange (i.e., other than cheques).
4. Combined cheques and receipt forms marked 'R'.

5. Travellers' cheques.
6. Promissory notes.

The millions of cheques each year which prior to the Act had to be indorsed by the payees before they paid them into their accounts, thus no longer have to be indorsed. The Act also did away with the habit of asking for a receipt when paying by cheque, because s.3 of the Act says that 'An un-indorsed cheque which appears to have been paid by the banker on whom it is drawn is evidence of the receipt by the payee of the sum payable by the cheque'. To overcome the problem of those bank customers (such as insurance companies) that still require a receipt, the banks started the practice of requiring that when a form of receipt on the back of the cheque is to be signed the cheque must bear a large 'R' on the front. This serves as a warning to the collecting and paying bankers to check that the receipt has been signed, even though the cheque may have been paid in by the payee to his or her own account.

Discharge

The subject of discharge is covered by ss.59–64, Bills of Exchange Act, which state that a bill of exchange (including both a cheque and a promissory note, as appropriate) is discharged by payment in due course by or on behalf of the drawee or acceptor. The term 'payment in due course' is defined as payment made at or after the maturity of the bill to the holder thereof in good faith and without notice that his or her title to the bill is defective.

When the acceptor of a bill is (or becomes) the holder of it at or after maturity, in his or her own right, the bill is discharged. A bill is also discharged if the holder unconditionally renounces any rights against the acceptor of the bill in writing, or does so by delivering up the bill to the acceptor. The bill is similarly discharged if the holder (or his or her agents) intentionally cancels the bill by indicating this on the bill. The liability of any party to a bill may be renounced by the holder by notice of renunciation, or the party may be discharged by the intentional cancellation of the holder's signature. In such a case, any indorser who would have had a right of recourse against the party whose signature is cancelled is also discharged.

A bill must not be materially altered without the approval of all the parties thereto; a 'material alteration' is stipulated in the Act as being an alteration to the date, the sum payable, the time of payment, the place of payment, and (where a bill has been accepted generally) the addition of a place of payment without the acceptor's assent. Where such an alteration is made the bill is not valid except against a party who has personally made, authorised, or consented to the alteration, and subsequent indorsers. However, where an alteration is not apparent a subsequent holder in due course may use the bill as if it had not been altered.

When a bill is paid by the drawer or an indorser (i.e., instead of the acceptor), it is not discharged.

An accommodation bill is discharged when it is paid in due course by the party accommodated. Such a bill is one drawn on a drawee and accepted by the drawee in order to provide temporary finance for the drawer. The drawer, if he or she is able to discount such a bill (which there should be no difficulty in doing if it is drawn on a person or business of repute such as a bank), is able to obtain the full value of the bill, less the discount, and has use of the money until the date of maturity of the bill.

S.60, Bills of Exchange Act protects the banker who pays a cheque in good faith and in the ordinary course of business, and states that it is not incumbent on the banker to show that the indorsement of the payee (or any subsequent indorsement) was made by or under the authority of the person whose indorsement it purports to be, and the banker is deemed to have paid the cheque in due course, although such indorsement has been forged or made without authority. This section of the Act has been very largely replaced by the Cheques Act 1957 but, nevertheless, where indorsements are still necessary s.60 is still important in that it protects the banker who pays against a forged indorsement.

The banker's duty and authority to pay a cheque ceases once payment has been countermanded in writing by the drawer or immediately notice of the death of the drawer is received. A drawer of a cheque which has been backed by the use of a cheque card cannot countermand payment because − provided the cheque has been properly signed in the presence of the payee, that the payee has written the number of the cheque card on the back of the cheque, and that the amount is within the limit set for each transaction − the bank has guaranteed payment.

9.4 RIGHTS AND DUTIES OF PARTIES TO A BILL

Holder of a bill

The holder of a bill (including a cheque, of course) is defined in s.2, Bills of Exchange Act as 'The payee or indorsee of a bill who is in possession of it, or the bearer of a bearer bill'. This can include an unlawful holder (such as a thief) or someone who has obtained the bill by fraud.

A holder may be a *holder for value*, or a *holder in due course*. A holder for value is a holder of a bill for which value has at any time been given. He or she is holder for value as regards the acceptor and all parties to the bill who became parties prior to the time that value was given. 'Value for a bill' means any consideration sufficient to support a simple contract or an antecedent debt or liability. Every party whose signature appears on a bill is *prima facie* deemed to have become a party to it for value.

A holder in due course is a holder who has taken a bill complete and regular on the face of it, under two conditions:

1. That he or she became a holder of it before it was overdue, and without notice that it had been previously dishonoured, if such was the fact.
2. That he or she took the bill in good faith and for value, and that at the time the bill was negotiated he or she had no notice of any defect in the title of the person who negotiated it.

To be 'complete and regular on the face of it', a bill must be properly dated and signed, with no discrepancy as to the amount, and the indorsement(s) must appear to be in order. A defect in the title means that the bill, or an acceptance on it, was obtained by fraud, duress, force or fear, or other unlawful means, or for an illegal consideration, or that the bill was negotiated in breach of faith or under such circumstances as amount to a fraud.

A holder of a bill who derives a title to it through a holder in due course, and who is not personally a party to any fraud or illegality affecting it, has all the rights of that holder in due course as regards the acceptor and all parties to the bill prior to that holder. Every holder of a bill is *prima facie* deemed to be a holder in due course.

The concept of a holder in due course has been tested in the courts on many occasions, but it is considered beyond the scope of this book to look into the ruling of the court in particular cases. A more thorough examination of the law is of course required in preparation for the subject Law Relating to Banking in Stage II of the Institute of Bankers Diploma examinations.

The reader will appreciate that the concept of the holder in due course is vital in the context of negotiability. Such a holder takes a bill free from defects in title, and can therefore acquire a better title to the bill than that held by the person who transferred the title, and he or she can transfer the title as holder in due course provided the person to whom he or she transfers it is unaware of any previous defect in title. A holder in due course has the maximum possible protection in a court of law, because it is incumbent upon anyone taking an action to prove that he or she is not a holder in due course.

Liability of parties

The parties to a bill of exchange are the drawer, the acceptor (usually the drawee) and any indorser. They are all liable on a bill as signatories to it. Such a signature must of course be genuine and s.24, Bills of Exchange Act makes it clear that a forged or unauthorised signature is wholly inoperative.

To be liable on a bill the drawer or indorser must deliver it, i.e. there must be an actual or constructive *transfer of possession* of the bill from one person to another. The drawer, acceptor or indorser must have the capacity to contract, e.g. must not be a minor, and must receive consideration.

The drawer of a bill engages that on due presentation it will be accepted and paid and that if it is dishonoured he or she will compensate the holder or any indorser who is compelled to pay it, provided that the requisite proceedings on dishonour are taken. He or she cannot deny to a holder in due course the payee's existence or capacity to indorse the bill. Until the bill is accepted the drawer is the principal debtor and if the bill is negotiated any indorsers incur secondary liability as surety for payment by the drawer.

The drawee (the person on whom the bill is drawn) is not liable on a bill if he or she does not accept it. Once he or she does accept it he or she engages that he or she will pay it according to the tenor of the acceptance. The drawee is precluded from denying to a holder in due course:

1. The existence of the drawer, the genuineness of his or her signature, and the capacity and authority to draw the bill.
2. In the case of a bill payable to the drawer's order, the then capacity of the drawer to indorse, but not the genuineness or validity of the indorsement.
3. In the case of a bill payable to the order of a third person, the existence of the payee and the then capacity to indorse, but not the genuineness or validity of the indorsement.

By his or her acceptance, the acceptor becomes the principal debtor and the drawer and indorsers become sureties for payment by the acceptor.

An indorser of a bill promises that the bill will be duly accepted and paid and that if it is dishonoured he or she will compensate the holder or a subsequent indorser who is compelled to pay it, provided that the requisite proceedings on dishonour are duly taken. An indorser is precluded from denying to a holder in due course the genuineness and regularity in all respects of the drawer's signature and all previous indorsements and from denying to the immediate or subsequent indorsee that the bill was at the time of the indorsement a valid and subsisting bill, and that he or she had then a good title to the bill.

9.5 DISHONOUR OF A BILL

A bill of exchange may be dishonoured by non-acceptance or by non-payment. When a bill is dishonoured for either reason *notice of dishonour* must be given to the drawer and any indorsers, otherwise they are discharged from liability. Such notice of dishonour must be given without delay, but the delay will be excused if it is caused by circumstances beyond the control of the party giving notice. Notice of dishonour can be dispensed with if the person to whom it is to be given cannot be found, or it has been waived. Notice of dishonour need not be given to the drawer when he or she and the drawee are the same person; where the drawer is a fictitious person or lacks contractual capacity; where the drawer is the person to whom the bill is presented for payment; where the drawee or acceptor is as between himself or herself and the drawer under no obligation to accept or pay the bill; or where the drawer has countermanded payment. Notice of dishonour need not be given to an indorser where the drawee is a fictitious person or lacks contractual capacity and the indorser was aware of this when he or she indorsed; where the indorser is the person to whom the bill was presented for payment; or where the bill was accepted or made only for the indorser's accommodation.

If a dishonoured bill is an inland bill, the holder may have it noted for non-acceptance or non-payment if he or she wishes but noting and protesting is not necessary in order to preserve the recourse against the drawer or indorser. A foreign bill, on the other hand, must be duly protested for non-acceptance or non-payment, as appropriate, otherwise the drawer and indorsers are discharged. *Noting* is the formal process whereby a notary public (or if one is not available, a householder in front of two witnesses) re-presents the bill for acceptance or payment. If it is then dishonoured the reply is noted on the bill. *Protesting* is a further stage in the process, and involves the preparation of a formal document (a protest), which contains a copy of the bill and a declaration by the notary public giving the facts concerning the dishonour. The noting and the protest are evidence which can be used in a court of law when taking action against the acceptor of the bill or, if necessary, the drawer and indorsers.

9.6 PROTECTION FOR THE BANKER

All that has been considered so far in this chapter concerning bills of exchange in general affects the banker equally as well as any other person who becomes a party to a bill of exchange. A banker may well be the drawee and/or acceptor of a bill and certainly in the case of a cheque the drawee must be a banker, for it must be drawn on a bank. It is quite common practice for a bank to accept a bill of exchange – for example, a bill of exchange drawn by an exporter against a documentary credit where the credit specifies that the bank will accept bills drawn against it – or a merchant bank may accept a bill drawn by its customer as a means of acquiring accommodation.

The Bills of Exchange Act and the Cheques Act, however, provide some special forms of protection for a banker handling both cheques and other bills of exchange. We shall be looking at those parts of these Acts which specifically concern the handling of cheques in the next chapter, which is concerned with the use of cheques, but it is appropriate in the context of this chapter to look in general terms at the protection provided for both the paying and collecting banker.

A paying banker who pays a bill of exchange (including a cheque) *in due course*, discharges the bill. 'In due course' means payment made at or after the maturity of the bill to the holder in good faith and without notice that the title to the bill is defective (Bills of Exchange Act, s.59). S.60, as we saw above, protects a banker who pays a cheque which bears a forged or unauthorised indorsement, provided the banker pays in good faith and in the ordinary course of business. If the banker *knew* that an indorsement was forged, he or she would not be acting in good faith. To pay a cheque in the ordinary course of business the banker would have to do so during normal banking hours and within normal banking practice. The protection of s.60 is necessary only in respect of cheques which require indorsement, because Cheques Act, s.1 protects a banker who pays a cheque which is not indorsed.

A paying banker is also protected by s.80, Bills of Exchange Act, which states that if he pays a crossed cheque to a banker in good faith and without negligence he or she is placed in the same position as if payment had been made to the true owner of the cheque.

A collecting banker acts as agent for the customer when collecting the proceeds of a bill of exchange. As such he or she is in danger of incurring a breach of contract if he or she does not follow established banking practice when presenting a bill of exchange for payment, or fails to give notice of dishonour. The banker is also in danger of committing conversion if he or she collects payment of a bill of exchange for anyone who has no title to it.

S.4, Cheques Act 1957 protects a banker who in good faith and without negligence receives payment of a cheque and certain other instruments (see below) or who, having credited a customer's account with the amount of such an instrument, receives payment thereof for himself. The banker incurs no liability to the true owner of the instrument where the customer has either a defective title or no title at all to the instrument merely because he or she receives payment. The instruments referred to in s.4 are:

1. Cheques.
2. Any document issued by a customer of a banker which, though not a bill of exchange, is intended to enable a person to obtain payment from that banker of a sum mentioned in the document (for example, an interest or dividend warrant).

3. Any document issued by a public officer which is intended to enable a person to obtain payment from the Paymaster General or the Queen's and Lord Treasurer's Remembrancer of the sum mentioned in the document, but is not a bill of exchange.
4. A banker's draft.

A banker who gives value for a bill of exchange (i.e., credits the customer's account) and then collects it in his own right could also claim protection under s.38, Bills of Exchange Act as a holder in due course.

TOPICS FOR DISCUSSION

1. Consider the importance of the concept of negotiability in the use of cheques and other instruments of payment.
2. If the acceptor of a bill of exchange undertakes to pay it at maturity, why should the drawer and indorsers also be liable on the bill?
3. Discuss the reasons why the Cheques Act 1957 was necessary.
4. What is the procedure for protesting the non-acceptance or non-payment of a bill?

CHAPTER 10

THE USE OF CHEQUES

10.1 TYPES OF NEGOTIABLE INSTRUMENT

Bills of exchange

In Chapter 9 we identified the concept of negotiability, and examined some of the negotiable instruments by looking at the law which governs their use. In this chapter we need to examine the characteristics of some of these instruments more closely, and especially the cheque which is of course the main negotiable instrument used today.

Up to the middle of the 19th century when the cheque came into its own the main method of settling debts was to use a bill of exchange, and as far as international trade is concerned it is still a main method of payment. Bills have been used as a method of payment since the 14th century both in international trade and for domestic settlements. When the UK was on the gold standard, bills of exchange were a much more convenient means of settlement than having to transport gold from one country to another, or from one part of a country to another.

Bills of exchange were at first a device which enabled debts to be married up against one another, but with the development of the international banking system bills are seldom used in this way now, and instead each transaction is settled on its own. Merchants married up debts by offsetting debts due to residents abroad for goods imported into Britain, for instance, against payments due to British exporters. If someone in Italy who had a payment to make to a merchant in Britain accepted a usance bill for, say, 90 days drawn on him by the merchant, he had that period of time in which to find an Italian exporter(s) who had a bill(s) which had been accepted by an importer in Britain. If he bought this bill for Italian lire he could then send it to an agent in Britain with a request that he presented it for payment in sterling and used the proceeds to pay his own bill when due.

Today the use of agents in this way is no longer necessary, and instead bills of exchange and the shipping documents (if any) to which they relate are sent through the banking system which collects bills on the instructions of its customers. In addition, the banks provide finance for exporters in anticipation of the proceeds of bills by discounting them – i.e., buying them at the face value less discount. In the case of foreign bills this process is referred to as 'negotiating' a bill, and involves more than the simple purchase of the bill as we shall see in Chapter 12.

For our present purposes, let us look at the inland bill of exchange illustrated in Figure 10.1.

This bill has been drawn by Jones & Brown (the drawer) on Lombard Credit plc (the drawee), possibly as a means of obtaining temporary accommodation. The payee is Jones & Brown because they have made the bill payable to the 'Order of ourselves'. The bill has been accepted by Lombard Credit plc, who are thus the acceptor of the bill. It is payable on 20 April 1984, which is 90 days after date.

What are the advantages to the parties concerned of using this method of settlement? Firstly, the bill is evidence of a debt and as it has been accepted by Lombard Credit plc it is *legally enforceable* against them. Secondly, it allows the drawee a period of time in which to make the payment, and lastly the drawer, if he requires it, can obtain immediate finance. The provision of this finance cannot be forced upon anyone, of course, and if the bill had been drawn upon some unknown small firm Jones & Brown might have had difficulty in getting it discounted. However, Lombard Credit plc, let us assume, is a well-known financial institution in the City of London, and as such its acceptances are undoubted. It may also be listed amongst the 'eligible banks' whose acceptances the Bank of England is willing to buy: let us assume this is so. The drawer should then have no difficulty in persuading a bank or a discount house to buy the bill for its full value less discount. If the market rate for bank bills (bills drawn on and accepted by banks) is 10 per cent, then Jones & Brown will secure approximately £2925 (£3000 *less* interest for roughly three months at 10 per cent). If it is an accommodation bill on which Lombard Credit have 'lent their name' to Jones & Brown in order that they may in effect borrow the money from the institution which discounts the bill, then Lombard Credit will charge a commission for their services – which will add to Jones & Brown's costs of borrowing – i.e., will have to be added to the £75 they have to pay in interest in order to arrive at the net proceeds of the bill.

Once discounted, the bill will be included in a bundle of commercial bills which is bought, sold or pledged as security in the money market and thus may form part of the bills market in which the Bank of England operates (see Chapter 7).

If having had the bill accepted Jones & Brown decide not to discount it but to use it as a means of paying a debt to some other firm, then they

Fig 10.1 *inland bill of exchange*

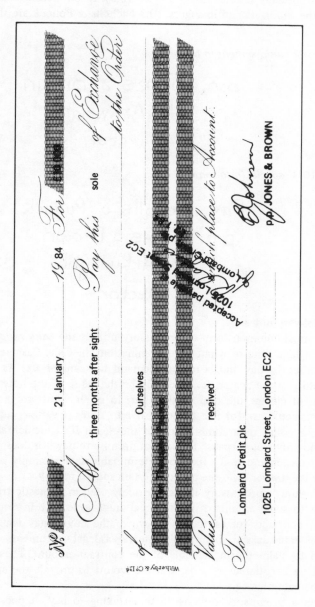

will simply indorse the bill in blank (see Figure 10.2). They could alternatively specially indorse it (see Figure 10.3). In both cases, Jones & Brown are the indorsers and in Figure 10.3 Nicholls & Pollock are the indorsee.

Fig 10.2 *indorsement in blank*

p.p. Jones & Brown
      K.Arkwright
         Director

Fig 10.3 *special indorsement*

Pay Nicholls & Pollock
p.p. Jones & Brown
      K.Arkwright
         Director

Promissory notes
The most common form of promissory note is the *bank note*. On a Bank of England note of whatever denomination, the Chief Cashier of the Bank promises to pay the bearer on demand the sum of £x. As to what he would pay the bearer, it could only be the value of the note in whatever form of change the bearer asked for. In other words for a £5 note the bearer could ask for five £1 coins, five £1 notes or various cupro-nickel or bronze coins, or a combination of these. An IOU incidentally, is not a promissory note because it does not promise to pay nor does it promise to do so on demand or at a fixed or determinable date; it simply acknowledges that the drawer owes the payee a certain sum of money.

Although promissory notes are rarely used in domestic trade they are used to some extent in international trade especially in respect of long-term contracts for capital goods where the buyer may issue a series of notes dated at, say, six-monthly intervals as legal instruments which can be used to claim the instalments of the contract amount. These notes may well be negotiated by a bank at a discount to provide the exporter with immediate finance.

As a promissory note is an undertaking to pay, it does not require acceptance. Unlike a cheque, it must be indorsed by the payee or indorsee even when he pays it into his own account.

Bankers' drafts

A bankers' draft is a draft drawn by a branch of a bank on the bank's head office. It is not a cheque, and is not generally covered by the Bills of Exchange Act. However, it is covered by s.80, as extended by s.5, Cheques Act 1957, to provide protection for a banker who pays a crossed draft. S.4, Cheques Act also protects a collecting banker, and s.1 protects a banker who pays a draft in good faith and in the ordinary course of business even though the draft has not been indorsed or is *irregularly* indorsed. Protection against a *forged or unauthorised* indorsement is provided by the Stamp Act 1853.

Dividend warrants

Dividend and interest warrants are now usually drawn in the form of a cheque, so that the normal provisions that relate to cheques in the Bills of Exchange Act and the Cheques Act 1957 apply. Even if it were not drawn in the form of a cheque, a warrant that is crossed would be covered by the Bills of Exchange Act to some extent in that s.95 states 'The provisions of the Act as to crossed cheques shall apply to a warrant for payment of dividend'.

10.2 HISTORY OF THE CHEQUE

Cheques first came into use in the 17th century as a rather special form of bill of exchange, in that they were drawn on a banker. A cheque was (and still is) an instruction by a depositor of a bank to pay over a sum of money from the depositor's account to a specified person, or to bearer. In the 18th century the private banks grew rapidly and in 1773 they found it necessary to establish the London Clearing House through which cheques could be exchanged. This greatly increased the ease of transfer of cheques, and paved the way for the development of the large joint stock banks once the 1833 Act permitted the establishment of them in London. The banks overcame the restrictions on the issue of notes in the London area contained in this Act, and the further restrictions on note issues contained in the Bank Charter Act 1844, by encouraging the use of cheques to transfer balances rather than by the use of notes for the purpose.

In 1853 the Stamp Act abolished the *ad valorem* duty on order cheques and replaced it by a fixed stamp duty of a penny for each cheque, thus greatly stimulating their use. The Stamp Act was followed by the Bills of Exchange Act 1882 which as we know established a code of law for cheques and firmly protected drawers of crossed cheques.

Possibly the main development in the 19th century which encouraged the use of cheques was the establishment of a sound banking system comprising only a few large banks with networks of branches. The increased use of banks by the public led to the recognition of the cheque as a convenient (and safe) means of settling transactions.

In the 20th century, the increasing affluence (especially subsequent to the Second World War) extended the use of bank accounts to people who previously did not feel the need to have them, and the Wages Act 1960 (which legalised payment of wages by cheque) encouraged this development. The introduction of *cheque guarantee cards* has enabled shopkeepers and other traders to accept cheques without fear of loss, making the cheque an even more convenient means of payment. Bank service till cards which enable account holders to obtain cash at times when the banks are closed has encouraged the opening of current accounts, and with them the futher use of cheques. Another development which encouraged the use of cheques was the abolition of the stamp duty on cheques in 1971.

10.3 CROSSINGS ON CHEQUES

By crossing a cheque, the drawer greatly increases the protection afforded by the Bills of Exchange Act, in that the cheque can be paid only to a banker. This means that the holder must pay it into an account so that the bank will obtain payment for it, and cannot obtain payment for it in cash at a bank counter. If therefore a crossed cheque is stolen the thief cannot obtain cash for it, and if he or she pays it into an account he or she may be traced. The thief may, of course, transfer title to the cheque to some other person who pays it into an account having taken the cheque in good faith and for value. Provided he or she had no knowledge of the defect of title, this transferee may claim to be a holder in due course.

S.79(2) of the Bills of Exchange Act stipulates that:

> Where the banker on whom a cheque is drawn. . . pays a cheque crossed generally otherwise than to a banker, or if crossed specially otherwise than to the banker to whom it is crossed, or his agent for collection being a banker, he is liable to the true owner of the cheque for any loss he may sustain owing to the cheque having been so paid.

A general crossing involves drawing two parallel transverse lines across the face of a cheque. If the drawer wishes to do so he or she may add the words 'and company' (or an abbreviation thereof) between the lines, but this practice is seldom adopted today: it is a relic of the past when banks were private companies. Also (or instead) if he or she wishes, the drawer may write the words 'Not Negotiable' between the lines which (as we saw in Chapter 9) means that anyone who takes the cheque cannot receive a better title to it than that of the person transferring it. The addition of these words does not make the crossing a special one, and it is still a general crossing.

A cheque is crossed specially when the name of a particular bank is written across the face of a cheque, with or without two transverse parallel lines. The words 'not negotiable' may be added.

The Bills of Exchange Act stipulates who has authority to cross a cheque:

1. A cheque may be crossed generally or specially by the drawer.
2. Where a cheque is uncrossed, the holder may cross it generally or specially.
3. Where a cheque is crossed generally, the holder may cross it specially.
4. Where a cheque is crossed generally or specially, the holder may add the words 'not negotiable'.
5. Where a cheque is crossed specially, the banker to whom it is crossed may again cross it specially to another banker for collection.
6. Where an uncrossed cheque, or a cheque crossed generally, is sent to a banker for collection, the banker may also cross it specially to the bank itself.

A crossing is a material part of a cheque, and it is not lawful for any person to obliterate or add to or alter a crossing except as mentioned above.

Sometimes the words 'Account Payee' or 'Account Payee Only' are written between the crossing on a cheque, but they have no statutory significance in that they are not mentioned in either the Bills of Exchange Act or the Cheques Act. A cheque bearing such words can still be negotiated or transferred, and the paying banker is not affected by the restriction. However, a *collecting* banker might be considered negligent by a court if he or she collected a cheque for a person other than the payee without seeking (and getting a satisfactory explanation from) the person paying it in.

Usually cheque books contain crossed cheques these days, and if a customer wishes to use such a cheque to draw cash at the counter, he or she will be allowed to do so. This is strictly speaking contrary to the law, but it will be appreciated by the reader that the bank runs little risk when paying cash to its own customer.

The various types of crossings are illustrated in Figure 10.4.

10.4 RESPONSIBILITIES OF PARTIES TO A CHEQUE

Who are the parties to a cheque?

As we saw in Chapter 9 when we were dealing with bills of exchange, there are generally three parties to a bill – the drawer, the acceptor (usually the drawee), and the indorser(s). The situation is rather different for a cheque, in that it is always drawn on a banker, does not need to be accepted

142

Fig 10.4 *crossings on cheques*

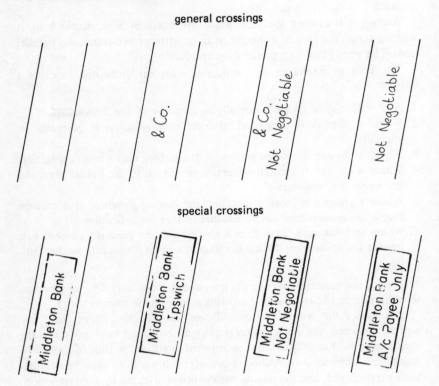

because it is always payable on demand, and may not need to be indorsed. Bankers are much more involved in collecting payment for cheques than they are in collecting payment for bills because far more of them are drawn and because the majority of cheques are crossed (whereas other bills of exchange are not crossed) and therefore can be paid only to a banker.

The parties to a cheque are the drawer, the drawee (a bank), the payee and, possibly, an indorser(s). In the specimen cheque in Figure 10.5 the drawer is A. Specimen, the drawee is National Westminster Bank, and the payee is Peter Burke who has specially indorsed the cheque over to Paul Conrad. Burke is the indorser as well as payee, and Conrad is the indorsee.

A. Specimen, as drawer of the sample cheque, has engaged that on due presentation it will be paid and that if it is dishonoured he will compensate the holder or any indorser who is compelled to pay it, provided that the proper procedure for dishonour is followed. He is the principal debtor and, as indorser, Burke is surety for payment by the drawer. Specimen cannot deny Burke's existence to a holder in due course nor his

Fig. 10.5 *a cheque*

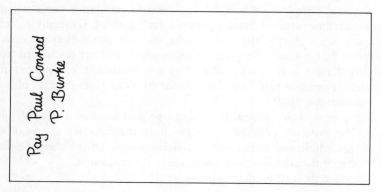

(a) *face*
(b) reverse

capacity to indorse the cheque (s.55(1), Bills of Exchange Act). As indorser of the cheque, Burke promises that the cheque will be paid when presented, and to compensate any party who has had to pay as a result of dishonour, provided the proper procedure for dishonour is followed. He cannot deny to a holder in due course the genuineness and regularity of specimen's signature (or if there had been any, an indorsement prior to his own). He cannot deny to Conrad, as a subsequent indorsee, that it was a valid cheque when he indorsed it, nor that his title to it was good (s.55(2)).

The sample cheque in Figure 10.5 has been negotiated and must therefore be indorsed by the indorsee (Conrad) before it is paid into his account (assuming that he does not further negotiate it). This applies even though he is paying the cheque into his own account (see Chapter 9).

The other party to the cheque, the National Westminster Bank which is the drawee, has special responsibilities, and so too has the collecting bank which presents the cheque for payment. The responsibilities of both the paying bank and the collecting bank have been discussed to some extent in Chapter 9, and the reader is advised to re-read the section on protection for the banker at this juncture before we look at these responsibilities in further detail.

The paying banker

The paying banker must pay a customer's cheque provided it is properly drawn and there are sufficient funds on the account or the customer has made appropriate arrangements for an overdraft facility which covers payment of the cheque. However, the cheque must not be a stale cheque or post dated, nor must there be any legal barrier to payment.

A 'stale' cheque is one which has been in circulation for a lengthy period of time without being presented for payment. Generally bankers will not pay a cheque after six months from its date unless the drawer confirms that it should be paid. Indorsees are completely discharged from liability if there is an unreasonable delay in presentment for payment, but the drawer remains liable on a cheque for six years from its date of issue (Limitation Act 1939).

If a cheque is post dated, it must not be paid until on or after the due date. The customer's mandate is to pay it on the due date and he or she would be within his or her rights to stop payment of the cheque before that date, or the customer may fail or die in the meantime.

There are six legal barriers to payment:

1. *Customer's death*. Immediately a bank receives notice of a customer's death, no further cheques may be paid.
2. *Mental incapacity*. If it is known that the customer's mental condition is such that he or she cannot manage his or her own affairs then cheques should not be paid. If there is doubt concerning the customer's condition then it may be necessary for a court order to be obtained under the Mental Health Act 1959. If an order is issued under the Act there cannot be any further transactions on the customer's account without the court's approval.
3. *Notice of bankruptcy*. Immediately (but not until) notice of a bankruptcy petition against the customer is received no further payments must be made from the account.
4. *Receiving or winding-up order*. Once a receiving order or a winding-up order against a customer *has been made* - not when notice of it has been received - the account must be stopped and cheques returned unpaid.

5. *Garnishee order*. If a creditor has obtained a judgement against the bank's customer, he or she may obtain a garnishee order and serve it on the bank. The bank must then pay over the customer's balance to the creditor – which, of course, means that any of the customer's cheques received after the order has been served must not be paid.

6. *Court injunction*. Where there is some dispute about the ownership of the funds held in an account it is possible that a court injunction may be served on the bank preventing it from making further payments from the account until the dispute is settled.

Quite apart from these legal barriers, the paying banker must be careful not to pay a cheque if he or she is aware of a defect in the presenter's title to the cheque or right to be dealing with it – if, for instance, it is apparent that the presenter is misapplying a company's funds or is an undischarged bankrupt. If the banker is aware of any defect, then he or she cannot claim to have paid the cheque in due course, i.e. in good faith and in the ordinary course of business without any notice of defect of title (s.60) and, if it is a crossed cheque, without negligence (s.80).

A banker must also not pay a cheque which has been materially altered unless the drawer appends his or her initials to the alteration. 'Materially altered' means an alteration to the date, the amount in words and/or figures, the payee's name, or any crossing.

The paying banker must pay or dishonour an open cheque presented at the counter immediately it is presented, and similarly an open or crossed cheque presented at the counter by a banker must be dealt with immediately. Cheques presented through the clearing or by post from another bank are usually paid (or dishonoured) on the day of receipt, notification of an unpaid cheque being sent off by post to the presenting banker that day. If the presenting banker requires immediate notification this may be given by telephone on the day the cheque is received by the paying banker.

A paying banker who wrongly debits a customer's account with a cheque which has been stopped by the customer, or which is post-dated, or which has an unauthorised alteration, or on which the customer's signature is forged is liable for damages to the customer. The banker is also liable for damages if he or she wrongfully dishonours a cheque and such damages could be quite substantial if it could be shown that the banker was liable for libel as well as breach of contract. Banks must therefore be very careful when stating the reason for the dishonour of a cheque.

If a paying banker pays a person not entitled to a cheque, the banker is liable to the true owner for conversion of the cheque. 'Conversion' is a tort committed when one person wrongly interferes with the property of another in such a way as to show that he or she denies (or is indifferent to) the title of the other. However, a paying banker is unlikely to know whether the presenter of a cheque has a good title to it and therefore the banker is provided with adequate protection by ss.59, 60 and 80, Bills of Exchange Act, and s.1, Cheques Act (see Chapter 9).

The collecting banker

A collecting banker's liability is to the customer for whom he or she acts as agent when he or she collects a cheque, and to the true owner if he or she commits the tort of conversion by collecting a cheque on behalf of a customer who has no title to it.

S.4, Cheques Act protects a banker who collects payment of a cheque in good faith and without negligence and stipulates that the banker is not negligent by reason only of a failure to be concerned with the absence of (or irregularity in) indorsement of the cheque. The cheque must be collected for a customer, i.e. a person for whom an account has been opened by a bank, and for the collection to be done in good faith within the context of s.90, Bills of Exchange Act it must be done honestly, whether it is done negligently or not. The banker must act with reasonable care if he or she is not to be accused of negligence, and in this connection following the 'usual banking practice' is obviously of importance. This fact was clearly established in the case of *Marfani and Co. Ltd* v. *Midland Bank Ltd* (1968), when in the Court of Appeal Lord Justice Diplock expressed the view that the facts which ought to be known to the banker must depend on current banking practice, and change as that practice changes. Cases decided 30 years ago, when the use of banking facilities was less widespread, might not be a reliable guide to what the duty of a careful banker is today. The courts should examine current banking practice and decide whether it meets the *standard of care* required from the prudent banker.

There have been many cases in which collecting bankers have been accused of negligence, and it would not be appropriate to examine them in detail in this book. However, there are some acts in the past of bankers that have been held to be negligent and which have resulted in changes in banking practice:

1. Failure to obtain the name of the customer's employers: *Savory and Co.* v. *Lloyds Bank Ltd* (1932).
2. Failure to obtain references in respect of a new customer unknown to the bank: *Ladbroke and Co.* v. *Todd* (1914), and failure to check on the authenticity of a reference: *Guardians of St John's Hampstead* v. *Barclays Bank* (1923) and *Lumsden and Co.* v. *London Trustee Savings Bank* (1971).
3. Collecting a cheque for an official of a company, i.e. paid into his private account: *Underwood* v. *Bank of Liverpool and Martins Bank*

(1924) and *Orbit Mining and Trading Co. Ltd* v. *Westminster Bank* (1963).

4. Collecting for an agent's private account cheques payable to him in his capacity as agent, or cheques drawn by him as an attorney: *Marquess of Bute* v. *Barclays Bank* (1955) and *Midland Bank Ltd* v. *Reckitt and Others* (1933).

5. Collecting for a company's account cheques payable to another company: *London and Montrose Shipbuilding and Repairing Co.* v. *Barclays Bank* (1926).

6. Collecting cheques inconsistent with the customer's business or private activities: *Nu-Stilo Footwear Ltd* v. *Lloyds Bank* (1956).

7. Collecting third party cheques without appropriate enquiries:

   (i) where customer's account has been unsatisfactory: *Motor Traders Guarantee Corporation Ltd* v. *Midland Bank* (1937);

   (ii) cheques marked 'account payee': *House Property Co. of London Ltd and Others* v. *London County and Westminster Bank* (1915);

   (iii) where circumstances warrant enquiry – cheques payable to partnership: *Baker* v. *Barclays Bank* (1955).

In the case of *Lumsden and Co.* v. *London Trustee Savings Bank* (1971), the defence of contributory negligence was allowed for the first time to a banker sued for conversion. This decision in favour of the bank might in effect have been reversed by the Torts (Interference with Goods) Act 1977, which came into effect in 1978, but s.47, Banking Act 1979 restored the situation to what it was before 1978. This section of the Act reads 'In any circumstances in which proof of absence of negligence on the part of a banker would be a defence in proceedings by reason of s.4 of the Cheques Act 1957, a defence of contributory negligence shall also be available to the banker notwithstanding the provisions of s.11(1) of the Torts (Interference with Goods) Act 1977'.

A collecting banker does not need to rely on the provisions of the Cheques Act for protection if he can demonstrate that he or she is the holder for value of a cheque presented for payment. To demonstrate this the banker would have to show that he or she has given value for the cheque and therefore is collecting it in his or her own right and not as agent for the customer. If the banker can establish himself or herself as the holder in due course (see Chapter 9) the banker can claim this in defence to an action for conversion.

A banker is deemed to be a holder for value:

1. Where he or she cashes a third party cheque for a customer or cashes a cheque for a customer of another bank or branch and there is no open credit arrangement.

2. If the banker has a lien on a cheque which, for instance, has been returned unpaid and to debit the customer's account would cause it to be overdrawn.

3. Where the banker takes a cheque as a *specific* reduction of an overdraft – this would *not* apply if a cheque was paid in in the normal course of business for the credit of an overdrawn account.

4. Where the customer is allowed to draw against the cheque before it is cleared, provided there is an implied or expressly declared contract for him or her to do so.

10.5 USE OF CHEQUE CARDS

Plastic guarantee cheque cards bear a number allocated specifically to the holder and they bear (or should bear) his or her signature. These two features of the card serve to identify the customer to whom it is issued and the card enables him or her to cash cheques up to a set maximum amount (at January 1984 £50) at any branch of the bank and also at branches of other banks, though they may charge the customer for the facility. The card also enables the customer to buy goods more easily because the seller is guaranteed payment of the cheque (again up to the maximum amount) provided that the drawer signs the cheque in the presence of the payee, that the signatures on the card and the cheque correspond, that a proper cheque form of the drawee bank and branch is used, that the number of the cheque card is written on the back of the cheque, and that the cheque card is not out of date. These and other conditions of use – such as keeping the cheque book and card in separate places – are notified to the bank customer when the cheque card is supplied, and repeated when the card is renewed, and the customer agrees to use the cheque card in accordance with these conditions.

Once a cheque has been drawn with the backing of a cheque card payment cannot be countermanded, nor can the banker on whom it is drawn refuse to pay it on presentation provided the terms of the card's use printed on the card have been observed, because the banker has guaranteed payment.

The customer to whom a cheque card has been issued must not use it to overdraw the account without prior agreement and to do so may be a criminal offence under s.16, Theft Act 1968. This section stipulates that 'A person who by any deception dishonestly obtains for himself or another any pecuniary advantage shall on conviction on indictment be liable to imprisonment for a term not exceeding five years'. The decision that the customer was guilty of an offence under this section was made in two cases concerning the use of cheque cards – *R.* v. *Kovacs* (1974) and *R.* v. *Charles* (1976). In the first case, the customer overdrew her account and was warned that no further cheques would be met. She did not return her cheque card as requested, and drew further cheques against it to buy goods. In the second case, the customer had an overdraft limit of £100 but drew in one evening 25 cheques, totalling £750.

Cheque guarantee cards are not usually issued to a customer unless he or she has established a record in which the account has been run on responsible lines (or, if it is a relatively new customer, he or she is known to be of good integrity or is willing to put up appropriate security).

10.6 POWERS OF AGENTS

The relationship of agent to principal is of importance to a bank in three different ways. Firstly, the bank itself acts as agent for its customer in a number of ways - for instance, in collecting cheques and in dealing with securities. Secondly, the customer may appoint an agent to draw cheques on the account and, possibly, to negotiate an overdraft or to deposit security. Thirdly, the customer may be an agent for another person.

We have referred elsewhere in this book to the role of a bank as agent; suffice it to say at this juncture that in acting as agent the bank must act with due care and within the scope of normal banking practice. It is the consequences to a banker which result from the customer appointing an agent to operate the account that we must mostly concern ourselves with in the context of this chapter, and to some extent the bank's responsibilities when the customer is an agent.

A principal may appoint an agent by word of mouth, but a bank will wish to see the authority in writing before acting upon it. A bank customer may authorise another person to operate the bank account, either by completing the bank's form of delegation or as part of a general power of attorney. If the bank is presented with a power of attorney, it must examine it very carefully to see that the agent's powers cover all the acts which are likely to affect the operation of the account and the bank's services related to it. In either case, the bank will wish to be introduced to the agent and will require a specimen signature. The agent is responsible to the principal - the bank's customer - for all actions and must act within the stated powers. As a third party, the bank must know what these powers are, and make sure that they are not exceeded because the principal is not bound by the agent's actions if they exceed these powers.

When signing cheques and other documents on behalf of the principal, the agent must do so *by procuration* - i.e., sign 'per pro'. As far as cheques and other bills of exchange are concerned, this is covered by s.25, Bills of Exchange Act, which reads 'A signature by procuration operates as notice that the agent has but limited authority to sign, and the principal is only bound by such signature if the agent in so signing was acting within the actual limits of his authority'.

If an agent exceeds the authority in borrowing money from the bank, the bank cannot enforce repayment against the principal unless the principal agrees, or is in some way unable to deny the agent's lack of authority. This is particularly important in the context of borrowing by the directors of a company, and is referred to again in Chapter 14.

If a bank's customer is an agent for some other person, the relationship is unlikely to affect the bank very much, but the bank may be put on enquiry if the customer draws cheques on the principal's account and pays them into his or her own (*Midland Bank Ltd* v. *Reckitt & Others* 1933). If, however, the bank is principal, and the customer its agent (as does happen occasionally), then clearly the bank may be considerably affected by the agent's actions. This relationship exists, for instance, when the bank holds the shipping documents in respect of goods which the customer has imported, as security for an advance. In order that the customer (if he or she is reliable enough) can have access to the goods in order to resell them, the bank may be prepared to release the documents against a trust receipt. The customer then handles the documents and the goods as agent for the bank.

The banks use other banks as their agents abroad when sending bills of exchange for collection, and when opening documentary letters of credit. They are responsible for the agent's actions but they are protected against negligence or unauthorised acts on the part of these agents to a very considerable extent by two international codes of practice, the *Uniform Rules for Collections* and *Uniform Customs and Practice for Documentary Credits*, both of which were drawn up in conjunction with bankers by the International Chamber of Commerce. These are not codes of law, of course, only of practice, but if the bank abides by them then it is likely that a court of law would decide in favour of the bank in a legal dispute.

10.7 THE CHEQUE AS A METHOD OF PAYMENT

To complete this chapter let us look at the merits of a cheque as a method of payment. Safety and convenience are two crucial aspects here.

The dangers of carrying too much cash around have become only too apparent in recent years, and to the extent that cheques can be used instead these risks can be reduced. A cheque is a safe way of transferring money, especially if it is crossed, when it can be paid only through a bank account and can thus be traced if it is stolen. Furthermore if a cheque is lost, payment can be countermanded. From the point of view of businessmen – retailers for example, who handle a great deal of cash – their activities would be much safer if they could persuade the majority of their customers to pay by cheque and in this connection the introduction of the cheque guarantee card has been very helpful. To the extent that more and more firms are paying wages by cheque, there is less need for large amounts of cash to be transported.

From the aspect of convenience, a cheque book is much easier to carry around than a large amount of cash, and cheques can be written out for any amount so that change does not have to be given. Cheques can be sent through the post, which is more convenient than having to meet the beneficiary in order to hand over the cash. Furthermore, transactions can be settled by cheque at any time, as it is not necessary to wait for the banks to open in order to obtain cash. Time is saved in counting cash and in taking it to and from banks. The fact that a cheque can be stopped is also convenient to the drawer, in that if he or she is dissatisfied with a purchase he or she can take it back to the supplier and, if still not satisfied, stop payment. Cheques are also convenient in that they can be post-dated and handed to the payee to make claims for payments as they become due.

Another merit of a cheque is that it is negotiable (unless marked otherwise) and can therefore be passed from hand to hand provided that it is indorsed. It also serves as evidence that a payment has been made, so that no receipt is necessary and a record of the transaction appears in the drawer's bank statement.

The cheque can be cheap to use in comparison with some other means of payment such as a postal order or money order, provided that the drawer does not incur bank charges. It also delays the time of actual payment - i.e., provides a period of credit - in that it takes three business days for a cheque to be cleared quite apart from any delay on the part of the payee in paying the cheque into his account.

TOPICS FOR DISCUSSION

1. Discuss the usefulness of a bill of exchange as a means of settlement.
2. Consider the developments since the 17th century which have stimulated the use of cheques.
3. Consider the usefulness of the various types of crossings that can be made on cheques.
4. Discuss the various circumstances in which a paying banker is absolved from the obligation to pay a customer's cheque.
5. Consider what is meant by the tort of conversion, and the extent to which (i) a paying banker, and (ii) a collecting banker might be held liable for the tort.
6. Discuss the circumstances in which a bank might be sued by a customer for libel as well as breach of contract when returning a cheque unpaid.

7. Under what circumstances does a banker act as agent for the customer in connection with a cheque, and what are the banker's responsibilities as agent?

8. Why should a bank be particularly careful when a customer appoints someone to run the account for him?

9. When a bank uses a bank abroad as agent in collecting a bill drawn under a documentary credit, how is it protected?

10. Discuss the use (and possible misuse) of a cheque guarantee card.

PART IV
BANKING OPERATIONS –
PAYMENTS AND SERVICES

CHAPTER 11

INTERNAL METHODS OF PAYMENT

11.1 PROVISION OF NOTES AND COIN

A very unrewarding and yet vital service which the banks provide for their customers is to make available to them the notes and coin which they need for making payments in cash. The customer expects to be able to draw cash at any time the bank is open (and to some extent when it is closed) in whatever denominations of notes and coin he or she requires. This is a particularly necessary service for the firm or company which has wage packets to make up on a Thursday or Friday, and usually to make it convenient to the bank (and to speed up the process when the cash is collected) the larger business customer will notify the bank a day or so before what mixture of cash will be required. In addition to drawing in cash, some business customers – especially retailers – will wish to change notes into coins and vice-versa. At the end of the day or early next morning these customers will wish to pay in their day's takings, most of which may well be in a mixture of notes and coins of all denominations which the bank has got to count and sort out. Dirty and worn notes have to be separated from the good ones and bundled up for despatch by security van or bullion van to head office to be presented to the Bank of England for withdrawal from circulation and destruction. Worn coins have similarly to be withdrawn from circulation, and when a branch has sufficient of them they must be sent through the bank's bullion office to the Bank of England.

Some branches of the banks are net receivers of cash, more being paid in by customers (retailers, maybe) than is withdrawn. In consequence such a branch must dispose of its surplus cash from time to time, possibly to other branches or banks in the locality or by security van to bullion department. If a branch is short of notes or coin it may be able to obtain supplies from other branches, or will need to be supplied by bullion department. New notes are obtained from the Bank of England by that department and distributed to branches.

Where it is considered necessary, branch banks have night safes fitted into the wall of the bank into which customers may deposit their daily takings after hours. These takings are placed in a special wallet that is locked before it is placed in the safe. The following day the wallet can either be collected by the customer and the contents paid into the account or (by agreement) the wallet will be opened by a cashier of the bank, the contents checked against the paying in slip and then credited to the account. The second of these alternatives is preferred by the banks, because the wallets can be opened and checked at times when the counter is not active and so avoid the congestion which would otherwise be caused by the customer paying in at a busy time.

A growing number of branches of the banks now have cash dispensing machines at which customers can obtain bank notes up to agreed limits after the bank is closed – and even when the bank is open if the customer prefers not to queue up at the counter. By inserting a special plastic card and keying in the customer's own personal number and the amount required, the customer can draw the cash needed (the amount he or she may draw varies from bank to bank and from customer to customer). Some of the machines can be used by a customer in order to find out the account balance, order a new cheque book or order a statement. The extent to which these and other machines are being installed will be discussed in Chapter 17.

All of these cash services are very costly to provide, and yet they produce no income to the banks. The banks must therefore rely on the rewards they receive for other services to cover the cost involved. To the extent that the community can be encouraged to receive payments (especially wages and salaries) by cheque or by credit to an account, and to use cheques rather than cash as much as possible, the need for cash, the use of cash, and the problems and expense of handling it can all be reduced.

11.2 PAYMENT BY CHEQUE

The use of cheques as a means of payment has already been discussed in Chapter 10, and it is only necessary at this juncture to examine the procedure through which cheques are cleared. This is greatly facilitated by the existence of the Bankers' Clearing House in London through which the member banks are able to clear both debit and credit items with one another both for themselves and also for non-member banks for which they act as agent.

When a cheque drawn on another bank is paid into the payee's account receipt of it by the bank is given by a rubber stamp and an initial on the counterfoil of the paying-in book. At the end of that day, the bank will dispatch that cheque to its clearing department together with all other cheques paid in by customers that are drawn on other banks or other branches. Any cheques paid in that are drawn by other customers of the branch do not need to be cleared, of course, and remain on the premises if they are paid (or are returned unpaid through the post to the customers who paid them in if they are dishonoured). In the specimen cheque in Figure 10.5, one set of magnetic characters along the bottom of the cheque is missing. This is the amount of the cheque, a fact which is not known when the cheque book is prepared for the drawer's use. Before the cheques are sent off to the bank's clearing department this amount is encoded on the cheque so that it can be read by a computer at a later stage.

On Day 2, the clearing department of the bank receives all the bundles of cheques sent to it by the branches the day before and they are checked against the tally slips that are sent with them. The cheques are sorted into bank and branch by an electronic reader/sorter machine and batches prepared of cheques to be presented to other banks at the Clearing House. Cheques on other branches are sent to those branches concerned by the clearing department as there is no need for them to go to the Clearing House. At the Clearing House, each bank hands over to other banks bundles of cheques drawn by customers of those banks and receives bundles of cheques from the other banks.

The clearing department posts the cheques it receives to the debit of its customers' accounts (including those received from branches that are drawn on other branches); this is done by an electronic reader which feeds the account number, cheque number and amount into the computer. These items are not actually debited to the accounts until the next day, by which time the branches on which the cheques are drawn will have been able to notify the clearing department if any of the cheques are not to be paid. The computer produces lists of all the items debited to customers' accounts, and these lists accompany the bundles of cheques that are sent off to the branches at the end of Day 2.

On Day 3, the bundles of cheques received from the clearing department are listed manually at the branch and the total checked against the computer list. The process of payment then begins. Each cheque has to be inspected to ensure that there is nothing technically wrong with it – do the words and figures differ? is cheque stale or mutilated? has the cheque been signed by the drawer? The clerk who is paying the cheques will also have to make sure that payment has not been countermanded. Provided that the drawer has an adequate balance on the account, or that the overdraft limit has not been exceeded, the cheque will be paid. This involves cancelling the cheque with a rubber stamp which impresses 'Paid' on the cheque, or a squiggle through the drawer's signature. If the manager decides to return a cheque unpaid – whether it be for a technical reason, or because it has been stopped, or because there are insufficient funds on the account –

the reason must be written on the cheque. The words 'Cheque out of Date', 'Payment Countermanded', 'Words and Figures Differ' or 'Drawer's Signature Required' cause no difficulties for the paying banker in that the customer (the drawer) can hardly object. However, if there are insufficient funds this must not be stated and, instead, the words 'Refer to Drawer' or 'Refer to Drawer – Please Re-present' will be used. An unpaid cheque is returned through the post direct to the branch of the bank which presented it for payment, as shown by the rubber stamp across the face of the cheque.

Assuming there are no delays in the post, an unpaid cheque will arrive back at the collecting bank's branch office on the fourth day and that branch will send it by post to the customer who paid it in. It will therefore be Day 5 before the customer who paid the cheque in is aware that the cheque is unpaid, although he or she may possibly be informed on Day 4 by telephone. The account will be debited with the unpaid cheque on Day 4, and it is for this reason that the banks expect their customers to allow four clear working days before drawing against cheques that have been paid in for collection, and reserve the right to send cheques back unpaid marked 'Effects Not Cleared' if they are drawn prematurely.

To expedite clearance of a cheque a customer may ask for it to be specially cleared, for which he or she will be charged a set fee. A special presentation involves sending the cheque direct to the bank on which it is drawn through the post, or by hand if it is local. The collecting bank then telephones the paying bank next day to ascertain whether the cheque is paid or not. If it is paid, the paying bank remits the amount of it to the collecting bank through the credit clearing.

Within the City of London a special Town Clearing operates (as distinct from the General Clearing which we have been looking at so far). Banks within walking distance of the clearing house in Lombard Street bundle up cheques of £10 000 or more that are drawn on other Town branches and send them to the clearing house by messenger. These are handed over to representatives of the banks concerned and delivered by them to the branches on which they are drawn. Cheques can be presented at the clearing house up to 3.50 p.m. and any unpaid cheques must be returned by 4.45 p.m.

The Town Clearing greatly facilitates the operation within the London money market, and those of the large companies in the City. Very large sums of money are involved and the total value of the Town Clearing is about 90 per cent of all daily clearings, although the total number of items is relatively small. To some extent the work of the Town Clearing has been taken over by CHAPS (see p. 222).

Settlement between the banks for cheques and for the credit clearing (see below) is made by offsetting money owed by a bank to other banks against money owed to it. The net amount is paid to (or by) each individual bank by a cheque drawn on the Bank of England. Settlement for the General Clearing takes place the day after the cheques have actually been exchanged because the cheques are not paid (or returned unpaid) until that day.

11.3 CREDIT TRANSFERS

As an alternative to drawing a cheque a person who has a debt to settle can do so by using the bank giro system, provided he or she knows the bank and branch and the account number of the creditor and that the creditor is in agreement with this method of payment.

The person initiating the payment writes out a credit transfer form indicating the name of the account holder to be credited and the account number plus the bank and branch at which the account is kept. The amount to be transferred can be paid to the bank which is to send the transfer or, alternatively, the debtor can write out a cheque payable to that bank. The credit transfer is then sent up to the bank's clearing department and taken to the Clearing House where batches of credit transfers are handed over to the banks whose accounts are to be credited. A giro credit paid in on Day 1 reaches the Clearing House on Day 2, and is handed over to the recipient bank which then sends it to the appropriate branch to arrive on Day 3.

The reader will appreciate that credit giros move through the clearing in the opposite direction to cheques – whereas a cheque is a *claim for money*, and passes via the clearing from the beneficiary's bank to the debtor's bank, a credit transfer represents a *payment of money* and passes, again through the clearing, but from the debtor's bank to the beneficiary's bank. The cheque clearing is the debit clearing and the giro system the credit clearing.

The bank giro system saves a debtor the effort of writing a cheque and sending it with the invoice (or some other indication of what it is for) to the beneficiary. The beneficiary is saved the trouble of having to visit a bank to pay in the cheque. However, the debtor has to visit a bank to initiate the transfer, but if when he or she does so a number of credit transfers are sent off (maybe all bills are saved up until the end of the month), the journey may seem more worthwhile and, furthermore, the debtor will need to write out only one cheque in respect of the total value. The beneficiaries receive notification of giro payments into their accounts by means of their statements of account.

The bank giro must be distinguished from the giro system operated through the Post Offices by the National Girobank.

11.4 STANDING ORDERS

Where a customer of a bank has payments to make on a regular basis – such as rent, mortgage payments and insurance premiums – he or she can arrange for them to be paid automatically by the bank as they fall due. The customer can forget about the payments – provided, of course, that he or she has sufficient funds on the account for them to be paid.

A standing order is an instruction to a bank to pay a stipulated sum of money to a stated beneficiary's account with a given bank and branch at a particular date (or dates) each year until further notice, or for a set period of time. The mandate has to be signed by the customer, of course, and any alteration or cancellation must be given in writing to the bank.

11.5 DIRECT DEBITS

As an alternative means of making regular payments a customer can authorise the bank to meet direct debits initiated by the beneficiary. The beneficiary claims the sum required through the bank and when the claim is received by the bank that is to make the payment on behalf of its customer it will be paid and debited to his account, provided that it is within the terms of the direct debit instructions. The instructions may stipulate a fixed sum that is to be paid, or the amount may be left open so as to avoid having to adjust the instructions when the sum changes. The timing of the payments is usually fixed, however.

To the building society, insurance company or other firm or institution which has thousands of payments due to it monthly on a regular basis, the direct debit is a very satisfactory way of obtaining payment. The beneficiary takes the initiative and, unless a direct debit bounces back unpaid, knows that payment has been effected. Under the alternative system of standing orders, the beneficiary has to check through its bank statements to ascertain whether each of the very many payments has been received.

11.6 AUTOMATED CLEARING SERVICES

The Bankers' Automated Clearing Services Ltd (BACS) was set up by the London and Scottish clearing banks to facilitate the transfer of funds by computer. Claims on (such as direct debits) and payments to (such as standing orders) other banks are fed into a bank's computer and this information is then transferred to the BACS system. This obviates the need for thousands of vouchers to be handwritten or typewritten, and where payments are to be made on a regular basis the computer can be instructed to feed them into the system. Large customers of the banks pay their wages and salaries by putting the information on to their own computers and handing over the computer tapes to their banks to be put through BACS.

The BACS system has opened the way for many developments involving the payment of money by computer including CHAPS (Clearing House Automatic Payment System) and this and many other developments will be considered in Chapter 17.

11.7 TRANSFERS BY TELEPHONE

Transfers of funds between branches of the same bank can be made relatively easily by telephone. Each bank has its own internal code system to authenticate messages and it can follow up telephone transfers with appropriate book-keeping transactions through the agency of head office. Between banks such transfers are more difficult but, nevertheless, they can be carried out quite speedily. It is necessary for the paying bank to contact its head office by telephone and arrange for the payment to be transmitted through the head office of the beneficiary's bank. That head office telephones its branch and instructs it to make the payment concerned.

Telephone transfers are a quick means of payment for the bank customer who has insufficient time to obtain and send a bankers' draft but in view of the work involved – especially for payments between banks – the charge is relatively high. Between banks the minimum amount that can be transferred in this way is £5000. No doubt telephone transfers will be largely replaced by the CHAPS system in due course.

11.8 BANKERS' DRAFTS

A bankers' draft is regarded as a very safe method of payment in that it is a 'cheque' drawn by a bank upon itself (and, as such, is unlikely to be dishonoured). Such drafts are used for making payments between solicitors in respect of house purchases, the legal conveyance being handed over in exchange for the draft. They are also used for other relatively large transactions such as the purchase of a car. Small transactions up to the limit of the cheque guarantee card can be settled by cheque, of course, with the bank's guarantee and do not warrant the use of bankers' drafts.

Between the banks themselves a special form of draft is used, called a *bankers' payment*. It is a simple form of debit slip which is passed through the clearing house like a cheque when it is received by a bank in payment for some transaction such as providing notes or coin to the other bank concerned.

11.9 CREDIT CARDS

Growing use is being made in the UK of the credit cards such as those issued by Access, Barclays Bank and the TSB. Access is owned jointly by the Midland, Lloyds and National Westminster Banks.

A credit card holder need not be a customer of a bank, but the majority are. Each holder is given a credit limit up to which he may purchase goods from retailers, garage owners and other companies who are members of the particular scheme. These suppliers have to pay a commission to the credit card company which is an agreed percentage of each transaction. This charge should not be passed on to the customer.

As far as the card holder is concerned, he or she pays nothing for the service unless he or she does not settle the monthly account by the stipulated time. This statement lists all the purchases during the month and is prepared from the copies of the slips presented by the suppliers of the goods when claiming payment from the credit company. These slips are prepared for and signed by the card holder when the purchases are made. When the holder receives the monthly statement he or she may, if preferred, pay only a proportion of the sum due – provided it is equal to or greater than the minimum amount stated on the account. The holder is then charged interest at around $1\frac{1}{2}$–2 per cent per month on the outstanding balance. He or she may also draw cash from one of the banks in the scheme within the credit limit and up to a stipulated amount each day, but interest is charged on such encashments from the day they occur. Access has a link internationally with Mastercard and both Barclaycard and Trustcard with Visa International. This enables a card holder to buy goods abroad which are ultimately paid for when the slips reach the UK, and are debited to the card holder's account.

Other credit cards used in Britain are those of American Express and Diners Club, both American organisations. The card holders have to pay annual subscriptions for these and they have to settle their accounts each month in full. The only credit they receive is from the date of purchase until the date by which the monthly account has to be settled.

TOPICS FOR DISCUSSION

1. Discuss the usefulness to the community of the services the banks provide in connection with notes and coin.
2. Follow the progress of a cheque drawn on another bank from the point where it is paid in by the payee to the point where it is returned unpaid.
3. Distinguish between the debit clearing and the credit clearing.

4. Discuss the differences between a standing order and a direct debit, and consider the advantages and disadvantages of each to the company which receives large numbers of payments on a regular basis.
5. Consider the usefulness of credit cards from the points of view of the card holder and of the supplier.

CHAPTER 12

INTERNATIONAL METHODS

OF PAYMENT

12.1 PAYMENTS BETWEEN BANKS

Customers of banks are able to effect payments to beneficiaries overseas in a number of different ways, and all of them result in book-keeping transactions between the banks concerned. These could be between a bank and its own international bank – i.e., between National Westminster and National Westminster International – but in addition the banks in the UK have accounts with banks abroad denominated in the currencies of the countries concerned, and similarly the overseas banks have accounts with the UK banks that are denominated in sterling. These relationships with banks abroad have been established through contracts made in the past and the particular banks which a UK bank holds accounts with are known as its 'correspondent banks'.

To a UK bank its accounts with other banks located abroad are its *nostro* ('our') accounts, whilst the accounts of those banks which it holds are called *vostro* ('your') accounts. The foreign currency balances held on nostro accounts are regarded virtually as cash in the way that a current account customer of a UK bank regards his or her balance as cash. These are the bank's holdings of the foreign currency concerned apart from whatever stock of currency notes it may hold at its branches. Receipts of foreign currency paid in (as various forms of claim for currency), by the bank's customers go into these accounts and payments made on their behalf in foreign currency come out of these accounts. From time to time it may be necessary for the bank to dispose of some of its surplus holdings of currencies on these accounts, or to build them up if they get low, and this is done by respectively selling and buying in the London foreign exchange market. It is only the bank's 'wholesale' transactions which involve the market, its 'retail' transactions with customers simply affect its stocks of currencies.

If then a customer of, say, Midland Bank wishes to make a payment of

DM5000 to a German exporter he or she can ask the bank to effect that payment in a number of ways, as we shall see, the result of which will be that a German correspondent bank will pay over that sum in local currency to the beneficiary and debit Midland's nostro account. Midland Bank debits its customer with the sterling equivalent of DM5000 plus the charges involved, unless he or she happens to hold a Deutschemark foreign currency account, in which case that account will be debited with the currency amount. Midland Bank will keep a nostro mirror account as a record of its transactions on its nostro account in the books of the German bank, and this it will credit with the DM5000.

Should the UK importer have contracted to pay for the goods in sterling a similar process is involved, but the German bank will have its sterling account credited with the amount, say £1250, instead of debiting the Midland nostro account with Deutschemarks. To Midland Bank, the German bank's sterling account is of course a vostro account. This account is credited, and the customer's account is debited with the £1250.

The reader will appreciate that what is a nostro account to Midland bank is a vostro account to the German bank, and the vostro account in Midland's books is a nostro account to a German bank. To avoid confusion the two terms have been used in this chapter only as they would be seen by Midland Bank.

We need now to look at the various alternative devices that can be used as methods of payment to bring about this end result of debiting a nostro account, or crediting a vostro account.

12.2 TT, SWIFT AND MT

The quickest means of transferring funds abroad is by *telegraphic transfer (TT)*. For the payment of DM5000, Midland Bank will send a cable (or telex) message to a correspondent bank in, say, Frankfurt, instructing it to pay (or to advise and pay) that sum to a specified beneficiary. The message will include an authenticating code and it will be the German bank's mandate to debit Midland's nostro account. Although this method is speedy it is expensive, because a cable message is involved and, therefore, if the payment is not urgent the importer (or whoever it is that is wanting to make a payment abroad) may be well advised to use a cheaper but slower method.

To a considerable extent the TT system has been replaced by *SWIFT (Society for Worldwide Interbank Financial Telecommunication)*, but there are still some parts of the world in which the system does not operate. Member banks now exceed 750 and they are located in Western Europe, Canada, the USA, Japan, New Zealand, Australia, Singapore, Hong Kong, and some South American countries. The system is a closed one involving the use of cables and computers and obviates using the normal cable and telex system available to the public at large (with the possible additional risks which that could entail). Messages can be sent through the system on either an urgent or non-urgent basis, the less urgent ones being dealt with at times when the system is less busy. Unless a customer especially asks for a telegraphic transfer, a bank would use SWIFT for transmitting the payment. It is of course equally as quick, and the charges to the customer are the same.

Less urgent payments can be sent by *mail transfer (MT)*. The payment instructions are the same as for a telegraphic transfer, but they are sent by airmail instead of cable and consequently the method is cheaper.

For all three of these methods of payment the bank will require its customer to complete an application form giving the same details and this also serves as a mandate to debit the customer's account. The details required are the amount; the name and address of the beneficiary; whether the beneficiary is to be advised that the payment is waiting at the overseas bank involved or that the bank is to await a call; and whether the charges are to be paid by the customer initiating the payment, or deducted from the amount to be paid over.

12.3 BANKERS' DRAFTS AND CHEQUES

Our customer of Midland Bank might prefer to make the payment by bankers' draft (indeed this might be stipulated in the contract of sale that was negotiated between him and the German exporter). We have already seen (p. 139) that an internal bankers' draft is one drawn by a bank upon itself and the same might apply if an international payment is to be made in sterling. Where the payment is to be made in foreign currency, however, the draft needs to be drawn on another bank. Midland Bank would draw a draft on its nostro account with the German correspondent bank for DM5000, and hand it to its customer, debiting the account with the sterling equivalent plus charges. At the same time, it sends a notification to the German bank by airmail that the draft has been drawn.

The customer then sends the draft to the beneficiary by airmail, together with the invoice (or some other indication of the reason for the payment). When it is received the German exporter pays the draft into the account and the bank debits Midland's nostro account. If the draft is for £1250 – i.e., in sterling – Midland will have drawn it upon themselves (though possibly this could be upon another bank) and the German beneficiary will either negotiate it – i.e., sell it to his or her bank – or ask the bank to collect the draft and pay the Deutschemark proceeds into the account. In either case, the German bank will send the draft by airmail to

Midland Bank and ask for its vostro account to be credited with the £1250.

As an alternative to asking the bank for a bankers' draft, the Midland customer may decide to write out his or her own cheque and send it to the beneficiary. The latter may not be best pleased with this method of payment, but nevertheless it is a method which can be used – and all the more easily since the abolition of exchange control in the UK. The reasons for the German supplier's displeasure are two fold. Firstly, irrespective of whether the cheque is made out in sterling or in DM the beneficiary will have to wait for the cheque to be collected by the bank before he or she receives payment; secondly, he or she will have to bear the expenses involved. The collection of the cheque will be done by airmail between the German bank and Midland Bank (possibly through the agency of another bank if they are not correspondent banks) and the German bank must await notification that the cheque has been paid (or that it has been dishonoured). Reimbursement will be by credit to the German bank's vostro account in sterling, or authority may be given by Midland Bank for its nostro account to be debited with DM.

For sums of up to £500 or $1000 *international money orders* issued by Barclays Bank may be used as a means of paying money abroad. These may be purchased by both customers and non-customers of the bank and at January 1984 the bank's commission was £2 per order. These orders are in effect bankers' drafts, and are dealt with by banks abroad as such. For quite small sums international postal orders may be obtained at British Post Offices.

12.4 BILLS OF EXCHANGE

We are already familiar with bills of exchange from our study in Chapter 9. In the context of this present chapter we need to look at the procedure involved in obtaining (or making) payment internationally by this means.

A bill of exchange is drawn by the creditor upon the debtor, which means that in international trade it is drawn by the exporter upon the importer (or possibly, in some circumstances, upon the importer's bank). The exporter is the drawer, the importer the drawee, and the payee as often as not is 'Ourselves' – i.e., the drawer is payee.

Bills of exchange are either 'clean' or 'documentary'. A clean bill has no documents attached, whereas a documentary bill has the shipping documents relating to the bill attached to it. These will generally be the bill of lading, invoice and marine insurance documents plus one or two others.

When a documentary bill is sent for collection through the banking system it becomes either a D/A bill or a D/P bill depending upon the instructions given to the banks concerned by the exporter. If the instructions are that the documents may be released against acceptance of the bill it is a D/A (documents against acceptance) bill; if the instructions are that they may not be released until the bill is paid it is a D/P (documents against payment) bill.

A bill of exchange may be a sight bill or a usance bill. If it is payable at sight it is payable on presentation, whereas a usance bill as we know is payable at a number of days or months after sight or after date. Usance bills are sometimes referred to as 'term' or as 'tenor' bills. A bill which is payable at, say, 90 days after sight is payable 90 days after the date of acceptance, it being assumed that a bill is accepted on the day it is sighted by the drawee. A bill that is payable 90 days after date is payable 90 days from the date of the bill. Where a bill is payable at a number of days after sight or date the date of maturity must be calculated precisely – for example, a 120 days' after date bill which is drawn on 14 March is payable on 12 July, whereas if the bill had been payable four months after date it would be payable on 14 July. In calculating the maturity date no allowance is made for days lacking in a month, so that a two months' after date bill drawn on 31 December would be payable on the last day of February, i.e. 28 or 29 February, as we saw in Chapter 9.

An exporter who has drawn a bill on an importer can do one of two things with it – assuming that he or she is going to involve the bank, and not send it to someone as agent in the importer's country to present it for acceptance and/or payment. Most bills are in fact presented through the banking system, and the two alternatives are to ask the bank to negotiate the bill or to collect it. If the bill is drawn on an importer, it is quite likely that the bank will prefer to collect it rather than negotiate it (buy it), whereas if it is drawn on a bank it would be willing to negotiate it because in the latter case there is little doubt that it will be paid at maturity.

When a bank negotiates a bill (and the documents attached, if there are any), it purchases the bill at its face value less discount, and then proceeds to collect it in its own right as a holder for value. However, the bank usually requires the customer to sign a document giving the bank the right to debit the account should the bill be dishonoured.

Bills of exchange are collected by the banks with the protection of the *Uniform Rules for Collection*, an international set of rules drawn up by the International Chamber of Commerce with the help and co-operation of banks in various countries. These rules are not a code of law, but inasmuch as a bank specifies in its documents that it is carrying out the collection within the rules, provided it does not in any way contravene them a court of law is almost certain to favour the bank in any law case. The exporter, as drawer of the bill, is required to give the bank detailed instructions when asking it to collect the bill. The bank has its own standard form for the exporter to complete which guides the customer in giving the right instructions. For instance, the first two instructions would most likely be 'Documents Against Acceptance' and 'Documents Against Payment', and the customer would be required to delete one of these. Other instructions would be concerned with whether the acceptance or payment may be deferred pending the arrival of the goods; whether charges may be waived if refused by the drawee; how notification of acceptance and payment are to be sent (i.e. airmail or cable); whether there is someone who can be referred to in the importer's country if there are any difficulties in collecting the bill (a 'case of need'); whether the bill should be protested if dishonoured; and what action should be taken in respect of the goods should they not be taken up by the buyer. These instructions are copied on to a *collection order* which, under the Uniform Rules, must accompany the bill when it is sent for collection in order that all bankers handling the bill with its shipping documents may be fully aware of the exporter's wishes.

The remitting bank sends the bill and commercial documents to a correspondent bank in the buyer's country, and that bank in turn may send them to a correspondent bank of its own. Both of these banks are known as *collecting banks*, and the last bank involved as collecting bank is known also as the *presenting bank* – it actually presents the bill for acceptance and/or payment. Once a bill has been accepted (if it is a usance bill, of course), the presenting bank retains it and presents it for payment on the due date. The shipping documents will, of course, have been handed over to the buyer against acceptance if the bill is a D/A bill, or will be held until payment if the instructions in the collection order are for documents against payment. If payment is obtained the presenting bank informs the remitting bank and indicates how reimbursement is to be made. If the bill is dishonoured, then the presenting bank will protest the bill if the instructions are to do so.

The banking system thus offers a safe means through which the bill of exchange can be used as a method of payment, in the sense that control of the shipping documents can be vested in the banks until the importer accepts liability for paying the bill by adding an acceptance to it, or until he or she actually pays the bill. Once it is accepted, the bill is legal evidence of a debt and can be used as such in a court of law. The device enables the exporter to give the buyer a period of credit by making the bill a usance bill, and yet the exporter may be able to get immediate finance by negotiating the bill or borrowing from the bank against the bill that is being collected. There can be no guarantee that he or she will take delivery of the goods and accept and pay the bill, of course, and if the exporter is not prepared to take this risk he or she must endeavour to persuade the buyer to instruct a bank to open a documentary credit in the exporter's favour.

12.5 **DOCUMENTARY CREDITS**

A documentary credit is a letter addressed by a banker to a beneficiary (usually an exporter) undertaking to make a payment to the beneficiary or to pay, accept or negotiate a bill drawn on the importer, against stipulated shipping documents and provided that all the terms of the credit have been met. The importer's bank issues such a letter of credit at the importer's request, but will do so only if it is satisfied that the importer will reimburse the bank for the payment it has made or the undertaking it has given to pay the bill, by adding its acceptance to it. The bank in effect 'stands in the shoes' of the importer, and says that the goods that have been ordered will be paid for.

From the point of view of the exporter, a documentary credit is an excellent method of payment. The exporter is assured of either immediate payment once the goods are despatched or the promise of such at the maturity of a usance bill drawn on the importer (or possibly on the issuing bank direct). If the payment is to be immediate it will either be against the shipping documents on their own or against a documentary sight bill, which as such is payable immediately it is presented for payment. Alternatively, the exporter may obtain immediate finance by negotiating a usance bill drawn on the buyer if the documentary credit undertakes to negotiate it, but the exporter will have to bear the discount cost of doing this. If the documentary credit is an acceptance credit then the exporter is assured that his or her bill on the importer will be accepted by the issuing bank and payment at the maturity of the bill is therefore not in doubt.

All this assumes, of course, that the exporter is able to fulfil all the terms of the documentary credit. This means that he or she must get together all the shipping documents listed in the credit, and see that they are all in order. For instance, the bill of lading must be clean – and thus not state that the goods and/or the packaging have been damaged. Apart from ensuring that the documents are in order, the exporter must meet other requirements stipulated in the credit, such as ensuring that the goods are shipped by the last date of shipment indicated, that the goods are not transhipped if the credit says they must not be, and that the goods are insured for the specific risks listed in the credit.

A credit may be *revocable* or *irrevocable*. A revocable credit may be cancelled or amended at any time, but a bank is protected for any payments made up to the time that notice of cancellation is received, or if it has accepted a bill of exchange. An irrevocable credit cannot be cancelled or amended without the approval of all parties to the credit, and clearly this type of credit is much more satisfactory from the exporter's point of view.

If the exporter can persuade the buyer to open a *confirmed irrevocable credit*, this is even more satisfactory because it means that the advising bank in the exporter's country has confirmed the credit and in doing so takes on all the same responsibilities as the issuing bank. The exporter has an assurance of payment from a local bank in addition to that of the issuing bank and he or she is able more easily to deal with any problems that arise in fulfilling the stipulation in the credit in that he or she can discuss them with the confirming bank. An added advantage is that even if exchange control restrictions are imposed in the buyer's country which prevent the issuing bank from meeting its obligations in the credit, they will not hold up the payment because the confirming bank is obliged to pay the exporter.

From the importer's point of view a documentary credit does ensure that payment is not made to the supplier (or a bill drawn by the supplier accepted) until the goods have been despatched, as evidenced in the bill of lading. This does not give the importer any guarantee that the goods will be precisely of the type and quality ordered, however, because the banks involved with the credit handle only the *documents*, and not the goods themselves. Not that the banks could be expected to be experts in any particular type of commodity, even if they were handling the goods – all that the banks are required to do is to ensure that the goods purport to be those ordered by the buyer, and to this end they must ensure that the description of the goods in the invoice matches the description in the credit. The importer can endeavour to ensure that the goods are of the quality expected by requiring that the shipping documents include a certificate of quality or a certificate of analysis. The first of these is a certificate issued by a business organisation in the exporter's country which is nominated by the importer to inspect the goods and certify as to their quality. The second is a somewhat similar arrangement, but the organisation concerned will analyse the goods (chemicals, maybe) after putting them through various tests.

As for bills of exchange sent for collection, the International Chamber of Commerce has produced a set of rules for documentary credits, *Uniform Customs and Practice for Documentary Credits*, which have been adopted by the UK banks and by banks in many countries of the world. They set out in considerable detail the terms and conditions under which the banks issue and handle documentary credits and they serve to protect all the parties involved with them.

TOPICS FOR DISCUSSION

1. Consider the usefulness of the international banking system in the settlement of transactions between importers and exporters.

2. Discuss the actions of the banks involved in transferring funds by TT or MT systems.
3. 'The bill of exchange is a convenient and comparatively safe method of obtaining payment from a buyer abroad, provided documents are attached to it.' Discuss this statement in the light of the procedure involved in collecting a bill of exchange.
4. Consider why it is preferable that a bill should be drawn under a documentary credit rather than stand on its own.

CHAPTER 13

BANKING SERVICES

13.1 SERVICES TO PERSONAL CUSTOMERS

Current, deposit and other accounts

The majority of bank accounts are personal accounts, as distinct from business accounts - they are accounts of individuals (or combinations of individuals) opened in order to carry out their own personal affairs. Some business transactions - such as those of the small businessmen - may pass through these accounts but, generally speaking, the transactions are those of the person who receives an income, possibly direct to the account, which is spent by drawing cheques on the account in respect of the normal expenditures as householders. The joint accounts are mostly between husband and wife, but there is no reason of course why any two or more persons should not open a joint private account. The joint account mandate must indicate whether one, all, or some of the account holders are to sign on the account, and it will also establish joint and several liability in respect of any borrowing that may occur on the account.

Unless a potential private account holder is already well known to the bank, through business connections maybe, the bank will need to take up a reference and will also want to know his or her employer's name and address. If the bank does not do these two things, it could at a later date be accused of negligence - if, for instance, the customer paid in one of the employer's cheques to his or her own account.

The opening of a current account provides the customer with the facilities of drawing cheques, arranging for regular payments by standing orders or direct debits, and having payments such as salary or dividends credited direct to the account. He or she is provided with a cheque book free of charge, and if he or she maintains a minimum credit balance (normally £100, though in the case of one or two of the large banks, no minimum balance is required) can avoid paying charges in respect of the work involved for the bank in clearing and debting all the cheques drawn.

Most banks now publish a tariff of charges on private accounts, so that the customer should be aware of the expense being incurred, if such is the case. The tariff indicates the charge for cheque and standing order debits and that a notional rate of credit interest (worked out on the average credit balance) is set off against these charges. On ordinary current-accounts net credit interest is not paid to the customer if the notional interest exceeds the charge for cheques drawn.

As yet the clearing banks have not been deflected from their policy of not paying interest on ordinary current accounts, but some clearing banks, merchant banks, foreign banks and licenced deposit-takers do, however, offer special types of account on which interest is paid and cheques can be drawn, but these are not strictly speaking current accounts. The normal requirement is for a substantial minimum balance of, say, £2500 to be maintained on such accounts against which money market rates of interest are paid.

The current account holder is sent a statement of account at regular intervals on which the paid cheques are listed by their numbers and the nature of credit items is briefly indicated. Used in conjunction with the cheque book and paying in book, this statement serves as a record of all personal transactions.

In addition to (or instead of) a current account the customer may wish to maintain a deposit account. If the amount to be placed on such an account is modest (less than £10 000) it would be placed on an ordinary seven-day deposit account. This means that the balance (or part of it) can be withdrawn in cash or transferred to a current account, subject to seven days' notice. Banks can, of course, insist on this period of notice but in practice they will usually allow a customer to withdraw the money immediately but deduct seven days' interest in lieu of notice. The rate of interest on ordinary deposit accounts is related to the bank's base rate and is usually about 3-4 per cent below that rate. Cheques may not be drawn on deposit accounts.

To help the individual plan his annual household expenditure more easily, the banks run budget accounts. These accounts are designed to overcome the problems that arise from the uneven incidence of expenditure during the year caused, for instance, by heavy fuel bills in the winter. The customer estimates his total outlay for the year, and arranges for $\frac{1}{12}$ th of this to be debited to the current account and credited to the budget account each month. The budget account balance will most likely be in credit some months and overdrawn for others, and debit interest will be charged and credit interest allowed appropriately.

For children, there are special savings accounts on which favourable rates of interest are paid and, possibly, a home safe provided to encourage saving.

The banks provide a number of different schemes for customers as variations on normal current accounts, deposit accounts and budget accounts, and the reader would be wise to obtain information about the specific types of schemes which his or her own bank provides.

Other personal services

The private customer may from time to time have occasion to make a status enquiry concerning an individual or firm with which he or she is going to have dealings. He or she may, for instance, be letting furnished accommodation, and would need to have some assurance concerning the future tenant's ability to pay the rent and, if possible, concerning respectability. He or she needs to ascertain the name and branch of that person's bank and pass this information to his or her own bank with an indication of the monthly or annual rent. As we saw earlier (p. 112) the reply from the tenant's bank will be a guarded and unsigned one, but it should help the customer to decide whether to go ahead or not.

Personal account customers with deeds and stock exchange securities may deposit them with the bank for safe custody and other valuables may be deposited in a locked deed box or sealed up in a parcel. Boxes and parcels are numbered by the bank to identify them, and receipts are issued which usually state 'Contents Unknown'. The banks do not want to know the contents, and usually advise the customer to take out appropriate insurance. The banks tend now to charge for safe custody services and thus are paid bailees (but, as we saw in Chapter 8, their legal position may well be unaffected by the fact that they are no longer gratuitous bailees).

The purchase and sale of stocks and shares is likely to be of interest to personal rather than business customers, and those who wish to buy or sell may ask the bank to arrange it. The banks pass on the orders to a stockbroker and share the broker's commission. If the customer wants advice on investments the request will also be passed on to a stockbroker, unless the amount of money to be invested justifies an approach to the bank's own investment department. That department in responding to a request for help will be guarded in its approach, mentioning the various types of investments which may satisfy the customer's needs, but without giving too firm a recommendation concerning the purchase of particular stocks or shares. They would prefer to help the customer make his or her own decision and to accept responsibility for the actions taken. However, they will look after a customer's investment portfolio for an annual management charge, and if the customer is willing to give them the authority, will buy and sell securities as they consider appropriate in order to maintain or improve the income and/or capital value of the investments.

Customers wishing to make payments abroad, or who are travelling abroad, may use the foreign services of the bank. Payments of the type dealt with in Chapter 12 will be made on the customer's behalf against an appropriate mandate, and for the traveller a supply of foreign currency plus travellers' cheques can be arranged. Travellers' cheques are made out in convenient denominations of sterling or foreign currency and are signed by the customer in front of an officer of the bank before he or she takes them away. When cashing a travellers' cheque at a bank abroad, the customer must sign it again in front of the cashier in order that the two signatures can be compared; similarly, if he or she cashes a travellers' cheque at a hotel abroad he or she must sign it when doing so. Lost cheques may be stopped by notifying the issuing bank.

If the customer wishes to cash cheques at a bank abroad, he or she can arrange for an open credit to be established with a correspondent bank. It is no longer possible for normal bank guarantee cards to be used when cashing cheques at banks in Europe, but some of the banks now issue special cheque cards for the purpose (and, in some cases, special books of cheques).

When travelling within the UK, the customer may use the cheque guarantee or service till card to obtain cash at bank counters or at cash dispensers, and the cheque guarantee card can be used, of course, when making purchases at shops, paying hotel bills, etc. He or she may, if desired, arrange for an open credit to be opened at a bank in the area to be visited.

A credit card may be used both at home and abroad to obtain cash up to a certain limit at banks, and to buy goods at shops which are members of the particular credit card scheme.

Travel insurance, and most forms of insurance services, are available to the personal customer through the bank's insurance department. Similarly, the services of other departments of the bank and of its subsidiary or associated companies, such as hire-purchase facilities, are available. The services of two of the bank's specialist departments (executor and trustee department and income tax department) are likely to be of particular interest to the private individual. The first of these departments will, if desired, act as executor and, if appropriate, trustee of the will made and relieve the customer of the problem of finding a relative or friend who is willing to take on the task. The income tax department will prepare and submit an income tax return and, hopefully, by being more knowledgeable about the allowances that can be claimed, save more in tax than the cost of the bank's service!

Banks offer special inducements to students, realising that although their accounts will not be very remunerative from the bank's point of view whilst they are students, they will hopefully have good steady incomes in later years and will want to make use of the full range of banking services. In addition to an initial gift, students are given free banking facilities for the duration of their course, and provided their grant is paid into the account may be allowed a cheque guarantee card and possibly a small overdraft facility.

Little has been said as yet about borrowing by personal customers. This is deliberate because the subject of bank advances is dealt with in Chapters 14 and 15, and it is more appropriate to look at personal borrowing in the context of bank lending in general.

13.2 SERVICES TO BUSINESS CUSTOMERS

Current, deposit and other accounts

Business customers in general obviously make much more active use of their accounts than private customers, whether they be sole traders, partnerships, limited companies or other institutions. They may have more than one current account to meet the particular needs of the business, and will make all their disbursements by cheque other than small petty cash items (and, maybe, wages). There will be frequent payments into the account, possibly once or more each day, and credit transfers may well come into the account in large numbers. The volume of cheques being paid into the account (and hence the use of the debit clearing), is likely to be heavy. The night safe facility may well be used, and the use of counter facilities for obtaining change and maybe a large weekly sum for wages is also a strong possibility. In view of the volume of work that business customers entail bank charges are the rule rather than the exception, and they are usually agreed by negotiation.

The larger business customers including local authorities and public corporations pay salaries and wages direct to the employees' bank accounts and use the banks' credit transfer service for this – possibly in the case of very large companies putting the information on computer tape to be fed into the BACS computers. Where employees are paid by cheque special facilities may have to be arranged by the company's bank for the staff concerned to be able to cash their cheques if they do not wish to pay them into a bank account.

Business customers, generally speaking, are likely to find a deposit account more useful than private account customers, in that they may have a fluctuating cash flow which makes transfers from current account to deposit account (and vice-versa) beneficial. They are also more likely to make use of deposits – at money market rates, of course – and also of certificates of deposit.

Help and advice

Whereas small business customers such as sole traders and partnerships are likely to look to their bank managers for help and advice on problems concerned with running their businesses and (especially, for instance, should they become involved in importing or exporting for the first time), larger businesses would employ their own experts in particular spheres of activity and have less need of such advice. However, larger businesses are likely to need help in other ways, particularly with financing their activities, with arranging mergers and takeovers, arranging performance bonds if they are involved in the construction industry, relationships with foreign subsidiary companies, and maybe help when going 'public'. Larger organisations are also likely to make fuller use of the services of the bank's subsidiary and associated companies such as those concerned with leasing and factoring.

13.3 MANUFACTURING AND EXPORTING

Business customers involved in manufacturing are the most likely ones to be concerned with the foreign services of the bank as exporters, and possibly also as importers. Let us therefore look at the services required by manufacturers with this fact in mind.

Manufacturers produce goods mostly in anticipation of demand, and therefore need working capital in order that they can purchase the raw materials they need and keep adequate stocks of them and of the finished goods to be able to meet orders. The banks provide the majority of their working capital and about a fifth of their advances are to manufacturers. We shall need to look at this more closely under the heading of advances in Chapter 14.

The raw materials, if they are imported, will involve the use of the bank's services in a number of ways:

Sources of supply and names of suppliers
The bank's economic intelligence department or commercial information department may be able to help in both connections. They hold information about commodity markets, and lists of suppliers.

Status enquiries on suppliers
Before placing orders with a new supplier, the importer should make a status enquiry through the bank.

Method of payment
The method of payment to be used will probably be stipulated by the supplier but, in any case, the bank will be able to advise on this and to make the necessary arrangements, e.g. open a documentary credit.

Foreign exchange

If payment for the goods is to be made in foreign currency, the bank will provide this when required. A forward exchange contract will fix the rate of exchange at which the currency is to be sold to the customer at some future date.

Finance

The bank may be willing to provide finance to pay for the imported goods (or, alternatively, the supplier may allow a period of credit by drawing a bill of exchange on the importer).

If a manufacturer sells goods abroad, a variety of banking services for exporters would also be available:

Advice on markets

The bank will help the exporter to find the best markets for the goods and may be able to suggest contacts with potential buyers.

Status enquiries

Enquiries concerning the creditworthiness of particular buyers abroad can be made through the bank, and should certainly be made in respect of any new customer.

Method of payment

The banks are able to advise on the usual method of settlement in particular trades (or for particular countries), and will advise on the advantages and disadvantages of the various means of payment.

Collection of bills

If payment is to be by way of D/A or D/P bill, the bank will undertake to collect the bill for the exporter.

ECGD facilities

The bank can advise on the protection available through the Export Credits Guarantee Department (ECGD) against the risks of non-payment by the buyer.

Post-shipment finance

When goods are despatched, the bank may be willing to advance money to the exporter pending receipt of the proceeds of sale. This may be by way of negotiating a bill of exchange drawn on the importer, or by way of an advance against a bill sent for collection, or simply a loan against goods sold on a cash against documents basis or on open account. The existence of an ECGD guarantee direct to the bank may make the bank more willing to lend, because of the added security provided.

Similar facilities are also available when capital goods are sold on medium- or long-term credit, but here an ECGD guarantee may be essential rather than optional.

Foreign exchange

Whatever means of payment is to be used the bank will assist the exporter in obtaining it, and if the sale proceeds are to be in foreign currency the bank will undertake to buy it on the spot or by forward exchange contract, at the market rate of exchange.

Exchange control

Although exchange control restrictions have been lifted in the UK they are still in force in some countries and may make it difficult for the exporter to obtain payment due. The banks are able to advise about these restrictions.

Manufacturing customers often find it expedient to use the services of a *factoring house* whether the goods are sold at home or abroad, and the banks have subsidiary companies which offer these services. A factoring house buys the invoices of the supplier and collects the accounts in its own name. It will either pay the manufacturer immediately the orders are despatched or at an agreed time after despatch and, of course, its charges will be greater for the former than the latter.

Most of a manufacturing company's plant and machinery is likely to have been purchased from proprietor's capital if the company is a substantial one, but smaller businesses may opt to acquire machinery through the bank's leasing company subsidiary, paying an annual rental for it rather than paying for it outright.

13.4 RETAILING

The banks' services to retailers have already been referred to in connection with their cash requirements and the daily paying in of their takings. Whether they are large retailers or small they are likely to receive substantial quantities of cash (and, to an increasing extent, cheques), and these need to be taken to the bank at frequent intervals. After hours, takings can be paid into a night safe if there is one at the branch.

Apart from this, the retailer will make use of the account with the bank to pay suppliers, and if trade is seasonal may require bank finance to enable stocks to be built up for a main selling period, such as Christmas.

The use of cheque guarantee cards by customers will enable the retailer to supply goods immediately which he or she might otherwise not release until the cheques were cleared, and he or she may choose to join one or more of the credit card schemes and pay the appropriate percentage fee in order to get the extra customers which should then be forthcoming.

13.5 PROFESSIONAL CUSTOMERS

Professional partnerships such as doctors, solicitors, accountants, architects and estate agents have joint accounts at the banks and the partners will usually have their own private accounts as well. The business account is likely to be in credit, and the range of bank's services called for is likely to be rather limited. In that they hold clients' funds, solicitors need to have a separate clients' account in which these funds can be kept apart from the practice's own finances. Where substantial sums are involved, these may be placed on deposit account.

When making large payments in respect of house purchases, solicitors require their banks to issue bankers' drafts which are handed over to the vendor's solicitor on the day of completion. There may therefore be substantial movements of funds through solicitors' accounts.

13.6 CONSUMER CREDIT ACT 1974

Since the passing of the Consumer Credit Act 1974, all institutions which are concerned with consumer credit services - including banks, finance houses, credit rating organisations, and debt-collecting agencies and brokers arranging credit terms for customers - have to be licensed by the Director General of Fair Trading. Each licence has to be renewed every three years, but can be withdrawn if the licensee does not comply with the terms of the licence. A wide range of businesses such as retailers, car dealers and double-glazing firms are involved in arranging credit terms for their customers, and are therefore covered by the Act.

The Act was designed to protect all borrowers who are not limited companies up to a maximum of £5000. It does not apply to ordinary trade credit, nor to credit in respect of foreign trade or house mortgages. All consumer purchases must now indicate the cash price of the goods or the amount of the loan, the total charge for credit (TCC), the number and amount of instalments, and the total sum payable. True rates of interest as an annual percentage rate (APR) must be given for all types of trans-actions, so that purchasers are both aware of the real cost of buying goods by instalments, and able to compare the terms with those offered else-where. When a borrower enters into an agreement he now has a period of three days in which to change his mind. Where a borrower repays before the end of the credit period, he is now entitled by the law to a rebate of some of the credit charges.

Banks are now required (as a result of the Act) to provide customers who borrow with a written agreement in the way that they have always done for personal instalment loans. In certain circumstances, a customer may cancel the agreement even though funds have been lent. Customers with overdrafts must be sent a statement shortly after interest has been debited to their accounts.

Under the Act it is an offence to canvass loans outside bank premises. This means actually physically canvassing (but not writing or telephoning), and it does not apply to soliciting for an agreement with an existing customer to overdraw the account.

The Office of Fair Trading under a Director General, which issues the licences to institutions registered under the Consumer Credit Act, was established by the Fair Trading Act 1973 which was passed with the declared intention of strengthening the machinery of promoting competition. The Director General took over the functions of the Registrar of Restrictive Trading Agreements and has the added responsibility for discovering potential monopoly situations or uncompetitive practices. The Office of Fair Trading provides ministers with information and advice on consumer protection, monopoly, mergers and restrictive practices.

13.7 MARKETING BANKING SERVICES

Marketing is a management function which – through the collection and interpretation of data concerning the markets and competition for the company's products or services – aims to ensure that the company's activities are aimed in the right direction. The marketing department works in conjunction with other departments to ensure that collectively they are achieving the best possible performance in promoting the products or services, and they monitor the results to see how they compare with the targets set. The banks are, of course, concerned with selling services rather than physical products, and the benefits of these services are not always immediately apparent to the purchaser. It will, for instance, take time for the customer who opens a budget account to appreciate the benefits of having done so. He or she needs to experience a whole year of freedom from worry in meeting seasonally heavy bills to realise the full advantages of the account (and to weigh the cost against the benefits).

The responsibility for promoting new banking services lies with the general management, under advice from the marketing specialists, and the bank will carry out a considerable amount of research before the launch. The banks also have an Inter-Bank Research Organisation which looks into the need for such services as those of the Clearing House Automated Payments System (CHAPS) which are run on a mutual basis, and also produces data on which the banks can base the introduction of services on an individual and competitive basis.

Marketing a bank's services is by no means only the concern of head office, however, and much of the success (or otherwise) in persuading customers to buy the services offered rests with the branch manager and his staff. There are no middlemen or distributors for the marketing man to convince, as there would most likely be if goods were concerned, and the customer's point of contact is the cashier or clerk at the counter (and, possibly, the manager). The attitude and knowledge of the facts of the person the customer meets is thus vitally important, for he or she is the *marketor*. This ignores one very important line of communication between the marketing department and the customer – advertisements in the press, on television, or maybe at the local cinema. But when the reader or viewer responds to the advertisement he or she goes to the local branch, and it is then that contact with the promoters of the service(s) is made.

TOPICS FOR DISCUSSION

1. Discuss the range of banking services used by personal customers.
2. All businesses are likely to need help and advice from their banks at some stage; consider the types of assistance that a bank might give respectively to small firms and large companies.
3. Discuss the range of foreign trade facilities provided by the banks.
4. Draw a comparison between the likely banking needs of retailer and professional partnership customers.
5. Discuss the purposes of the Consumer Credit Act 1974, and its implications for the banks.
6. Consider and contrast the role of head office and the branch in the marketing of a new banking service.

PART V
BANKING OPERATIONS -
LENDING AND SECURITIES

CHAPTER 14

BANK LENDING

14.1 BASIC CONSIDERATIONS

When a bank manager receives a request for an advance there are a number of questions he or she must personally consider, and many that must be asked of the customer before the manager is in a position to make a decision as to whether to lend the money or not (or to recommend approval if he or she has to put the request to district or area office). Some of the questions will not be difficult to answer if the customer has been known for years and the banker is therefore aware of how well or badly the customer has managed his or her finances. If the customer is a relatively new one, however, the banker may well have to ask some searching questions in order to be satisfied that if he or she lends the money there is every likelihood that it will be repaid, and in the time agreed. Let us look at each of these basic considerations in turn.

How much, and for what purpose?

Obviously the customer must indicate how much he or she wants to borrow and why he or she needs the money. The manager is going to be happier with the proposition if the customer has worked out requirements in a businesslike fashion, and can demonstrate quite clearly how the flow of funds is going to affect borrowing needs (during at least the first year and, preferably, beyond that). If the customer is vague about requirements, and virtually leaves the manager to do the calculations, he or she is not creating confidence and may well have the request rejected simply on the basis that he or she lacks perception as to what the advance is going to mean in terms of setting aside sufficient funds each year to service the debt, and to repay some of it. The manager may well even so have to ask some searching questions, however succinctly the customer has put together the proposition, because the manager will need to decide whether or not the customer is likely to achieve the plans. If the advance is a straightforward personal one for the purchase of a car, or to modernise a kitchen or something of that nature, the manager has to look at the customer's income to consider whether or not he or she is likely to repay as quickly as suggested.

If the advance is for business purposes, then figures will have to be produced by the customer which demonstrate how the extra capital is going to increase the turnover and profits of the business, and enable the loan to be repaid. The manager may decide that the customer is underestimating the needs and, if he or she is willing, recommend a larger advance which is more realistic and which will prevent the customer from running into difficulties and through having to cut back on the scale of activities, not achieve the desired targets. The manager must also be satisfied that the purpose for which the advance is required is appropriate to the customer – if the customer is wanting the advance to stock up a shop with toys for the Christmas period, what are the chances that he or she will in fact be able to sell toys in the particular shop, bearing in mind its position and the degree of competition in the area?

How, and when, is the advance to be repaid?
It may be easy for the customer to borrow money, but repayment can so often turn out to be more difficult than expected. The bank will want an advance to be reduced from year to year, and for the customer to demonstrate how this is going to be achieved.

There are exceptions to this principle of gradual reduction, of course. The borrower may, for instance, require an advance in anticipation of receiving a lump sum which will completely repay the borrowing, or, if the business is expanding more rapidly than expected may come back to the bank during the period of advance and say that he or she wants to borrow more, rather than make the expected repayments. Each application must be judged on its merits, of course, but what must be clear at the outset is the *source* of repayment. If it is to come from, say, the maturity of an assurance policy, the bank may require the customer to sign an instruction to the assurance comapny that the funds should be paid direct to the bank. If it is to come from the profits of the customer's business then the bank will want to see sound projections of the firm's income and expenditure, based on reasonable assumptions rather than over-ambitious ones.

The bank manager must also ask what would happen if the project was a disaster. What would be the bank's position? Would the customer still have sufficient resources to fall back on with which to repay the bank? Are there assets on security which can be sold?

What the bank will want to avoid is a dormant loan or overdraft, and therefore it will need to examine very carefully the customer's ability to make expected reductions, or to repay at the end of an agreed period. It is also essential, of course, that the customer should be able to service the debt – i.e., to pay the interest and charges as they fall due.

Creditworthiness

'Creditworthiness' really means 'Is the customer a suitable person to borrow from the bank?' In other words, it calls for an assessment of *character*, and this is something which the bank manager has to do from the customer's past history and/or by making judicious enquiries. The manager will know, for instance, whether the customer has borrowed from the bank before (and, if so, whether he or she repaid on time and without any difficulties from the bank's point of view). Also whether the customer has run the account in a satisfactory manner. Have cheques ever been returned through lack of funds? Has a reasonable balance been maintained; an active account been operated? What have been the sources of income? Has the account ever been overdrawn without prior arrangement?

If the customer is a new one, it may be necessary to make enquiries from a previous bank, or through a credit-reporting agency.

The manager may know his customer socially, or through business contacts and thus have built up a picture. The manager may have visited the business premises (or, if not, would possibly make a point of doing so in order to form a judgement as to the customer's business acumen).

If the customer has a personal account, the manager may be able to form an opinion as to whether or not he or she lives beyond existing means. If the account suggests that means are modest, yet the customer drives around in a very expensive car and generally appears to be living extravagantly, the manager may well doubt suitability for an advance.

The creditworthiness of business customers must be assessed not only on their own personal characters, but also on the performance of their businesses. A number of years' balance sheets and profit and loss accounts will indicate how successful (or otherwise) the customer has been in running the business. We shall look at balance sheets again later on.

The customer's stake

Quite reasonably, a bank may expect a borrowing customer to put up some of the funds required for any business proposition. Unless the customer is willing to put some of his or her own money into it, and thus bear some of the financial risk, he or she cannot expect the bank to do so. The customer must demonstrate confidence in the venture, and will, of course, have a greater incentive to succeed if he or she is financially involved. At one time it was considered reasonable to expect the customer to put up at least half of the money required, but this was never more than a very rough rule of thumb and the tendency now is to consider each case very much on its own merits. The term 'gearing' is used to describe the ratio between the amount of capital put into the business by the businessman and the total borrowing by the business. Where borrowing accounts for more than 50 per cent of the total resources, the business is said to be 'highly geared'.

For a completely new venture, the bank is more likely to insist on a reasonable participation in it than if the business has been running successfully for some time and simply needs additional working capital in order to hold larger stocks – for instance, to increase its sales. If, too, the customer lodges ample security, such as the deeds of a house, but prefers not to liquidate the asset in order to put more cash into the business, the bank may be more inclined to lend a greater proportion of the funds required.

Security for advance

If a borrower is prepared to lodge some security for an advance, the bank is more likely to agree to it (or more likely to agree to lend a larger sum than would otherwise be forthcoming). However, the bank does not want to rely on the security, in the sense that the last thing it will want to do is *foreclose*. The security is there as a last resort, and therefore the bank will look just as closely at the facts and figures concerning the source of repayment as it would do if no security was to be lodged. By no means all advances are secured, instead they may be based entirely on the creditworthiness of the borrower, but obviously a banker is going to be happier if there is security to fall back on should some event occur (e.g., a bad harvest where a farmer customer is involved) which stops the borrowing from following its predicted course. There are a variety of forms of security, as we shall see in Chapter 16, but whatever type is offered for a particular advance the bank will want to ensure that it has the authority to dispose of the asset, or that instructions are given to ensure that the proceeds of it are sent to the bank.

National interest

As we saw in Chapter 7, the Bank of England gives guidance to the banks from time to time as to which advances are (or are not) in the national interest. For instance, loans to exporters have always been given top priority whereas lending for speculative purposes has generally been considered to be against the national interest. If a customer wishes to borrow money in order to speculate on the Stock Exchange the bank must bear this directive in mind in making its decision. On the other hand, an exporter or a business which is concerned with producing defence equipment might well be given more favourable treatment than the facts and figures suggest because of the importance of such activities to the nation.

So far, we have looked at general considerations which must be taken into account in deciding whether (or not) to agree to any request for an advance. There are particular considerations which apply to the various types of borrowers, however, and also particular types of advances which are appropriate for various purposes.

14.2 TYPES OF ADVANCE

Overdrafts and loans

An *overdraft* is particularly suitable to the private or business borrower whose needs fluctuate. An overdraft limit is granted, and the borrower may draw cheques on the account which cause the balance to become a debit balance up to that limit. As credits are paid into the account – whether they be the borrower's salary in the case of a personal account, or sales proceeds in the case of a business account – the debit balance is reduced and may even swing into credit and then, as further cheques are drawn, the balance swings back again towards the overdraft limit. Ideally, the overdraft diminishes over the course of time as income is used to reduce the borrowing and the overdraft limit is reduced each year as agreed (or, alternatively, is reviewed each year or at some more frequent period, and a new limit fixed in the light of circumstances).

For businesses an overdraft, if there is one, may be used to provide *working capital*, whereas for longer-term purposes a *loan* would be more appropriate. There has been a tendency since about 1975 for the percentage of bank lending to industry on a fixed-term basis to rise as the banks have provided a greater proportion of the development advances required by industry, in addition to the more traditional overdraft for working capital.

Not all loans are for the purchase of particular assets required for a business, and a proprietor might well decide to borrow his working capital by way of loan rather than by overdraft. He might prefer to have an agreed sum which is actively employed in the business on a continuous basis (subject to agreed reductions), and this would be more appropriate where the business is not subject to seasonal fluctuation of trade. An ordinary loan account is opened in the name of the customer and the agreed amount is debited to the loan account and credited to the current account. From time to time (or, possibly, at an agreed time or times each year), an amount is debited to the current account and credited to the loan account by way of repayment. Interest is charged on the outstanding balance on the loan account on a daily basis, and is debited to the current account. Interest on an overdraft is also calculated on a daily basis and debited to the current account, but the balance fluctuates much more freely than a loan and the borrower gets the advantage of the reduced average borrowing figure brought about by credits paid into the account in the ordinary course of the firm's business.

A loan may be more appropriate than an overdraft where the finance is required on a medium- or long-term basis, and where the advance is to be reduced regularly over the period. Where the borrowing is kept quite separate from the customer's current account, the true extent of the borrowing is much clearer to both the bank and the customer.

Business development loans

These are loans to smaller businesses normally for periods up to five years (though they may be for 10 years), and for amounts ranging between £2000 and £250 000. The purposes of the loans vary, but the most usual reasons for them are the purchase or extension of a property, the purchase of a professional practice or business, the purchase of plant and equipment, and additional working capital.

The interest for the whole period of the loan is added to the principal sum at the outset, and the combined figure is divided by the number of months to arrive at the amount of the monthly repayment. In addition, a commitment fee of about 1 or $1\frac{1}{2}$ per cent of the sum that is borrowed has to be paid at the commencement of the period.

Business development loans may be secured or unsecured, each application being dealt with on its own merits. The main advantages of the loans are that the business proprietor knows the extent of the commitment to repay and to service the debt, in that both principal and interest is paid on a regular monthly basis. The rate of interest is fixed for the whole period of the loan, so the borrower will not be burdened with a greater outlay should interest rates move up during the period of the loan.

Business development loans are very suitable for borrowers under the government's Small Business Scheme through which, in addition to obtaining bank finance if the proposition warrants it, the small business proprietor may be awarded a government grant.

Finance for exporters

In addition to normal working capital, business customers who are involved in exporting may obtain bank finance pending the arrival of the proceeds from selling their goods. If the method of payment is a bill of exchange drawn on the importer, the exporter may possibly persuade the bank to *negotiate* the bill and the documents (to buy them at face value less discount) or – as is more likely – to advance money against the collection of the bill. Even if there is no bill of exchange and payment is to be simply against documents or even an open account, the bank may be willing to lend money on the strength of the shipment.

The exporter will find the bank willing to lend a larger amount (and at more favourable terms) if he or she has an ECGD *comprehensive guarantee*, which gives protection against non-payment by the buyer. Any claims under this guarantee can be assigned to the bank. If, in addition to the basic form of ECGD guarantee the exporter takes out an ECGD comprehensive bills guarantee or an ECGD comprehensive open account guarantee, the terms would be even more favourable. These supplementary guarantees are direct between ECGD and the exporter's bank, and cover 100 per cent of the amount lent. In return for this first-class security, the banks agreed with ECGD that they would provide the finance to exporters at only $\frac{5}{8}$ per cent above base rate (which is, of course, a very favourable rate of interest).

Where an exporter sells capital goods or embarks on capital projects overseas, and is obliged to give medium-term credit (up to five years) or long-term credit (more than five years) to the buyer there are special forms of ECGD guarantees which again encourage the banks to provide finance, and at favourable terms. The rates of interest for this type of finance are agreed internationally and vary according to the type of country to which the goods are sent (i.e., a poor or a prosperous country). At January 1984 they range from about 10–12 per cent.

Discount of bills

Quite apart from the negotiation of bills for exporters, the banks also provide finance for their customers involved in domestic trade by discounting bills for them. When discounting a bill of exchange a bank is in effect buying the bill, which it can then present for payment in its own right. It pays the customer the full value less a discount which is calculated at a rate of interest for the period of time up to maturity.

Many of the bills which are discounted by the banks are in fact accommodation bills, and as such are drawn on a drawee (most likely a merchant bank) who is willing to accept the bill as a service to the drawer for which a commission is charged. The drawer's obligation is to put the drawee in funds before the maturity date of the bill.

Finance from subsidiary and associated companies

The large banking groups are able to employ the services of their subsidiary companies (such as those which are concerned with factoring or hire purchase) if their customer's request for an advance can more reasonably be satisfied by the type of finance offered by a subsidiary. It may be that the customer has fully utilised the normal loan and overdraft facilities, and the bank would prefer to see any further finance provided with the stricter control over the customer's sale proceeds or over the goods purchased which the subsidiary would have. The services of a leasing company might well be appropriate if the customer cannot afford to buy the equipment and could better afford an annual rental.

If medium- or long-term finance is required, the bank may consider it appropriate to put the customer in touch with one of the associated companies (or corporations) in which it has a shareholding. The Agricultural Mortgage Corporation, for instance, provides long-term mortgage finance for farmers, and Finance for Industry provides medium- and long-term finance for industry generally, as does Equity Capital for Industry. Both Finance for Industry and Equity Capital for Industry will, where appropriate, take up an actual shareholding in the company it is financing and will thus be able to participate in the running of the company (or, at least, bring its influence to bear as a shareholder). The British banks do not as a general rule take up shares in their customers' companies but this tradition has been broken in recent years, and the banks to a modest extent have followed the example of banks elsewhere in Europe, especially in West Germany, which are much more directly involved in their customers' businesses.

As a member of the EEC, the UK is entitled to apply for loans from the European Investment Bank, and this is becoming an important source of development finance for customers of the UK banks.

14.3 THE COST OF BORROWING

The rates of interest on bank loans and overdrafts are quoted to customers in three different ways:

1. At a margin over base rate.
2. At a margin over LIBOR.
3. At a fixed rate.

Of these methods of quoting, the link with base rate is the most common. As we have seen earlier, each of the banks declares its own base rate which (although it can no longer be directly compared with the Bank of England's MLR because it is no longer published) reflects market rates of interest generally. The banks' base rates are all very similar in amount, and they tend to lead market rates. The most favoured of the banks' borrowing customers are the 'blue chip' companies of national repute, and they would probably be able to command a rate of interest as low as 1 per cent above base rate. Smaller business customers may be quoted 2 or 3 per cent above base rate, and personal customers between 3 and 5 per cent above, and possibly even more. Smaller loans are more costly to the bank to service (and also tend to be more risky), hence the less favourable rates of interest. As we have seen, a business borrower, even a small one, can borrow at only $\frac{5}{8}$ per cent above base rate if he is exporting and has obtained appropriate ECGD cover.

The term LIBOR stands for London Inter-bank Offered Rate and is used for medium-term loans. 'Blue chip' customers may be quoted about 1 per cent or less above LIBOR, and smaller companies wider margins. Although the rate of interest is quoted in this way, it tends to be adjusted only when the loan comes up for renewal.

Fixed rates of interest – i.e., where the rate charged remains unchanged for the whole period of the loan – are used for personal instalment loans, business development loans, and medium- and long-term export loans backed by ECGD direct guarantees to the banks. They are also used by the hire-purchase subsidiary companies of the banks when lending to individuals, and in making finance available to industry and commerce. For personal instalment loans and small term loans to industry the rate of interest is charged on the whole amount of the loan for the full period, making the true rate of interest considerably greater than the nominal rate quoted. If, for instance, £1000 is borrowed over two years at 10 per cent per annum, the interest will amount to £200. The average loan over the period will be approximately only £500 and therefore the APR will work out at nearly 20 per cent.

Whereas a customer who borrows by way of overdraft pays interest on only his outstanding debit balances from day to day and gets the benefit of payments into the account (however, temporary), he does have to pay charges for cheques and other debit items, and sometimes credit items. A customer who borrows by way of loan, however, may avoid paying charges by maintaining a sufficiently high credit balance on his current account (if he is a personal customer, not a business customer). However, he has to pay interest on the whole of the loan, and cannot offset a credit balance on his current account against it.

14.4 SPECIAL TYPES OF BORROWER

Lending to minors

As we saw in Chapter 8, a minor should not normally be allowed an overdraft because the bank is not able to enforce repayment, in that any contract is void under the Infants' Relief Act 1874. However, banks do allow small overdrafts on an unsecured basis where circumstances warrant them and a secured advance is possible where a third party indemnifies the bank and becomes primarily liable for the debt. The security must be in the form of an *indemnity* rather than a guarantee because a minor cannot be a principal debtor (as he would be under a guarantee). If a form of guarantee has a clause inserted which makes the guarantor directly rather than indirectly liable, it serves the purpose, but has in effect been converted to an indemnity.

Lending to executors

Quite often executors need to borrow, as we saw above, in order to pay the capital transfer tax on an estate to obtain probate. If capital transfer tax is payable, the estate must be at the least reasonably substantial and there should be assets that can be realised after probate in order to repay the advance. The bank will enter into an understanding with the personal representatives of the deceased as to which assets will in fact be sold, and will require them to sign a form of charge which makes them personally liable for the borrowing.

Borrowing may also be permitted (unless the will stipulates otherwise) to enable the representatives to pay off the deceased's debts pending disposal of assets, but again they are jointly and personally liable for the borrowing although they are entitled to be indemnified out of the estate.

Lending to house buyers

When a customer is selling one house and buying another he or she will often require a *bridging loan* to cover the time gap between the receipt of the proceeds of sale and the payment for the house he or she is buying. Even when sale and purchase are synchronised he or she may require temporary finance to enable the 10 per cent deposit at the time of signing the contract for the house he or she is buying to be paid. Similarly, if the customer is awaiting a building society mortgage which has been agreed in principle, the bank may be willing to lend that amount pending the receipt of the mortgage funds.

Before agreeing to provide bridging finance a bank will normally require evidence that the customer has a contract of sale for the house being sold. The bank will require a solicitor's undertaking from the customer's solicitor to hold on loan the deeds of the property being sold, to forward the deeds of the new property to the bank on completion of the purchase (if the bank is providing the purchase funds) and to pay over the proceeds of sale to the bank, or return the deeds.

The bank will require written permission from the customer to act in connection with the sale and purchase, giving the bank authority to deal with the solicitor(s) and building society(s) involved.

If the bank is providing a mortgage loan, it will of course wish to control its security – i.e., the deeds of the property being purchased – and, as mentioned above, the solicitor's undertaking must include the forwarding of the deeds to the bank on completion of the purchase. The bank will also ensure that its own form of mortgage (usually legal mortgage) is completed by the customer.

Lending to sole traders

A sole trader is a person who is in business alone, though he or she may well have some employees. The business may operate under the customer's own name or there may be a business name. In either case, the bank would open the account in the trader's name adding 'Trading as . . .' if there is a business name.

The customer is fully responsible for the business and when opening the account there would be no additional formality than when an ordinary private account is opened (other than the need for the bank to see some evidence of the business name, if there is one). This could simply be a copy of one of the customer's invoices, or a piece of business notepaper, or the manager could visit the premises where the proprietor's own name must be exhibited in addition to the business name. Any advance would be to the customer personally, and if security is lodged it is deposited in the customer's own name and not in the name of the business.

A sole trader is not obliged to keep a set of accounts, but may well do so in order to produce them when settling any tax liability with the Inland Revenue. If the accounts exist and the customer has an advance the manager would wish to see the profit and loss account and balance sheet at the end of each year.

Lending to a partnership

As a partnership has no legal entity (except in Scotland) and all the partners are fully liable for the firm's debts, when lending to the firm a bank is in fact lending to the partners. The bank's mandate on opening the account will have clearly established that the partners were jointly and severally liable for the overdraft (or loan). Should the partnership fail to repay the loan, the bank can then look to each of the partners to repay it, suing the partners first jointly and then individually in turn if necessary. When the advance is negotiated all the partners should agree to it in writing (although legally any partner in a trading partnership can bind the other partners, and similarly can give securities to cover such borrowing). If it is a non-trading partnership (such as solicitors or accountants), an individual partner cannot bind his firm in respect of borrowing or pledging security, so that it is all the more necessary to have a written contract with *all* the partners.

Lending to a limited company

When lending to a limited company, a bank manager will need to examine the company's memorandum of association to see whether the purpose of the loan is in accordance with the company's objects and whether the amount is within its borrowing powers (*intra vires*). It is also necessary to examine the articles of association to confirm that the borrowing is within the directors' borrowing powers and the various other powers of the directors. If the advance is to be secured, the objects clause in the memorandum of association will usually give express power to charge security, and should be examined to ensure that this is so.

If an advance to a company exceeds the company's borrowing powers it is *ultra vires* and cannot be ratified by the members of the company. It may therefore be very difficult for the bank to obtain repayment. The company could pay the money back if it wished to (and, if necessary, the bank as a creditor of the company may be able to get an injunction to prevent the company from parting with the money if it still has it). The bank may possibly sue the directors for breach of authority and, finally, the European Communities Act 1972 may help the bank if it has acted in good faith. If the borrowing is within the company's borrowing powers but *ultra vires* the *directors'* borrowing powers it may be possible to persuade the company to ratify the borrowing in a general meeting, or to amend the articles of association retrospectively by special resolution where any type of *ultra vires* loan has been made.

In addition to examining the memorandum and articles, the bank will require to see the company's accounts (preferably for the last three years), in order to see if the profits figures warrant a loan of the size requested. In addition, if the company is willing to produce cash flow forecasts for the next year or more these will be helpful in making the decision as to whether to make the advance or not.

Where an advance to a company is to be secured, the bank's forms of charge must either bear the company's seal or be signed by officials of the company who are authorised to sign. The charge has to be registered with the Registrar of Companies within 21 days of the signatures.

14.5 SECURED AND UNSECURED LENDING

For small and temporary advances, the question of security usually does not arise – the overdraft or loan being granted to the customer on the strength of known character, and in anticipation of receipt of funds that will repay the advance. However, even the most respectable and honest customer may suffer some misfortune which makes it difficult to repay, and therefore if the advance is to be more than temporary it is advisable to take some form of security (and with an adequate margin to allow for any fall in market values during the period of the advance, if the security is one which fluctuates in value).

No hard and fast rules are laid down by the banks concerning security for advances, and each case is dealt with on its own merits. During the 1980s the banks have been much more liberal in their attitude towards firms which have run into difficulties, often lending beyond the security available and being very flexible about the dates of repayment.

Generally it can be said that where security is offered for an advance it is more likely to be granted. However, if the proposition is a good one (and in the event of failure the customer would have plenty to fall back on to repay the advance), it may well be granted without security. Where an advance is a secured one, the appropriate form of charge must be completed and the necessary procedures carried out before the advance is made.

The various forms of security, and the procedures involved, will be discussed in Chapter 16.

14.6 SUPERVISION OF ADVANCES

Each branch manager has a discretionary limit up to which loans and overdrafts can be granted to customers. Beyond that limit, control is vested in a district office with possibly its own directors' committee. Very large propositions would have to go to the Board of Directors at head office.

It is the branch manager's task regularly to review each borrowing customer's account and, if necessary, to report to district office or to head office. When reviewing an account (possibly yearly or half-yearly, depending upon the circumstances), he may find it necessary to interview the customer concerned in order to discuss failure or success in keeping within the prescribed borrowing limit, and needs for the succeeding period.

When a secured advance is granted, the manager is responsible for ensuring that all the necessary steps are taken to complete the security. If a charge is to be taken over a company's assets, for instance, it must be registered with the Registrar of Companies within 21 days. If the security is in the form of house property or industrial buildings, then the manager must check that it is properly insured (and that the premiums have been paid). If the security is an insurance policy, then again it is necessary to ensure that the premiums are paid. It is also necessary to *revalue* securities from time to time – this may, for instance, mean viewing a property in order to update its forced sale value, or writing to an insurance company for the surrender value of a policy, or valuing stocks and shares from the financial press.

Should a customer overdraw the account without prior arrangement, or exceed the overdraft limit, the cheque(s) concerned has to be referred to the manager for a decision as to whether it should be paid or not. If necessary, the manager will contact the customer by telephone or call to discuss the matter before deciding on a course of action.

TOPICS FOR DISCUSSION

1. Discuss the various points that a manager must consider when approached for an advance.
2. Review the various types of special schemes of finance available to bank customers.
3. How are rates of interest quoted to bank customers? Do they have any other charges to pay?
4. Discuss the ways in which the banks provide advances (i) to personal representatives, and (ii) to house buyers.
5. Discuss all the steps that a bank manager must take before lending to a limited company.

CHAPTER 15

CUSTOMERS' BALANCE SHEETS

15.1 SIGNIFICANCE OF FINAL ACCOUNTS

The final accounts of a business concern comprise the profit and loss account and the balance sheet, and may include a manufacturing account and a trading account. Their purpose is to show how successfully (or otherwise) the business has been run during the accounting period (usually a year), and also an account as at the last day of the period of the assets and liabilities of the business. To arrive at the profit or loss for the year it is necessary to deduct from the turnover (the total sales) the cost of materials and labour, and all the other expenses of producing and or selling the goods or services. By comparing a number of sets of final accounts it is possible to see a trend in income and expenditure figures – a trend which can say a great deal about the increasing (or decreasing) profitability of the firm's operations and point to the future likely situation.

A personal account holder will not produce a set of annual accounts, though he or she may well keep a very close check on income and expenditure, and will have a good idea of what any assets are worth. When he or she asks for an advance he or she is usually willing to indicate income, and say something about commitments. If he or she is asking for a personal instalment loan, the branch manager might ask the customer to fill in a form giving these details and in addition the values of any main assets, such as a house. The customer may offer one (or some) assets as security for the advance. Usually this information is asked for and given verbally during an interview, rather than written down in the form of a set of accounts.

The self-employed customer will need to keep some record of income and expenditure in order to satisfy the tax inspector, but these accounts may well be rather crude and lacking in the sort of detail which a bank might hope to see. Such a customer is unlikely to produce a balance sheet and if he or she did might exclude from it all personal assets and show only those actually used in the business. Yet the owner of a sole trading operation is personally liable for all of the debts of the business, and the bank will need therefore to know what the personal resources are. The self-employed person might pledge the deeds of a house as security, or any other personal asset.

Similarly the partners in a firm are jointly liable for the debts of the firm, and the bank's mandate will ensure that they are jointly and severally liable. As a partnership the customers are more likely to keep proper accounts, and will usually be prepared to produce annual accounts when presenting an application for an advance. Again the question arises as to what the partners' personal assets are, and the reader will appreciate that a great deal of tact and diplomacy may be required in trying to glean information.

The main use of final accounts to the banker is in respect of corporate borrowers - limited companies - which are entities in themselves quite apart from their shareholders. Invariably these days companies are limited, and the liability of the shareholders is thus restricted to the amount of their capital so that there can be no recourse to their personal capital (unless a personal guarantee has been given). Companies must by law keep proper sets of accounts, and because the affairs of companies are usually far more complicated than those of smaller businesses, the final accounts are especially useful to the bank. Usually, also, the larger company borrowers prepare careful budgets and cash flow forecasts which are used in presenting their case for additional credit. Most of what is said in the rest of this chapter relates to the affairs of companies, but the same considerations apply broadly to non-corporate customers also.

15.2 INFORMATION FROM ACCOUNTS

Simplified accounts
A set of simplified accounts is given in Appendix 2, which contains the basic information required by a banker when examining a company's accounts and omits any unnecessary detail. The banks have their own record forms on which they record information from their customers' accounts, on a somewhat similar basis to these simplified accounts. The modern tendency is to produce balance sheets in vertical form instead of showing liabilities and assets side by side and, in view of these different modes of presentation, it is perhaps even more necessary to extract what is required and record it in a standardised form.

This specimen trading and profit and loss account (Appendix 5) give us a dynamic picture of what profit was made during the year in question and how that was achieved, whereas the balance sheet (Appendix 5) shows us the amounts of assets and liabilities as they stood on 31 December - a very static picture. But even balance sheets produce a dynamic picture when a series of them is compared. The balance sheet for a particular year may appear to paint a good picture, but when it is compared with balance sheets for previous years it may show that although the present position is sound it is less satisfactory than, say, two years ago - for instance, stocks and debtors may have risen at a higher rate than one would have expected after allowing for rising prices and the increase in turnover.

Working capital

The working capital of a business is the amount of its *net current assets*. This figure is arrived at by deducting the amount of current liabilities from the total of current assets. In the example in Appendix 5 the net current assets are £170 000 (£290 000 − £120 000) and the current ratio is 2.4:1 which is above the ratio of 2:1 which is considered to be the desirable minimum. This ratio is calculated by dividing the total of current assets (£290 000) by the total of current liabilities (£120 000).

Expressed another way, the working capital of a business is the amount of stock, debtors and cash that would remain if all the creditors (including the shareholders to whom dividends are due) were paid. Ideally, a good proportion of the working capital will be in cash, the most liquid asset of all (in Appendix 5 at £65 000, cash - on account at the bank, of course - is nearly 40 per cent of the working capital, which is quite a high ratio).

Working capital must be sufficient for the company's needs from day to day. It is the capital that is used to buy materials or other stocks, pay wages, transport costs and other costs that arise from the manufacture and/or sale of goods. This is quite apart from the costs of using the fixed capital assets which in the long term must also be covered in order that they can be maintained and replaced.

Capital and reserves

The share capital and revenue reserves accrued from trading profits plus capital reserves (if any) that have arisen through (for instance) revaluation of capital assets, form the *proprietor's stake* in the business. If the total of these capital resources is high in relation to the total of the assets, it is a satisfactory state of affairs from the bank's point of view. It means that the proprietor(s) has not relied upon sources outside the business to finance the acquisition of assets. In Appendix 5 the fixed assets are more than covered by the proprietor's capital and there are no long-term debentures or other loans indicated in the balance sheet. Furthermore, there is little reliance upon short-term sources of finance - e.g., creditors - to provide assets.

Another satisfactory aspect of this balance sheet is that the company has been ploughing back its profits into the business, and not distributing them all to the shareholders. A comparison of balance sheets will show to what extent this has in fact happened in recent years.

Creditors

The amount outstanding to creditors needs to be looked at in relation to the total of purchases during the year, and can be expressed as a ratio which indicates the number of weeks' credit taken. This is calculated by multiplying the amount of creditors by 52, and dividing by the total of purchases. Extracting figures from Appendix 5 gives us:

$$\frac{70\,000}{375\,000} \times 52 = 9.7 \text{ weeks.}$$

This ratio can usefully be compared with similar ratios in previous years to see whether the business has been taking longer credit from its suppliers or not.

Debtors

Similarly debtors need to be looked at in relation to the value of sales and the debtors/sales ratio is a useful measure especially if it is compared with that of previous years. In Appendix 5, the debtors/sales ratio is:

$$\frac{80\,000}{625\,000} \times 52 = 6.7 \text{ weeks.}$$

If this ratio is higher than in the previous year(s), then there is additional pressure upon the liquidity of the company.

What is perhaps more important is the size (and spread) of the debtors and the provisions being made for bad debts. If the total is higher than would have been expected from the growth of business, the bank would have to enquire why this is so (and if there is one particularly large debtor, make some enquiries).

If the business is finding it difficult to secure payment from its debtors and is running into cash flow problems as a result, the bank may decide to advise that the services of its *factoring house* subsidiary should be used. The factors would buy the company's invoices at a discount, and take responsibility for collecting the debts, thus converting the asset Debtors into cash.

Stock

Clearly any build-up of stocks of raw materials, work-in-progress and finished goods is a warning signal, and calls for enquiries. As the business expands so will stocks have to increase in order to be able to meet orders, but any excessive build-up could be the result of poor sales of some (or all) lines. There is another accounting ratio which could be useful to the banker – by multiplying the value of stocks by 52, and dividing by the cost of goods sold, the number of weeks taken to turn over stock can be ascertained (and compared with the same ratio for the previous year(s)). Extracting information from Appendix 5 gives:

$$\frac{145\,000}{375\,000} \times 52 = 20 \text{ weeks.}$$

Turnover and profits

The turnover (total sales) of the business should increase year by year at a higher rate than inflation if the business is prospering, and this information can be ascertained, of course, by comparing the trading accounts for a number of years.

The gross profit and net profit ratios should also be fairly constant year by year, because any deterioration would suggest that the business is having to cut its profit margin in order to sell its goods. Any substantial fall in margins would certainly call for investigation – but it must be borne in mind, of course, that a fall in margins may be more than amply compensated for by an increase in total sales and in the total of profits.

The gross profit ratio is the ratio of gross profit (sales *less* cost of sales) as a proportion of sales. In Appendix 5:

$$\frac{250\,000}{625\,000} \times 100 = 40 \text{ per cent.}$$

The net profit ratio is the proportion of net profit to sales, and therefore:

$$\frac{93\,750}{625\,000} \times 100 = 15 \text{ per cent.}$$

These profit ratios can be compared with ratios of similar companies in the trade, and the bank would have access to such information from its own records and from published sources such as the Census of Production and the Census of Distribution. There is nothing hard and fast about such figures, of course, but they do serve as a guide.

15.3 EFFECTS OF AN ADVANCE ON THE BALANCE SHEET

The banker must consider the effects of the proposed advance on the structure of the customer's balance sheet, because the advance will be used to acquire assets which may or may not be liquid. If the company borrows in order to buy new machinery that asset will appear in the total of fixed assets, and on the liabilities side a new current liability will appear – i.e., the bank loan (or overdraft). If the advance is by way of overdraft, the figure may well appear to be smaller than if it were a loan because any cash balance will be used to offset it. If the company in Appendix 5 arranged an overdraft limit of £150 000 to buy the machinery, the overdraft might at first stand at only £85 000 because of the cash in hand, and this figure would move up and down as the company employed its working capital. If the advance was by way of loan, a liability for that amount would arise and the cash balance would remain on the assets side of the balance sheet.

Whichever of the two forms of borrowing is employed, the fact is that the working capital has been greatly diminished and the business may need more of it to cope with the higher scale of production which (presumably) is going to materialise from the employment of the new machinery. By discussion with the proprietor(s), the bank must endeavour to obtain realistic projections as to the increases in turnover, stocks, debtors and creditors that are likely to occur, and from these projections the company's true borrowing needs.

These projections must take into account any seasonal or cyclical factors, and their consequences on the cash flow of the business. If the company manufactures toys, for instance, its main selling period is likely to be during the middle of the year as retailers stock up for the Christmas trade, and payments from these retailers may not be received for some weeks after the goods are despatched. The new machinery may not bring about an increase in turnover and in cash receipts for some months after its installation (and even for a year or so if a new line in toys is to be marketed).

If, for instance, the company produces machine tools used by other manufacturers, it may well suffer from the cyclical effects of upturns and downturns in the economy, and these could be quite severe and prolonged. Customers involved in other capital goods industries such as the building trade can both gain and suffer from substantial swings in their fortunes, and the bank in considering any application for an advance must do so in the light of the general economic situation – not only at the time of lending, but as far ahead as can be reliably forecast.

Banks pay increasing attention these days to the customer's *cash flow forecasts*. Large business concerns have always produced such forecasts, but for a smaller concern this is not the case. It can be a salutary exercise for the entrepreneur to have to sit down and write out his expected income and expenditure in detail month by month during the year ahead, and it is particularly desirable that the small businessman who is borrowing for the first time should do so. He or she will find that the balance on the account will fluctuate considerably month by month, and that the borrowing need may be greater than initially expected. Even within a month he or she may find that a larger overdraft is needed than the projected balances at the beginning and end of that month reveal. The banks have their own printed cash flow forms which they can supply to customers for completion.

15.4 VALUATION OF ASSETS

When making an advance to a business, the bank must look very carefully at the valuations given to assets in the customer's balance sheet, especially if the bank may have to rely on the sale of these assets to repay the advance should the business fail.

Usually the fixed assets are valued quite realistically on a 'going concern' basis at their cost *less* depreciation (and, in the case of buildings, their valuation may even be increased from time to time as market prices for property rise). Whilst the business is running profitably and there is no likelihood of any of the assets having to be sold off quickly at a knock-down price, the valuations give a true picture of the worth of the business. However, a banker must be cautious and will have to consider what would happen if the business failed during the period of the advance. The banker therefore must value the assets on a forced sale (a 'gone concern') basis. For the buildings, the balance sheet valuation may still be realistic especially if the property is not of a specialised nature and therefore more generally sought after. The manager will be aware of property prices in the area, and be able to judge the likelihood of getting the price asked, even if the property has to be sold quickly.

As far as machinery is concerned, it is unlikely to produce a good price unless it is in particularly good order and in demand – and, therefore, the balance sheet valuations should be written down. Tools, vehicles, furniture and fittings should be drastically written down. Stocks of raw materials and finished goods may need to be written down, but the banker must use his judgement as to how easily these could be sold, and at what price.

The debtors of the business may not pay up, and the bank must therefore ensure that in its own valuation of the assets adequate provision is made for bad debts.

Clearly not all businesses need to be valued on a 'gone concern' basis, and where the business has been run successfully and profitably for years and is likely to continue to do so, and all past borrowings have been repaid as agreed, there would be little point in adopting such a cautious attitude.

15.5 BANK ADVANCES BY SECTOR

It is important that the banks should spread their lending over industry and commerce, the nationalised industries, finance, distribution and private borrowing, so as to avoid being reliant upon the fortunes of any one or more sectors or industries. The extent to which the banks spread their advances is indicated in Table 15.1. From this it will be seen that Manufacturing accounts for 18 per cent of total advances and that advances to Agriculture, Forestry and Fishing, to 'Other Financial', Professional, Scientific and Miscellaneous, and to Personal Borrowers, account for much of the remainder.

Table 15.1 *advances by banks in the United Kingdom to UK residents, 17 August 1983 (£ million)*

Manufacturing	
Food, drink & tobacco	2 650
Chemicals & allied industries	2 548
Metal manufacture	1 001
Electrical engineering	1 567
Other engineering & metal goods	3 765
Shipbuilding	899
Vehicles	981
Textiles, leather & clothing	1 169
Other manufacturing	4 639
Total	19 218
Agriculture, forestry & fishing	5 034
Mining & quarrying	2 436
Construction	3 791
Hire purchase finance houses	1 563
Property companies	4 062
Other financial	14 731
Transport & communications	3 689
Public utilities & national government	706
Local government	1 462
Retail distribution	4 339
Other distribution	6 786
Professional, scientific & miscellaneous	14 154
Persons	25 567
	107 539

Source: *Bank of England Quarterly Bulletin*, December 1983

TOPICS FOR DISCUSSION

1. Consider the usefulness to a banker of the final accounts of his customer's business. What additional information is required from sole traders and partnerships?

2. What is the 'current ratio', and how may this be affected by a loan to buy a fixed asset?

3. Consider the usefulness of the creditors, debtors and stocks ratios to the banker.

4. Discuss the relationship between gross profit, net profit and turnover. Why is it that a reduction in the profit margin may not necessarily result in a fall in profits?

5. Distinguish between seasonal and cyclical fluctuations in business, and show how they can affect cash flow predictions.

6. Why should a banker consider valuing his customer's assets on a 'gone concern' rather than 'going concern' basis?

CHAPTER 16

SECURITY FOR AN ADVANCE

16.1 INTRODUCTION

When a customer lodges some form of security for an advance – whether it be title deeds, stocks and shares, an assurance policy, a debenture, or a guarantee or some other asset or instrument – he or she does so to encourage the bank to make the advance. The bank has no intention of relying on the security to repay the advance unless it is forced to do so, but in case this should happen the bank will want to ensure that it has a *legal title* to the asset or that written instructions are given by the customer for the proceeds of its sale or redemption to be sent to the bank.

We have already examined the concept of the banker's lien over a customer's property as it passes through the bank's hands in the ordinary course of business – such as cheques and bills of exchange paid in for collection (Chapter 8) – and we have compared a lien with a pledge or letter of hypothecation. The reader would be wise to reread that discussion before proceeding to look at other forms of security.

16.2 LAND

Title to land

The term 'land' refers not only to the land itself, but to the property built on it, and of course most of the mortgages of land to the banks rely more on the value of the houses, shops and/or other buildings constructed on it than the value of the land itself. Land is a good form of security in that there is no risk of losing control over it if the borrower has a good title and the security is properly charged. Furthermore the price of land, and the property on it, tends to appreciate over time. However, the law relating to land as security is very complex and we can do no more here than look at the general procedure for taking land as security. The comments that follow relate to the law as it stands in England and Wales; in Scotland, certain aspects of property law are quite different.

The customer who lodges land as security is either a freeholder or a leaseholder, and the title is either registered or unregistered. A freeholder owns an estate in the land and usually this is *estate in fee simple* which is the nearest approach to absolute ownership. A leaseholder, on the other hand, holds a legal estate for a term of years from the freeholder or from a sub-lessor. When the lease expires the land reverts back to the freeholder or sub-lessor. A new form of tenure of land was created in 1967 known as *crownhold*. This is land compulsorily acquired by the Land Commission and re-granted by the Crown on sale or by lease.

Most land is now registered land - i.e., the name of the owner is recorded by the Land Registry - but some still remains unregistered with the claim to ownership resting in the possession of a bundle of deeds. These deeds must show a chain of title over a period of at least 15 years, and if the land is sold the solicitor acting for the owner has to prove this title. Proof of title has become much simpler with the conversion to registered land because the registered land certificate is proof of title, and it is necessary only to send it to the Land Registry to have it brought up to date.

Charge by way of mortgage

A bank will always require its customer to give it a full legal mortgage rather than an equitable mortgage over land, unless the mortgagor is of the highest standing and the advance is only very temporary and repayment from other sources undoubted. An equitable mortgage involves simply depositing the title deeds or land certificate with the bank together with the bank's form of equitable mortgage which is signed by the mortgagor under hand. In the form the borrower undertakes to execute a legal mortgage if called upon to do so.

The creation of a legal mortgage can be achieved by deed in either of two ways - by lease to the mortgagee for a term of years, or by a legal charge. The first of these usually gives the bank a lease for 3000 years, but this ceases on repayment. If the land is leasehold then there is a sub-lease for a period which is a few days shorter than the head lease. The second type of legal mortgage gives the bank a charge over the land for an indefinite period and gives the bank the same protection and powers as a legal mortgagee for a set period of years. A legal charge is simpler than a lease for a term of years, and has the advantages that both freeholds and leaseholds can be mortgaged together and that a charge on leasehold property creates no sub-lease which might contravene a clause in a lease restricting sub-letting.

The procedure for taking a mortgage over unregistered land is first to obtain the deeds and get a solicitor's report on title. An abstract of title usually accompanies the deeds, and from this the solicitor is able to follow the chain of title through to the present owner. His report on title, in addition to establishing that there is a good title going back for at least 15 years, will state whether there are any *restrictive covenants* likely to affect the security and whether legislation such as the Town and Country Planning Act 1947 affects the security. The branch manager will need to value the property, and to search the local land charges register and the land charges register at the Land Charges Department. The latter search is usually made at the same time or after the date on which the customer signs the bank's mortgage deed. The bank must give notice to the insurers of the property of the bank's interest in it.

The bank retains the deeds as possession of them is protection for the mortgage. They give the bank first priority in any charges against the property, provided there were no existing charges on the land charges register at the time the mortgage deed was signed.

A mortgage on registered land is much more easily processed in that there are no title deeds to be investigated and reported on. A land certificate issued by the state replaces the title deeds, and when there is a change of ownership the name of the new freeholder or leaseholder is recorded on the land register and a new certificate issued by the Land Registry. The procedure for completing a legal mortgage on registered land is for the bank to examine the land certificate to satisfy itself that the customer has a title to it, and to make a search of the land register for any adverse entries (the reader should note that the search is made at the land register, and not the land charges register which is concerned only with unregistered land). The borrowing customer is then required to complete the bank's form of legal mortgage and this and a copy of it are sent to the Land Registry within 20 days of the date of the search, together with the search certificate, the land certificate and the appropriate registration fee. The Land Registry returns the original of the form of charge, which is bound into a charge certificate, and this certificate is the bank's security. The land certificate is retained by the Land Registry and is not returned to the owner of the land until the bank notifies the Land Registry that the mortgage is to be cancelled.

Where an equitable mortgage on registered land is to be taken, the land certificate is deposited with the bank together with a memorandum of deposit. Notice of the deposit of the land certificate is sent to the Land Registry to be entered on the land register. This then serves as notice to any prospective purchaser or mortgagee that the land certificate has been deposited as security. The land certificate is also sent to the Registry to be endorsed and returned to the bank.

16.3 GUARANTEES

A guarantee is a 'promise to answer for the debt, default or miscarriage of another person' (Statutes of Frauds 1677).

A guarantee is good security provided the guarantor is sound, and it is a simple procedure as no registration of the guarantee is involved. The bank can take action against the guarantor as soon as it has demanded repayment from the debtor and he or she defaults.

There are three parties to a guarantee – the creditor, the principal debtor, and the guarantor. The primary liability to pay is the principal debtor's and the guarantor becomes liable to pay only if the debtor defaults. There must be a valid debt between the creditor and the principal debtor, but the guarantor has no interest in the contract between them apart from an undertaking to pay if the debtor fails to do so. An existing overdraft is not strictly speaking consideration for a guarantee under hand and therefore it is necessary to bring about some change in the amount or availability of the overdraft to introduce the consideration which must support the contract. This adaptation is usually built in to the wording of the bank's guarantee form. Where a guarantee is signed before an overdraft is taken, the overdraft is clearly the consideration for the guarantee.

The value of the guarantee is, of course, dependent upon the financial standing of the guarantor, and therefore before agreeing to take a guarantee as security for an advance a bank must make a *status enquiry* through the guarantor's banker for the amount of the guarantee (and would be wise to renew this enquiry regularly each year). If more than one guarantor is involved, a status enquiry must be made against each one of them for the full amount of the guarantee and the form of guarantee is usually worded so as to give the bank joint and several liability. A bank is not obliged to accept a guarantee which is unsupported by a cash deposit or some form of security, and might therefore insist that the guarantor lodges cash or securities with it.

Completion of the guarantee should ideally take place at the branch where the customer's (the debtor's) account is held. Failing this it should be sent to the guarantor's bank with a request that the bank should obtain a signature to the form. In either case, the guarantor's signature should be witnessed by an officer of the bank concerned to confirm the validity of the signature.

A guarantor has the right to determine the guarantee by giving notice as stipulated in the guarantee and paying the amount due under it. Whether the guarantee is determined by the guarantor or by the bank demanding payment the guarantor is entitled to take over all the securities deposited to secure the debtor's overdraft, but if the debt is greater than the amount of the guarantee he or she can take only a proportionate share of these securities. Having paid up under the guarantee, the guarantor has a right of action against the debtor.

16.4 STOCKS AND SHARES

Stocks and shares are a good form of security from a bank's point of view, provided that in the case of company stocks and shares (as distinct from government stocks) they are quoted on the London or provincial Stock Exchanges. Quoted stocks and shares are more easily marketable, and their valuation can be ascertained easily from the daily press or the Stock Exchange Official List. Prices of stocks and shares fluctuate from day to day, of course, and therefore it is necessary to allow an appreciable margin when taking them as security.

Whilst it is possible to create a legal mortgage over stocks and shares which involves having them transferred into the bank's name (or in the name of one of its nominee companies), the most common practice is for the shares to stay in the customer's name and for the bank to have an equitable mortgage only over them. The danger of this practice is that the bank has no notice of any prior equitable title; but for the majority of customers this is very unlikely, and if there is any doubt a legal mortgage could be taken.

An equitable mortgage simply involves the deposit of the share certificates, together with a memorandum of deposit. In the memorandum, the customer undertakes to complete a legal mortgage if asked to do so, and to charge any bonus issues. If thought desirable, the bank could require the customer to complete a blank transfer form (leaving it undated) so that the bank could sell the shares at any time.

If the securities are not registered securities – i.e., they are bearer securities – they are fully negotiable and the bank taking them in good faith and for value obtains a perfect title to them, even if the customer has a defective one. The bearer securities are pledged to the bank, and are simply lodged with the standard memorandum of deposit.

16.5 LIFE POLICIES

A life assurance policy, whether a whole-life or an endowment policy, is a satisfactory form of security in that it can be easily assigned to the bank, has an increasing surrender value provided the premiums are paid, can easily be realised, and the amount of the policy (plus profits, if there are any) falls due if the assured dies, or earlier if the policy matures.

A whole-life policy provides a capital sum (plus profits, if it is a 'with-profits' policy) upon the death of the assured, whereas an endowment policy provides a capital sum (with or without profits) on a certain maturity date, or upon the death of the assured should he die earlier.

The procedure involved in taking an assurance policy as security is quite straightforward. The policy must be inspected to ensure that it contains no clauses (such as a suicide clause) which is likely to affect its security value, and the bank must ensure that the age of the assured has been admitted. The policy must have a *surrender value* which must be adequate for the bank's requirements, and this may possibly be ascertained from the policy itself although it is usual practice to ask the assurance company to supply this when the assignment of the policy is registered with them. Though it is possible to take an equitable assignment over the policy by simply accepting it on deposit (preferably with a memorandum of deposit), it is usual practice to take a legal assignment. This is completed by executing a legal mortgage under seal which is kept by the bank with the policy. A notice of the assignment is sent to the assurance company with any appropriate registration fee. A duplicate copy of the assignment is returned as an acknowledgement. In addition to the surrender value, the assurance company is asked to confirm that the premiums have been paid up to date, and that there are no prior assignments of the policy.

Unless the policy is to be converted to a paid-up policy, the bank will want to ensure that premiums are paid, and usually these are met by standing order or direct debit on the customer's account.

16.6 DEBENTURES

When a company borrows from a bank the most usual form of security is a debenture. This is a written acknowledgement of indebtedness by the company in favour of the bank incorporating a fixed and/or floating charge over the company's assets, present and future. The debenture is a continuing one, and thus covers amounts borrowed by the company at any time.

A fixed charge is over *specific property* (such as the company's land and buildings) and it is the banks' practice to take a legal mortgage over all the property specified in the charge.

A floating charge is an equitable one over assets (such as stock, work-in-progress and debtors) which are *continually changing*, and in fact it usually covers all the assets not specifically covered by the fixed charge. The value of such assets changes as the fortunes of the company change and, as we saw in Chapter 15, they are worth more to a 'going concern' than to a 'gone concern'. As a floating charge is not likely to be enforced until the company goes into liquidation or a receiver is appointed, the assets should be valued on a 'gone concern' basis and it must be borne in mind that by the time a company is forced into liquidation these assets are likely to have been run down anyway.

Quite often a bank will take a fixed charge over cash and debtors, and the company undertakes to pay all amounts received from debtors into its account and not to charge the debts elsewhere.

Before advancing money against a debenture the bank must ensure that the borrowing is within the powers of both the company and the directors. The charge(s) is executed under seal and has to be registered at the Companies Registry within 21 days of execution.

16.7 AGRICULTURAL CHARGES

A farmer who has not formed an incorporated company or society may create a fixed and/or floating charge over some or all of the farming stock and other assets.

As for a fixed charge created by a company borrower, the property to be charged must be specified, but it can include the progeny of livestock listed and any agricultural plant substituted for that listed.

Before a charge(s) is executed the bank applies for an official search at the Land Charges Registry to check whether any prior charges exist. The bank's form of charge is then executed by the farmer under seal, and this is registered at the Land Charges Registry within seven days. The bank notifies the farmer's insurers of its interest in the property.

TOPICS FOR DISCUSSION

1. Discuss what is meant by 'land', and the differences between freehold and leasehold property.
2. Distinguish between registered and unregistered land, and consider the advantages from a bank's point of view of taking registered rather than unregistered land as security.
3. What is the difference between an equitable and a legal mortgage of land. Why would a bank prefer to take a legal mortgage?
4. Consider the usefulness of a guarantee as a form of security.
5. Why are quoted stocks and shares a good form of security from a bank's point of view?
6. Discuss the procedure for taking a life assurance policy as security.
7. Distinguish between fixed and floating charges, and their value to a bank as security for company advances.

PART VI
BANKING OPERATIONS –
THE FUTURE

CHAPTER 17

DEVELOPMENTS IN BANKING

17.1 THE HIGH STREET CONGLOMERATE

In a speech to international bankers in 1983, Mr J. S. Fforde, an adviser to the Governor of the Bank of England, put forward the supposition that by the mid-1990s we would have some 15–20 independent, nationwide, competing chains of 'financial supermarkets'. Alternatively, perhaps there would be some six or seven nationwide chains consisting of nationwide clearers and building societies together with partnerships between clearing banks and building societies or perhaps also between foreign banks and building societies. We have seen in this book how banking is concentrated into the hands of a few banks and it is a fact that between 1955–80 the number of building societies was reduced from about 800–270 and further amalgamations have taken place since.

The rapid developments in both the banks and the societies and the 'High Street war' that has been going on to win personal deposits could well point to the eventual consolidation of financial services into the hands of a few conglomerates. Already Hambro Life has introduced a comprehensive package of services aimed at $1\frac{1}{2}$ million more wealthy people which offers an interest-bearing current account, an automatic credit limit, a Diners Club charge card, portfolio administration (and, possibly, management if assets are large enough), and a comprehensive statement every month of all transactions together with an evaluation of assets.

The banks are already offering a very wide range of services (both through their parent companies and their many subsidiaries), and each one of the large clearing banks including the TSBs has in a matter of only a few years built up a very large stake in the house mortgage market – a stake large enough to put one or two of these banks very much on a par with the top building societies in terms of total house loans. The building societies, for their part, have formed links with banks which enable them to offer cheque books to their depositors and some of the other banking services such as cheque guarantee and credit cards and the use of automatic teller machines (ATMs), but as yet they are restricted by the Building Societies Act 1962 from moving into more direct competition with the banks by buying their way into banks, insurance and hire-purchase companies which could be run as subsidiaries. At present building society depositors are not allowed to overdraw, and new legislation would be necessary for this to be permitted. Since the Finance Act 1983, however, the building societies have been able to compete with the banks for deposits in the wholesale money markets by the issue of certificates of deposit.

In the retail market, the building societies have been very successful in attracting personal deposits, very largely at the expense of the banks (who now have only 37 per cent of personal sector deposits, compared with the building societies' share of 48 per cent).

In the City of London the reform of the Stock Exchange has permitted incursions by the banks into the realm of stockbroking and stockjobbing, and also there have been links between stockbrokers and stockjobbers which eventually could do away with the distinction between the two. One of the merchant banks (Warburgs) has through its parent company acquired a large holding in one of the major stockjobbers which in turn has formed a joint company with a firm of stockbrokers.

Whether or not the hustle of activity in the financial sector will end up with the consolidation into a few large conglomerates as forecast by Mr Fforde remains to be seen, but what is certain is that the rapid development since 1974 will be more than outshone by the developments in the next 10 years, especially in the sphere of electronic data processing.

17.2 AUTOMATED TELLER MACHINES (ATMs)

At the beginning of 1984 the English and Scottish clearing banks including the TSBs had approximately 4600 ATMs installed, and by the end of 1984 this total is likely to reach 6500. In addition, it is likely that ATMs will be installed at Post Offices for the use of National Girobank customers. Midland and National Westminster banks will have 2000 ATMs between them to serve their 6000 branches, and customers of both banks can use machines at either bank to draw cash, check on their balance, order a statement or order a cheque book. A similar link is about to be forged between Lloyds, Barclays, Bank of Scotland, Royal Bank of Scotland and Williams and Glyns which, when it is in operation in 1985, will offer their customers the mutual use of about 2500 ATMs. Experiments are already taking place in the siting of ATMs outside supermarkets and the logical extension of this is to place the machines in offices and factories which may well encourage the unbanked members of the public to open accounts.

The building societies are also proposing to install ATMs on a joint basis, and it is likely that up to 1000 of these will be available to building society customers before long.

Within the banks ATMs are being installed to speed up the cash service, and National Westminster Bank has set up an experimental self-service lobby at its branch at Basingstoke where, in addition to ATMs and till cash dispensers, it offers a day safe for traders' deposits and a quick deposit box for personal customers. Customers can also make use of an automated account information service through which they can search for specific cheques and for specific amounts and obtain a list of up to 20 entries since the last statement. We shall no doubt see the extension of such services to other branches (and elsewhere ?) in the future.

National Westminster has also been experimenting with a telecommunications network between groups of branches (and within the branches) aimed at the elimination of unnecessary paperwork.

17.3 ELECTRONIC FUNDS TRANSFER (EFT)

Electronic funds transfer (EFT) is already taking place through BACS and SWIFT and is about to be available between banks in Britain through CHAPS (see below) and within the next two years EFTPOS (Electronic Funds Transfer at the Point of Sale) will be under way.

Negotiations are already taking place between the banks and retailers concerning the installation of EFT terminals in supermarkets and large stores, but the main stumbling block appears to be who is to pay for them. Retailers have also expressed the need for a joint approach to the introduction of terminals by the banks and building societies together with British Telecom through which the transmission network would presumably operate.

The most likely development is an extension of the use of existing cash dispenser cards for the settlement of transactions at shops, although there is the alternative of extending the use of credit cards for this purpose instead of (or in addition to) ATM cards. Already about 20 million adults (or nearly 80 per cent of bank current account holders) have at least one credit card, cheque card or cash dispenser card, so that the population is well equipped with plastic cards which could be adapted for use at terminals in retail outlets.

Further developments are also likely in the sphere of home banking. Already the Nottingham Building Society in conjunction with British Telecom and the Bank of Scotland has made it possible for its customers to carry out transactions both with the building society and the bank and with certain retailers by a link through the telephone to their television sets. For a fee, customers are supplied with the Homedeck keyboard and adaptor and by subscribing to Prestel they have the necessary television/ telephone link with the building society, the bank and the retailers.

Customers can see their building society or bank account on the screen, can pay certain bills by operating the keyboard and these are debited immediately, and they can transfer funds from the building society to the bank and vice-versa. They can send messages to either the bank or the society by typing them on the keyboard.

17.4 CHAPS

The Town Clearing system was replaced in February 1984 by The Clearing House Automated Payments System (CHAPS). This system enables any of the member banks (Settlement Banks) to send funds to one another by electronic means for settlement on the same day (and, of course, they can carry out such transactions as agents for other banks and for their customers). Some of the banks' corporate customers have direct computer links with their banks, so that two such customers can settle transactions between themselves via a bank's computer and its links with CHAPS. Not only does the new system reduce the need for the Town Clearing, it also abolishes the old system whereby banks transferred funds telegraphically between themselves.

17.5 BACSTEL

The Bankers' Automated Clearing Services (BACS) extended its services in 1983 by permitting bank customers to send their payroll instructions, direct debits and trade payments through British Telecom direct to the BACS computer. This new service, called BACSTEL, enables a customer to transmit information to the automated clearing service at any time and the funds are available in the relevant bank accounts by 9.30 a.m. on the third day following the input of the information into the system.

Already BACS processes well over 500 million fully automated payments each year.

In 1984 it is intended that the credit clearing will be automatically processed, and to this end customers' paying in books have been standardised and bear encoded details.

17.6 CONCLUSION

By the introduction of new electronic methods of payment (and extending the existing ones) the banks intend to reduce the use of cash, cheques and paper credit vouchers which are to them very expensive and time-consuming. One estimate is that the volume of cheques will be reduced by 10 per cent by 1990. The use of notes and coin will never be completely replaced by the electronic transfer of funds – i.e., we shall never become a completely cashless society – but it is certain that by the turn of the century we will use cash much less than we do now.

As far as the competition for personal deposits is concerned, the banks have already made a concerted effort to attract them away from the building societies by offering new types of accounts on which interest is paid and cheques can be drawn, and on which there is an automatic borrowing provision. However, there is the danger that customers will switch from current accounts to these new accounts. The point of sale use of plastic cards may well help to attract customers to the banks, but it will be an uphill task to persuade manual workers to switch from the use of cash in managing their affairs to the use of a bank account, ATMs and EFTPOS. Perhaps this points the way to closer links between the banks and the building societies, and to the type of conglomerate envisaged at the outset of this chapter.

APPENDICES

APPENDIX 1 NATIONAL WESTMINSTER BANK PLC GROUP BALANCE SHEET

LIABILITIES	1982 £m	1981 £m
Ordinary shareholders' funds:		
Ordinary share capital	238	237
Reserves	2 301	1 969
	2 539	2 206
Preference share capital	14	14
	2 553	2 220
Loan capital	933	654
Minority interests in subsidiary companies	27	23
Deferred taxation	231	247
Current, deposit and other accounts	50 196	39 709
Other liabilities	547	451
	54 487	43 304

ASSETS	1982 £m	1981 £m
Coin, bank notes and balances with the Bank of England and with State banks abroad	708	621
Cheques in course of collection on other banks	921	900
Money at call and short notice	7 559	6 112
Bills discounted	711	776
Dealing assets	149	17
Certificates of deposit	632	799
Investments — other than trade	1 104	1 164
Customers' and other accounts	41 475	31 791
Trade investments	18	36
Investments in associated companies	147	101
Premises and equipment	1 063	987
	54 487	43 304

APPENDIX 2 NATIONAL WESTMINSTER BANK PLC OPERATIONS FLOWCHART

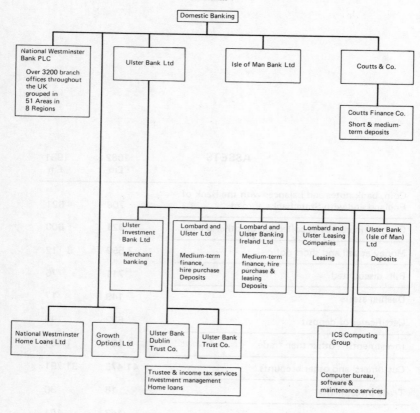

UK Business

Domestic Banking

National Westminster Bank PLC

Over 3200 branch offices throughout the UK grouped in 51 Areas in 8 Regions

Ulster Bank Ltd

Isle of Man Bank Ltd

Coutts & Co.

Coutts Finance Co.

Short & medium-term deposits

Ulster Investment Bank Ltd

Merchant banking

Lombard and Ulster Ltd

Medium-term finance, hire purchase Deposits

Lombard and Ulster Banking Ireland Ltd

Medium-term finance, hire purchase & leasing Deposits

Lombard and Ulster Leasing Companies

Leasing

Ulster Bank (Isle of Man) Ltd

Deposits

National Westminster Home Loans Ltd

Growth Options Ltd

Ulster Bank Dublin Trust Co.

Ulster Bank Trust Co.

Trustee & income tax services Investment management Home loans

ICS Computing Group

Computer bureau, software & maintenance services

Principal Associated Companies and Other Investments—UK

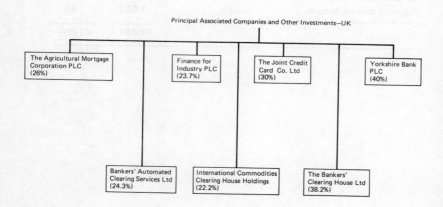

The Agricultural Mortgage Corporation PLC (26%)

Finance for Industry PLC (23.7%)

The Joint Credit Card Co. Ltd (30%)

Yorkshire Bank PLC (40%)

Bankers' Automated Clearing Services Ltd (24.3%)

International Commodities Clearing House Holdings (22.2%)

The Bankers' Clearing House Ltd (38.2%)

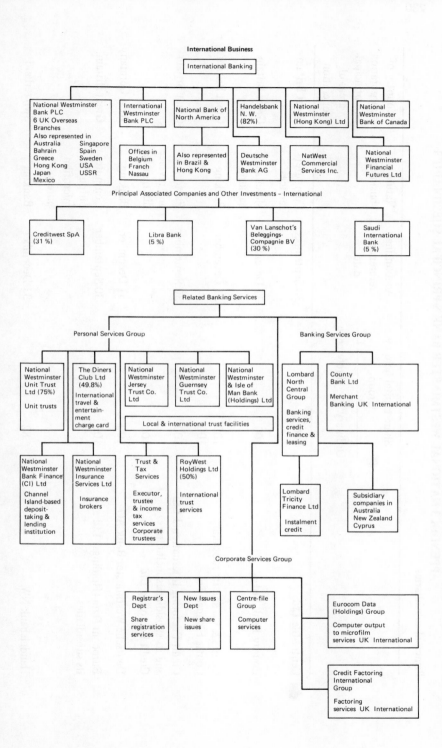

International Business

International Banking

National Westminster Bank PLC
6 UK Overseas Branches
Also represented in
Australia
Bahrain
Greece
Hong Kong
Japan
Mexico
Singapore
Spain
Sweden
USA
USSR

International Westminster Bank PLC

Offices in
Belgium
French
Nassau

National Bank of North America

Also represented in Brazil & Hong Kong

Handelsbank N. W. (82%)

Deutsche Westminster Bank AG

National Westminster (Hong Kong) Ltd

NatWest Commercial Services Inc.

National Westminster Bank of Canada

National Westminster Financial Futures Ltd

Principal Associated Companies and Other Investments – International

Creditwest SpA (31 %)

Libra Bank (5 %)

Van Lanschot's Beleggings-Compagnie BV (30 %)

Saudi International Bank (5 %)

Related Banking Services

Personal Services Group

Banking Services Group

National Westminster Unit Trust Ltd (75%)
Unit trusts

The Diners Club Ltd (49.8%)
International travel & entertainment charge card

National Westminster Jersey Trust Co. Ltd

National Westminster Guernsey Trust Co. Ltd

National Westminster & Isle of Man Bank (Holdings) Ltd

Local & international trust facilities

Lombard North Central Group
Banking services, credit finance & leasing

County Bank Ltd
Merchant Banking UK International

National Westminster Bank Finance (CI) Ltd
Channel Island-based deposit-taking & lending institution

National Westminster Insurance Services Ltd
Insurance brokers

Trust & Tax Services
Executor, trustee & income tax services
Corporate trustees

RoyWest Holdings Ltd (50%)
International trust services

Lombard Tricity Finance Ltd
Instalment credit

Subsidiary companies in Australia New Zealand Cyprus

Corporate Services Group

Registrar's Dept
Share registration services

New Issues Dept
New share issues

Centre-file Group
Computer services

Eurocom Data (Holdings) Group
Computer output to microfilm services UK International

Credit Factoring International Group
Factoring services UK International

APPENDIX 3 NATIONAL WESTMINSTER BANK'S PRINCIPAL SUBSIDIARIES

Principal subsidiaries

	Share capital held by Group		Accounting reference date	Nature of business	Country of incorporation and principal areas of operation
	Ordinary %	Preference %			
Centre-file Ltd	100		30 September	Computer services	Great Britain
County Bank Ltd	100		31 December	Merchant banking	Great Britain
Coutts & Co and its subsidiary Coutts Finance Co	100	100	31 December	Banking	Great Britain
Credit Factoring International Ltd and its subsidiaries including Credit Factoring Ltd	100	100	30 September	Factoring and invoice discounting	Great Britain
Deutsche Westminster Bank AG	100		31 December	Banking	West Germany
Eurocom Data (Holdings) Ltd and its subsidiaries	100		30 September	Computer output to microfilm bureau	Great Britain
Handelsbank NW	82		31 December	Banking	Switzerland

Company			Year end	Activity	Country
International Westminster Bank PLC[c]	100		31 December	Banking	Great Britain
Isle of Man Bank Ltd	100		31 December	Banking	Isle of Man
Lombard North Central PLC and its subsidiaries including	100	nil	30 September	Banking services, credit finance and leasing	Great Britain
National Westminster Finance Australia Ltd,	100	98			Australia
National Westminster Finance New Zealand Ltd and	100				New Zealand
Lombard Tricity Finance Ltd	100				Great Britain
NatWest Holdings Inc. and its subsidiaries including	100		31 December	Banking and factoring	United States of America
National Bank of North America and	100				
NatWest Commercial Services Inc.	100				
National Westminster Bank Finance (CI) Ltd	100		30 September	Banking	Channel Islands
National Westminster Channel Islands (Holdings) Ltd and its subsidiaries	100		31 December	Trustees	Channel Islands
National Westminster Financial Futures Ltd	100		31 December	Financial futures broking	Great Britain
National Westminster Home Loans Ltd	100		31 December	Home mortgage finance	Great Britain

232

Principal subsidiaries (*cont'd*)

	Share capital held by Group		Accounting reference date	Nature of business	Country of incorporation and principal areas of operation
	Ordinary %	Preference %			
National Westminster (Hong Kong) Ltd	100		31 December	Banking	Hong Kong
National Westminster Insurance Services Ltd	100		30 September	Insurance broking	Great Britain
National Westminster Unit Trust Managers Ltd	75		30 September	Unit trust managers	Great Britain
National Westminster Bank of Canada	100		31 October	Banking	Canada
Ulster Bank Ltd and its subsidiaries[a]	100		31 December	Banking	Northern Ireland

a Credit Factoring International Ltd and its subsidiaries operate world-wide.
b Subsidiaries of Eurocom Data (Holdings) Ltd also operate in Denmark, Finland, Sweden and West Germany.
c International Westminster Bank PLC also operates in Belgium, France and the Bahamas.
d Ulster Bank Ltd and its subsidiaries also operate in the Repulic of Ireland.

APPENDIX 4 SIMPLIFIED BANKING GROUP BALANCE SHEET

Fig A.3 *simplified group balance sheet as at 31 December 19. .*
£million

Capital & reserves	2500	Cash & balances with central banks	700
		Call money	8 000
Loan capital	1000	Bills discounted	700
		Dealing assets	200
Deposits	50 000	Cheques in course of collection	1 000
		Certificates of deposit	700
		Investments	1 000
		Advances	40 000
		Trade investments	20
		Investments in associated companies	180
		Premises	1 000
	53 500		53 500

APPENDIX 5 SIMPLIFIED PROFIT AND LOSS ACCOUNT AND BALANCE SHEET

Fig A.4 *simplified profit and loss account for the year ended 31 December 19. .*

Cost of sales	375 000	Sales	625 000
Depreciation	75 000		
Administration expenses	81 250		
Net profit	93 750		
	625 000		625 000

simplified balance sheet as at 31 December

Share capital	500 000	Fixed assets			
Profit & loss account	220 000	Cost			700 000
		Less depreciation			150 000
					550 000
Current liabilities		Current assets			
General 70 000		Stock	145 000		
Dividend 50 000	120 000	Debtors	80 000		
		Cash	65 000		290 000
	840 000				840 000

APPENDIX 6   BUSINESS AND TECHNICIAN EDUCATION COUNCIL – ELEMENTS OF BANKING MODULES

LEARNING OBJECTIVES

ELEMENTS OF BANKING 1

	Section references
A1. Briefly trace the evolution of money, identifying its functions and the characteristics required of whatever is used as money to enable it to perform its functions satisfactorily.	5.1, 5.2, 5.3
A2. Identify the shortcomings of money as an indicator of value and outline methods of protecting its value.	5.3
A3. Distinguish the forms that money takes in a modern society (coinage, notes, legal tender, bank deposits).	5.5
A4. Distinguish between money and 'near money'.	5.5
B1. Outline briefly the origins and development of the UK banking system.	2.1, 2.2, 3.1
B2. Briefly outline the development of the Bank of England, explaining its functions and including its role under the 1979 Banking Act.	2.1–2.5
B3. Distinguish between the short-term money markets, the loan and savings markets and the capital markets (including the Stock Exchange).	4.1–4.6, 6.5
B4. Within these markets, identify the functions, ownership and inter-relationships of the various types of institutions (banks, discount houses, acceptance houses, building societies, insurance companies, etc).	4.1–4.7
C1. Given the balance sheet of a major commercial bank:	
C1.1 Identify the nature and significance of the liabilities and assets.	3.2–3.7
C1.2 From this determine the main sources and uses of funds.	3.2–3.7
C1.3 Distinguish between liquid and other assets and appreciate the security and profitability of each.	3.6
C1.4 Identify relevant ratios: cash and balance at the Bank of England to deposits; liquid assets to deposits; capital to deposits; 'free capital' (i.e., capital minus fixed assets) to deposits.	3.7
C2. Explain the main methods of protecting depositors' funds (including reference to the 1979 Banking Act).	3.8
C3. Understand the basis of the creation of credit.	3.9
C4. Outline the purposes of and the methods used for official control of bank credit.	7.4

D1. Outline the nature of savings and their role in the economy, and identify who saves (personal, public and company sector savings). 6.1, 6.2

D2. Identify and compare major forms of saving (including banks, building societies, pension funds, insurance companies, unit trusts, National Savings) and their relative attractiveness to savers. 6.3, 6.4

D3. Specify the principal institutions which on-lend savings and their respective roles in the economy (banks, building societies, finance houses, etc.). 6.3, 6.4

E1. Define the meaning and role of the rate of interest. 7.4

E2. Identify the factors which influence interest rates. 7.4

E3. Describe the structure of interest rates including base rates, LIBOR, blue chip, etc. 14.3

E4. Appreciate in outline the effects of interest rate changes on banking business (domestic and international), competition for savings, investment and employment. 7.1-7.7

F1. Distinguish different types of bank customer and the different considerations which may apply to them, with particular reference to personal and corporate accounts including executor, trustee, church, club, etc. 8.5

F2. Understand the basic contractual relationship between banker and customer (e.g. debtor/creditor, agent/principal) with a basic understanding of the contractual capacity of different types of customer (including provisions related to limited companies). 8.1

F3. Explain the procedure for opening bank accounts and the main terms used in mandates and powers of attorney for operating bank accounts and in other bank documents whereby the customer gives instructions to the bank. 8.1-8.6

F4. Fully appreciate the bank's legal duties to the customer, e.g. secrecy, acting with due care. 8.1-8.6

F5. Differentiate between joint and several liability. 8.5

G1. Identify the different types of negotiable instruments and their particular characteristics. 9.1, 9.2

G2. Trace the development of a cheque as a method of payment. 10.2

G3. Appreciate the origins and current meanings of crossings on cheques. 10.3

G4. Explain the responsibility and rights of parties to cheques and bills of exchange. 10.4

G5. Explain the rights of banker, customer and holder of a cheque in the event of misuse of a cheque card. 10.5

G6. Identify and explain the consequences of conversion. 8.4, 10.4

G7. Describe conversion in respect of items held in safe custody. 8.4

G8. Identify unauthorised acts by agents and their effects on the bank. 10.6

H1. Identify the different inland methods of payment (including cheque, bank giro, banker's order, direct debit, etc.) and explain how they are processed.   11.1–11.9

H2. Explain the operation of the bank clearing system.   11.2

H3. Outline the methods of making international payments including mail and cable transfers, bankers' drafts and the settlement of sterling and currency payments between banks.   12.1–12.5

ELEMENTS OF BANKING 2

A1. Outline the link between the money supply and the level of bank and economic activity.   7.1–7.2

A2. Identify and evaluate the difference between various money aggregates, in particular those used for official control purposes.   5.5

A3. Appreciate the factors which bring about changes in the money supply, including private and public sector borrowing and external factors.   7.1–7.5

B1. Identify the broad objectives of government economic policy and the role of monetary policy as one of the methods of achieving those objectives.   7.1–7.5

B2. Identify the different techniques available for implementing monetary policy – money aggregates, ratios, interest rates, special deposits, quantitative controls, suggestion and request.   7.1–7.5

B3. Be aware of the effects of monetary policy techniques on the banks.   7.1–7.5

B4. Distinguish between short-term and long-term interest rates and appreciate the role of the government in influencing interest rates.   7.1–7.5

B5. Appreciate the relationships between balance of payments, exchange rates and interest rates.   7.1–7.5

C1. Identify the wholesale money markets, their origins and functions (local authority, inter-bank, company funds, certificates of deposit, Euro-currency markets and the financial futures market).   4.1–4.7

C2. Evaluate their role in the economy.   4.1–4.7

D1. Identify and outline the main services offered by the commercial banks to personal customers (e.g., executor and trustee services, credit cards, hire purchase, insurance, etc.).   13.1

D2. Identify and outline the main services offered by the commercial banks or their subsidiaries to business customers (e.g., factoring, leasing, etc.).   13.2

D3. Relate the range of services to the needs of specific types of customer (e.g. importers/exporters, manufacturers, retailers, professions, householders, students, etc.).   13.3–13.5

D4. Evaluate the methods adopted by banks for marketing their services. 13.7

D5. Recognise the constraints imposed upon banks by legislation such as the Consumer Credit Act and the Fair Trading Act. 13.6

E1. Identify the general principles governing bank lending and its supervision. 14.1

E2. Identify the various forms of bank lending and their suitability for the purposes of different borrowers. 14.2

E3. Outline the special features of contractual capacity that a banker needs to bear in mind in lending to minors, executors, house buyers, sole traders, partnerships and limited companies. 14.4

E4. Identify the circumstances in which security may be required. 14.5

E5. Appreciate the various types and attributes of security (e.g. land, stocks and shares, life policies, guarantees). 16.1–16.7

F1. Explain the liability of banks to persons affected by their activities (e.g. through negligence, breach of contract, vicarious liability, conversion, defamation). 8.1–8.5

F2. Differentiate between lien, hypothecation and pledge, and understand the meaning of safe custody. 8.6

F3. Outline the nature of wills, the appointment and duties of personal representatives and the duties of trustees. 8.5

G1. Interpret the final accounts and other financial statements of a business from the viewpoint of profitability, efficiency, liquidity, capital structure and investment. 15.1–15.3

G2. Interpret the accounts of a company on the basis of a 'going' and 'gone' concern through examination of the trading and profit and loss accounts and the balance sheet. 15.1–15.5

G3. Identify the significance of the data relating to stock (retail and manufacturing), debtors, creditors, borrowing, dividends and tax. 15.1–15.5

G4. Determine relevant factors relating to cyclical business, off balance sheet finance, plant and machinery, employees, etc. 15.1–15.5

G5. Understand and apply elementary accounting ratios and appreciate the importance of the cash flow position. 15.1–15.5

H1. Define the concept of negotiability and relate it to banking instruments. 9.1–9.2

H2. Explain the meaning of acceptance, endorsement and discharge. 9.3

H3. Name the principal statutes relating to negotiable instruments and outline in general terms their fundamental consequences. 9.1–9.6

H4. Describe the statutory protection for a holder for value, a holder in due course, the rights and duties of parties to a bill, presentation for acceptance and presentation for payment. 9.1–9.6 / 10.1–10.4

H5. State the position of the collecting banker and the paying banker with regard to statutory protection, negligence, negotiability and endorsement necessary to transfer. 9.1–9.6 / 10.1–10.4

H6. Explain the banker's position in the event of revocation of authority, material alteration and forgery.   9.1–9.6 / 10.1–10.4

H7. Identify the action following the dishonour of a bill of exchange or the non-payment of a cheque.   9.5–10.4

J1. Identify evidence of ownership (e.g. land certificate and title deeds, and means of checking title).   16.1–16.7

J2. Outline special factors concerning land ownership – freehold/ leasehold, registered/unregistered, prior charges and interest.   16.1–16.7

J3. Outline the obligations of mortgagor and mortgagee.   16.1–16.7

J4. Describe the appropriate instruments of transfer, e.g. conveyance, transfer, assignment.   16.1–16.7

J5. Outline the ways in which security may be taken and the respective rights of bank and customer relating to legal and equitable mortgage and assignment.   16.1–16.7

INDEX